Inclusive Education Theory and Policy

Inclusive Education Theory and Policy

Moving from Special Educational Needs to Equity

Sue Soan and Jeremy Monsen

 Open University Press

Open University Press
McGraw Hill
Unit 4
Foundation Park
Roxborough Way
Maidenhead
SL6 3UD

email: emea_uk_ireland@mheducation.com
world wide web: www.mheducation.co.uk

Copyright © Open International Publishing Limited, 2023

All rights reserved. Except for the quotation of short passages for the purposes of criticism and review, no part of this publication may be reproduced, stored in a retrieval system, or transmitted, in any form or by any means, electronic, mechanical, photocopying, recording or otherwise, without the prior written permission of the publisher or a licence from the Copyright Licensing Agency Limited. Details of such licences (for reprographic reproduction) may be obtained from the Copyright Licensing Agency Ltd of Saffron House, 6–10 Kirby Street, London EC1N 8TS.

Executive Editor: Eleanor Christie
Editorial Assistant: Phoebe Hills
Content Product Manager: Ali Davis

A catalogue record of this book is available from the British Library

ISBN-13: 9780335250394
ISBN-10: 0335250394
eISBN: 9780335250400

Library of Congress Cataloging-in-Publication Data
CIP data applied for

Typeset by Transforma Pvt. Ltd., Chennai, India

Fictitious names of companies, products, people, characters and/or data that may be used herein (in case studies or in examples) are not intended to represent any real individual, company, product or event.

Praise Page

"This book provides an insightful and accessible analysis of the current position of inclusion and SEND within the English stated funded educational system, its teaching workforce and possible futures. The thought-provoking, yet evidence-based arguments encourage critical reflection as well as self-reflection. I would highly recommend this book to any SEND specialist or educational leader."
Dr Jo Van Herwegen, Associate Professor at the
Faculty of Education and Society, UCL, UK

"This book is a wake-up call to us all to the 'liberation' of our current system... it invit[es] active engagement in change through review and reflection... I would recommend this book to my teachers"
Dr Stella Scharinger, Primary School Executive Head Teacher,
The Stour Academy Trust, UK

"This is a timely much needed book. The authors bring a wealth of experience of both research and practice to the work. Starting with the back story of special needs, the book leads on to recent trends in change and ends with updated highly useful suggestions for the future."
Dr Elaine Wilson, Fellow of Homerton College, former Professor at the
Faculty of Education, University of Cambridge, UK

"This book, co-authored by long time practitioners, brilliantly demonstrates that an inequitable, illiberal education system can be changed to become inclusive and equitable. With one part examining the system over the decades since the Warnock report, and a second part presenting policy and practice for a fairer system with an end to a SEND industry, it presents a state-maintained education system desperately in need of radical reform that can be renewed to serve all children and young people."
Sally Tomlinson, Emeritus Professor Goldsmiths
at the University of London UK, Honorary Fellow at the
Department of Education, University of Oxford, UK

"The authors don't shy away from razor-sharp analysis and critique of a SEND system in crisis even though their primary motivation is to offer 'real-world solutions'. Compassion for the children and young people that this book is about, as well as for the professionals who support them, and their families, permeates everything they say. The book provides an excellent overview for those who are new to the field or have *limited time to study; it also offers many surprising and thought-provoking insights for those well-versed in the challenges and opportunities of an inclusive education system. I highly recommend it."*

Beate Hellawell, Lecturer at the UCL Institute of Education, UK and Team Leader at EHC Needs Assessments, UK

"This is a scholarly, well informed and timely book. It arrives at a time of significant need within education for 'at risk' young people and offers clarity and insight to practitioners. If you are seeking a guiding light through the complex maze of SEND legislation and policy, this book is for you."

Dr Amelia Roberts, Associate Professor and Deputy Director of the UCL Centre for Inclusive Education, UK and Vice Dean (Enterprise), UCL Institute of Education, UK

Dedication

This book is dedicated to all those who have taught us over the years with wisdom, creativity and compassion, allowing us to become the people we are.

Stewart Clark
Mark Soan

Contents

Figures	x
Tables	xi
Foreword	xii
Acknowledgements	xv
Abbreviations	xvi
About the Authors	xvii
1 THE IMPORTANCE OF EDUCATION	1
2 THE JOURNEY SO FAR – A SELECTIVE CRITICAL ACCOUNT OF SPECIAL EDUCATIONAL NEEDS LEGISLATION AND GUIDANCE IN ENGLAND SINCE THE WARNOCK COMMITTEE REPORT (1978)	6
3 CLASSROOM-LEVEL INCLUSIVE EDUCATIONAL PRACTICE: QUALITY FIRST TEACHING FOR ALL LEARNERS	32
4 'TOO MUCH EDUCATIONAL CHANGE': LEADING EDUCATIONAL IMPROVEMENT THROUGH THEORY ENGAGEMENT BETWEEN SCHOOL LEADERS AND TEACHERS	53
5 TIME FOR A REVISIONING OF THE STATE SCHOOL SYSTEM: ACKNOWLEDGING WHAT IS NOT WORKING AND CREATING AN EDUCATIONAL PEDAGOGY THAT REFLECTS A NATION'S VALUES AND ASPIRATIONS	72
6 WHY BECOME A TEACHER: WHY NOT?	90
7 THE TWENTY-FIRST-CENTURY ENGLISH EDUCATION SYSTEM: CHOOSING A NEW PATHWAY	108
References	122
Index	144

Figures

Figure 3.1	Waves of intervention model	44
Figure 4.1	Single- and double-loop learning	63
Figure 4.2	The bypass and engage approaches to leading improvement	67
Figure 5.1	Some current disruptions to the further evolution of inclusion in current English state-run schools	88
Figure 7.1	Potential enforcers of inclusion in a liberated English state education system to meet parents' expectations	121

Tables

Table 2.1	A summary of the SEN terminology used in the 1994 (DfE), 2001 (DfES) and 2015 (DfE and DoH) Codes of Practice (adapted from Capper 2020: 30)	11
Table 2.2	Summary of key policy initiatives leading up to the 2014 Children and Families Act and subsequent 2015 SEND Code of Practice (adapted from Capper 2020: 2)	14
Table 2.3	A summary of the key changes made in the 2015 Code of Practice (DfE and DoH 2015) (adapted from Capper 2020: 6)	19
Table 3.1	Summary of the theoretical approach and key principles of Dewey's, Vygotsky's and Bruner's theories of learning	40
Table 4.1	A comparison between Elissa's current and possible future theory-of-action for teaching early literacy (adapted from Robinson 2018: 16)	65
Table 6.1	The government requirements of the 'teaching profession'	94
Table 6.2	Proportion of pupils with an autism spectrum disorder EHC plan, by primary type of need, as of January of each year (HM Government 2022b)	98
Table 6.3	Proportion of pupils with a speech, language and communication need EHC plan, by primary type of need, as of January of each year (HM Government 2022b)	99
Table 6.4	QTS national statistics for all routes into teaching (Gov.uk 2022)	101
Table 6.5	Difference in numbers of trainee teachers qualifying between 2012/13 and 2018/19 and between 2012/13 and 2020/21	102

Foreword

It gives me great pleasure to be able to give an informed outsider's perspective on a book which, though focused as it is on the English state education system, has enormous relevance for other countries and their educators and policy-makers as they commit to inclusive educational policies and practices.

Over many years since graduating as a teacher, working as an educational psychologist and national policy and strategy manager, in what was formerly known as Special Education (now known as Learning Support) in the Ministry of Education in Aotearoa, New Zealand, and in my current role as Director, Office for Disability Issues in Whaikaha, the Ministry of Disabled People, inclusion has been at the heart of the policy and practice discourse.

Additional context that underscores the importance of this book and its commitment to inclusive education is provided by the United Nations Convention on the Rights of Persons with Disabilities (the Convention), to which the United Kingdom and 164 other countries are signatories, and make a firm commitment to inclusive education. In 2016 the United Nations committee which monitors and champions the Convention provided additional guidance to signatories on implementation of Article 24 (the education article) of the Convention.

The easy-read version of this guidance provides real clarity on what signatories to the Convention have committed to, and I quote:

- Inclusive Education is when people with disabilities and people without disabilities learn together.
- This means people with disabilities are not sent to other schools or classrooms away from other people.
- Countries need to change how education works so that everyone gets a good education.

For children, young people and adults with learning differences and disabilities, their families and friends, inclusion is more than a policy or practice question – it is about the right to lead a 'good life that is right for me'. The opportunity to learn and achieve on my terms alongside others in my community, the opportunity to be part of and contribute to my community – to know that I belong. I am reminded of the words of a parent whose expression of what she wanted from the education system for her child 'with special educational needs' was: 'I will know progress has been made when I and other parents no longer hope for what every other parent expects from the education system'.

At Auckland University I had the opportunity and good fortune to work alongside Professor Jeremy Monsen as a fellow student over 3 years on the Diploma of Educational Psychology course. We graduated, and took different pathways in our careers, but have remained connected over the last 40 years as colleagues and collaborators on how we continue to learn as professionals and give effect, add value, contribute, innovate and continue to respond to the big ideas and challenges presented to us as graduate students.

My connection with Dr Sue Soan is more distant – we have never met. However her research, academic and professional roles create an instant connection and respect for what she has achieved and the issues that she has worked on over many years.

Both Professor Jeremy Monsen and Dr Sue Soan, as individuals and importantly as partners in jointly authoring *Inclusive Education Theory and Policy: Moving from Special Educational Needs to Equity*, bring together considerable experience and knowledge and in their book present important ideas and evidence for educators and education policymakers alike.

Three key ideas in this book, amongst the many, immediately resonated with me. The first is that better inclusive educational outcomes for pupils with learning differences and disabilities are not achieved through 'special' strategies but through sound, evidence-based teaching and learning approaches, and that all these approaches should be available in all educational settings. Thank you for presenting the work of influential educational thinkers – Dewey, Vygotsky and Bruner – and reminding us of their contemporary relevance to teaching, learning and inclusion.

The second, and this is particularly important for policymakers like me, is that effective policy is more than a technically sound paper that has been endorsed by decision-makers. Good educational policy and change must effectively engage those implementing it – teachers and school leaders – and those who are the potential beneficiaries – pupils with learning differences and disabilities, and their families. Thank you for detailing the work of Professor Viviane Robinson and the need for policymakers to step away from the assumption that their position of power and privilege creates effective educational change. Great educational outcomes for pupils with learning differences and disabilities are achieved through the many dedicated, reflective and reflexive teachers who deserve respect, appreciation and the opportunity to collaborate on change. Educational change is not achieved through compliance with new policy, but through a lived commitment to the new policy itself.

The third area is that progress towards inclusion is being made for pupils with learning differences and disabilities, yet there is much more to be achieved: the important position that education as a 'public good' must be good for all, that all pupils are learners and that potential realized and equity achieved are inextricably linked to removing the barriers to inclusion through effective policy, teaching and learning, and those many teachers who see themselves as learners on a journey. The social model of learning differences and disability creates the expectation that 'we get schools ready for kids, and not kids ready for schools'.

The authors make it clear that not everyone will agree with some of the ideas presented in their book. This is indeed their challenge to teachers, school leaders and policymakers, to take the opportunity to read, debate, discuss, critique, agree, disagree, think about and learn from the many important concepts presented in the book so that the state education system becomes a better place for all learners.

I conclude with a Māori proverb... Whāia te mātauranga hei oranga mō koutou – meaning 'seek after learning for your own well-being'.

Brian Coffey

Member of the New Zealand Order of Merit, Director of the Office for Disability Issues, Whaikaha, the Ministry of Disabled People, Aotearoa, New Zealand.

Wellington, January 2023

Acknowledgements

We would like to thank the following people for their enormous assistance and contributions, in many forms to, the development of this book.

Yasin Arslan, for his skilful and methodical approach in locating relevant literature and resources. PhD candidate, Postgraduate Teaching Assistant in the Department of Psychology and Human Development at UCL IOE and Senior Research Assistant (Westminster, Kensington & Chelsea Educational Psychology Consultation Service).

Dr Zoe Capper, for her invaluable historical insights as part of her thesis for the degree of Applied Educational and Child Psychology doctorate, School of Education, College of Social Science, University of Birmingham, 2020.

Dr Emma Kennedy, for her invaluable scrutinizing of the Viviane Robinson material, included in Chapter 4. Course Director for the Doctorate in Child Community and Educational Psychologist and Lifespan Autism and Learning Disabilities Team; Educational Psychologist at the Tavistock & Portman NHS Foundation Trust.

Dr Ed Baines, for his invaluable feedback on Chapter 3. Senior Lecturer in Psychology of Education, Psychology and Human Development, University College London, Institute of Education.

Abbreviations

ASD	Autism spectrum disorder
CTD	Continuing teacher development
CPD	Continuing professional development
DES	Department of Education and Science
DfES	Department for Education and Skills
DfE	Department for Education
DoH	Department of Health
ECF	Early career framework
EHC plan	Education, Health and Care plan
EP	Educational psychologist
EY	Early Years
ICT	Information and communication technology
ITE	Initial teacher education
ITT	Initial teacher training
LA	Local authority
LEA	Local educational authority
Ofsted	Office for Standards in Education
OT	Occupational therapist
Primary School	Equivalent to elementary school in the USA, covering ages of about 5 to 10
QTS	Qualified teacher status
SALT	Speech and language therapist
Secondary School	Equivalent to junior high and high school in the USA, covering ages roughly 11–18 years
SEMH	Social, emotional and mental health needs
SEN	Special educational needs
SENCo	Special educational needs coordinator
SEND	Special educational needs and disabilities
SLCN	Speech, language and/or communication needs
SpLD	Specific learning difficulty
SRP	Specialist resource provision
TA	Teaching assistant
UNESCO	United Nations Educational, Scientific and Cultural Organization

About the Authors

Dr Sue Soan gained her Bachelor of Education (Hons) in 1981 and went on to teach in nursery settings, primary mainstream and special schools for over two decades, as a classroom teacher, a subject coordinator (mathematics), a special educational need's coordinator (SENCo) and Senior Leader. In 2003 she gained a position, first as Senior Lecturer, in Enabling Learning for Continuing Professional Development in the Faculty of Education at Canterbury Christ Church University. Over the next decade she became a principal lecturer and then Faculty Director of Special Educational Needs and Inclusion. In 2015 Sue made the decision to focus on research and now works part time at the university, supervising doctoral students. Her doctoral thesis (2013) explored the education provision of looked-after children who had experienced early life abuse and neglect. She is also an educational advisor and panel member for fostering organiations, and undertakes clinical supervision with school leaders. Her research interests include the SENCo role, motor and coordination development, multi-professional working, looked-after children, autism and clinical supervision. As an authority in her field, she has published in peer-reviewed journals and presented her research at national and international conferences. Sue is a trustee of a national SEN organization.

Professor Jeremy J. Monsen is the Principal Educational and Child Psychologist, overseeing the delivery of psychological servcies to children and young people across two London boroughs (Westminster, and Kensington & Chelsea, as part of a bi-borough children's service). Jeremy is currently Visiting Professor at the School of Psychological Sciences and Health, University of Strathclyde, Glasgow. His other affliations include: Lecturer (Honorary) to University College, London, and to the UCL Insitute of Education, UK, and Senior Research Fellow at Canterbury Christ Church University.

1 The Importance of Education

Introduction

We have written this book hoping that what it proposes will generate active debate about whether the current English state education system offers our children and young people the quality, holistic education they will need as they move towards adulthood in what can only be described as a 'troubled world'. Relative economic success and ease of living over the last few decades has perhaps given the majority of the population a false sense of security about how good our national services actually are, including, we suggest, our state school system. When people criticize these services (e.g. the health service, schools, Early Years education and care), the typical response from government is 'we are providing more funding than ever before'. Such an answer is not good enough when it comes to the welfare and education of our future generations. Throwing more and more funding at a broken system is all too frequently just a short-term fix. A long-term, considered and evidence-informed plan to aid transformation is often the answer, but due to our 4-year cycle of politics, such plans are either never proposed, or if considered are not put into action. We argue here that we need to reflect on what can be learnt from the past and how, if we are brave enough, we can liberate education, so that our children and young people experience daily high-quality teaching and learning opportunities that are equitable and inclusive for all.

We do not claim that we have all the answers to such a complex and broad issue, but we do know what it is like to work, day in and day out, in various school- and education-based roles across a period of four decades – 80 years in total! As professionals committed to inclusive and equitable education, we have hoped to see so much more change than we now suspect is possible before we lose the 'right' to be change agents. There are so many 'stories' we could share where a pupil does not receive the teaching and learning environment they need to be successful learners because of the structural barriers, lack of funding and professionals who perhaps are not confident enough to take a stride outside of their usual practice. With every one of these stories our society has failed, and continues to fail, our children and young people in what, arguably, lays the foundations for their futures.

We are not saying that the teachers in our schools today are not passionate about children and their role, or are not excellent, proficient professionals. Most schools now provide good learning environments for pupils, and a flexible, non-prescriptive national curriculum has been beneficial for the majority. But we do feel that on a daily basis teachers' and other educators' ability to fulfil their roles as competently and inclusively as they could is hampered by politically influenced national and local policy, a long-standing lack of commitment to providing professional initial and continuing teacher education, and damaging economic and bureaucratic systems. It is undeniable that schools have become more inclusive, and that in principle teachers and parents/carers support inclusion, but when a school's reputation is on the line or a head-teacher or principal's position is at risk due to poorer than 'required' examination results, then inclusive practice is sidestepped until the risk is avoided. During these times our most vulnerable pupils are still continuing to be failed and excluded from a high-quality education fit for them. There should not be the need for 'additional' or 'different' provision if all pupils are considered an integral part of a school's responsibility and success. With a jointly funded, integrated health, social care and education service for children and young people, and a national inspection system which has at its core priority 'inclusion for all', a more just and equitable state-maintained education system could be within reach – *if* civil society demands it.

We know that to be a teacher you need to have a rich resource of underpinning theory and a wealth of skills and knowledge. A teacher needs to love learning and teaching, and to never lose their curiosity and their ability to explore and delve into new avenues of learning in an attempt to better support a pupil. Without doubt, however, the most important part of the role is to love being with children and young people and to have an unending wish to nurture children's wonder and curiosity as they watch, read or hear something they have never experienced before. Only last week one of the authors stood and smiled as they watched a young child mesmerized looking at raindrops fall into a drain, bouncing up and down on its decorative cover. What a moment to capture and to talk and think about! What a teaching and learning experience – provided by nature.

Despite the many difficulties, we have really valued and never regretted entering the field of education in all its different forms. We feel honoured to have been given the privilege of educating other people's children and young people, and still love entering a classroom full of fun, discussion and wonder.

The book

This is a book of two halves. Chapters 2, 3 and 4 look from the current time to past decades, while Chapters 5, 6 and 7 reflect on the issues the previous chapters have raised and propose new ways of structuring or 'liberating' our state-maintained education system so that it can become as inclusive, equitable and just as possible. We point out many difficulties that have arisen, especially concerning the special educational needs, disabilities and inclusion agendas and evidence why we think they do not work effectively for all pupils. It is important to note that we use the term 'pupil' to describe all children and young people engaged in educational activity when appropriate.

We want this book to be read by new practitioners, 'seasoned' teachers, other educators and the general public. We have therefore tried to make our writing as accessible as possible and have provided referenced evidence to support our thinking and proposals. It would also be great if local and national politicians across the spectrum engaged with our work. Even if our readers disagree with our views and thinking, we hope this book will generate the space for debate and change in inclusion and inclusive education. As Mary Warnock herself said, 'it is well overdue for a radical review' (Warnock and Norwich 2010: 11).

Chapter 2, entitled 'The Journey So Far – A Selective Critical Account of Special Educational Needs Legislation and Guidance in England since the Warnock Committee Report (1978)', provides a critical review and discussion of some of the major educational policies in England since 1978 and their subsequent impact on teaching and learning, and schools. This chapter highlights the driving ideologies, assumptions and inherent contradictions behind successive government reforms, including:

- the libertarian/neoliberal agenda
- marketization of education
- parental choice
- free schools and academies
- the myth of an inclusive society
- the narrow focus on academic attainment
- the impact of austerity
- the SEN/D 'industry'
- the Covid-19 global pandemic.

It also considers the nation's mental health and well-being, as well as wider social capital issues around growing inequalities and the stagnation of social mobility. The chapter concludes by arguing that a change in our state education in England is well overdue.

Chapter 3 is called 'Classroom-Level Inclusive Educational Practice – Quality First Teaching for All Learners' and posits that any reform of the English state education system must avoid the dual traps of reinventing the wheel and the blind adoption of the latest educational fad. We discuss the contributions of past seminal educational thinkers Dewey, Bruner and Vygotsky and encourage reformers to critically reflect on their contributions. This chapter also revisits and reminds people of some of the core educational ideas and approaches their educational thinking shared with us and whether they are relevant for today. It challenges all teachers to reconnect as scientist-reflective practitioners to core pedagogical principles (Kelly and Perkins 2012). This is an approach which emphasizes that all learners need to be thought about holistically, including their culture, background and lived experiences, and the need for more personalized and individualized approaches in an inclusive classroom.

The next chapter, **Chapter 4**, adopts a pragmatic approach and looks critically at why previous attempts at educational reform have largely failed. Drawing on the work of Robinson (and others), we describe an approach we think would be able to embed educational reform and the required crucial change.

Chapter 5 is the first chapter of the 'second' part of this book. It turns our readers' attention to the current time and the future. It asks the question whether inclusion and an inclusive system is actually possible in our current system, and if it is actually still desired as a strategic and aspirational goal. The existing inequalities still experienced in our SEND system are discussed next, asking the question, 'Is a perfect storm in waiting?' The importance of parental/carer engagement and the difficulties associated with trying to negotiate the SEND bureaucracy are also explored, before tackling the problematic issue of 'labelling'. Of course, pragmatically a label can gain extra support or provision for a pupil, but other implications are voiced. Having considered the role of parents/carers, attention is turned to the professionalization of teachers, and the disparate education provision available in England today. Finally, readers are challenged to ask themselves the question (and read our thoughts) about what the real purpose of education in twenty-first-century England could or should be.

The next chapter, **Chapter 6**, focuses on what, we strongly suggest, is the central core to a successful education for each and every pupil – the teacher. We ask questions such as who becomes a teacher and why do they make this career choice. We tackle the question about whether teaching is a profession, a semi-profession, a vocation or even a craft, which leads us to critically reflect on the current initial and continuing teaching education programmes available. Of course, the subject of retention and the employment of other practitioners in schools is also debated. This chapter aims to provide readers with a vision for the reinvigoration of the teacher's role and identity in a time when pupils need skills which will enable them to be flexible, critical, creative and also conservationists; to be able to succeed, to be future thinkers able to design, participate and be happy in a world where employment markets are as yet unknown. Here it is proposed that teachers will need to be able to facilitate the progressive development of learning through exploration, problem-solving and effective communication and debate, alongside a blended approach to knowledge acquisition. We consider that in order to fulfil these challenges teachers will need to be recognized as skilled professionals or craftspeople, and supported to follow through changes as society requires, free from constant policy and political change.

Chapter 7, the final chapter, attempts to draw together the significant issues and discussions raised throughout the book, which we consider are core to a truly holistic, fluid and flexible high-quality education system fit for all pupils in the twenty-first century. It suggests that there is a need for a national collective curriculum which every pupil is required to be taught, including in academies and independent/public schools. It confronts the subject of affordability, of the hindrance of our nation's party politics on education policy and change and asks whether society does want inclusion. It explicitly says that the separate SEND system should end. In order for this to be a viable option the routes into and throughout a career in teaching are debated further. Critically, a plan for enabling the embedding of partnership working throughout our services (or service) is proposed. Robust and consistent collaborative working has, up to this current time, been mostly unachievable and so we suggest it is another core element to the successful liberation of our education (and other child and young people's) services. The curriculum has not been overlooked, with suggestions which make purposeful use of technological advances in creating new opportunities and experiences.

We felt that it was important to provide a possible 'starting' point for collective discussion, and so on the final pages of the book there is an outline of *'Six Principles for an equitable and inclusive education system: Respectful of all; responsible for all'*. Then to complete our book we offer a visual presentation of potential enforcers of inclusion in a liberated English state education system able to meet parents'/carers' expectations.

Remember: As a teacher you have the ability to make or break a child with just one word. Use your precious position wisely.

2 The Journey So Far – A Selective Critical Account of Special Educational Needs Legislation and Guidance in England since the Warnock Committee Report (1978)

Introduction

This chapter presents some of the key special educational needs and disabilities legislation and associated guidance produced in England since the 1978 Warnock Committee report (Warnock 1978; Education Act 1981). It begins with the ground-breaking and hugely influential Warnock Committee report (Warnock 1978; Frederickson and Cline 2010; Lindsay et al. 2020; Waters and Brighouse 2021) and the resultant 1981 Education Act (Education Act 1981). It then outlines the subsequent main iterations (Education Act 1993; Code of Practice 1994; DfE 1994; DfES 2001; Special Educational Needs and Disability Act 2001; Children and Families Act 2014) and the associated Special Educational Needs Code of Practice (DfE and DoH 2015) and the *SEND Review: Right Support, Right Place, Right Time* (Green Paper) (HM Government 2022). The Green Paper does not, as some people had hoped for, represent a radical departure from the previous legislation but merely refines it around certain key areas – creating greater efficiency in the use of funds and staff, accountability and increasing workforce skills and competences.

The discussion highlights some of the main features, constraints and paradoxes that have emerged from these various reforms, as well as other factors that have influenced the direction of educational thinking and practice – including the confusion over what exactly 'inclusion' means, the national curriculum with its narrow focus on academic attainment, and the impact of a market ideology being applied to the state education sector.

The conclusion reached is that after nearly 45 years since the original Warnock Committee report (1978) it is now time to abandon the use of terms such as SEND and 'the SEN pupil' altogether, certainly in educational contexts. It is argued that it is now time to refocus policymakers', school leaders' and teachers' efforts on the classroom and school level, and on the needs of all learners, irrespective of their differences and uniquenesses.

For historical accuracy, the now problematic and discriminatory tone and language sometimes used in the original documents is referred to in this chapter. In no way do we support their contemporary usage.

The start of a new way of thinking about learning needs and individual difference – the Warnock Committee report 1978

Since at least the early 1960s in the United Kingdom (UK), as in other parts of the world, there had been a growing dissatisfaction with how children and young people with learning needs were being identified and supported, both in mainstream and special schools (Frederickson and Cline 2015; Capper 2020; Lindsay et al. 2020; Waters and Brighouse 2021). This dissatisfaction culminated in the UK with the commissioning by central government in 1974 of Lady Warnock and her committee to undertake one of the most comprehensive critical appraisals ever seen of the efficacy of educational provision for 'handicapped' children (Warnock 1978; Warnock and Norwich 2010; Frederickson and Cline 2015; Lindsay et al. 2020). The final Warnock Committee report (Warnock 1978) can be seen to represent a seismic conceptual shift in how children and young people with learning differences and other needs were perceived, assessed, understood, interacted with and worked with in an increasingly diverse society.

The term 'handicapped child' was replaced by 'children with learning difficulties' who present with 'special educational needs' (SEN). This move away from a diagnostic and medicalized model of individual difference in schools to a more functional description of need embedded in a teaching–learning framework was subsequently given legal status in the 1981 Education Act (Education Act 1981). Despite the intentions to move away from stigmatizing labels, a range of new terms were introduced ('emotional and behavioural disorders', 'learning difficulties: specific, mild, moderate and severe', 'speech and language disorders' and 'visual disability and hearing disability') (Norwich 2019a; Lindsay et al. 2020).

The descriptive term special educational needs (SEN) could be applied to *any* child or young person requiring additional or different teaching–learning approaches and support in mainstream classrooms, and at any point in their educational journey. The Warnock Committee (Warnock 1978) introduced for the first time the notion that in the mainstream state-maintained educational system at any one time about 20 per cent of all pupils presented with some form of 'special need', which changed over time in response to teaching and learning interventions and the pupils' maturation. Of this heterogeneous grouping, only about 1–2 per cent would present with needs that were so complex, long-term and severe that they would require specialist provision, and (after the 1981 Education Act) a formal Statement of SEN to legally protect such provision (Warnock 1978). Unfortunately, the 1981 Education Act had very little to say about the 18 per cent whose needs were less severe but still required purposeful support as part of regular, sound classroom teaching–learning practice (much later referred to as Quality First Teaching (DCSF 2008; Whittaker and Hayes 2019).

The Warnock Committee (Warnock 1978) advocated a more nuanced approach with a 'continuum of provision' model from the least to most restrictive and disenabling learning environments, irrespective of locational type – mainstream, unit or special school. Their view was that 'segregated' (given the term's negative connotation, the use of 'separate' was eventually adopted) special schools were for those pupils with the most complex, long-term and severe needs, requiring regular specialist multi-practitioner input (Warnock and Norwich 2010; Frederickson and Cline 2015; Capper 2020; Lindsay et al. 2020).

The Warnock Committee (Warnock 1978) proposed three pathways for the integration (given the term's negative connotation, this evolved into 'inclusion') of pupils with SEN and disabilities into mainstream schools – **locational**, **social** and **functional** inclusion. It offered the following criteria to inform local education authority (LEA) decision-making – parents and carers needed to be supportive of the proposed placement; the pupil's learning needs could be met in a mainstream educational setting; the LEA was using its financial and other resources efficiently; and the education of other pupils would not be adversely affected.

The Warnock Committee (Warnock 1978) recommended that mainstream schools were able to readily access external specialists to facilitate the integration/inclusion of pupils presenting with learning and other needs. Such external support was seen as being vital to the implementation of an inclusive approach (Monsen and Frederickson 2004; Monsen et al. 2014; Frederickson and Cline 2015; Lindsay et al. 2020). This included practitioners like specialist teachers (STs), educational psychologists (EPs) and school advisors, all employed directly by the LEA. The importance of teacher pre-training and continuing professional development (CPD) was stressed in the report.

A staged multidisciplinary approach to the identification and assessment of pupils with special needs was advocated, rather than focusing solely on within-child diagnostic or medical labels (F. Armstrong 2007; Armstrong et al. 2011). Such an approach involves drawing on multiple practitioner and parent/carer perspectives to clarify, define and analyse an individual's unique set of needs – the aim being to reach a more functional understanding of a child or young person's needs, with a focus on solutions in complex situations like home and school. For the first time there was acknowledgement of the vital role played by the quality of the teaching and learning experiences offered by teachers, settings and schools.

Such positions enabled the beginnings of a radical conceptual shift which sees learning for *all* pupils as being an interactive and social activity with needs changing over time in response to appropriate quality teaching, and for the vast majority of learners this could be achieved in mainstream school settings (Booth and Ainscow 2011; Norwich 2019a; Lindsay et al. 2020). This view challenged the assumption that a medical or similar 'diagnosis' was sufficient in and of itself to identify a pupil's unique needs, and that the default position was usually then separate special educational provision and support.

The 1981 Education Act (Education Act 1981) saw many of the Warnock Committee report's (Warnock 1978) core recommendations put into a legislative framework. The report has been hugely influential for future SEN policies right up to the present day, not only in the UK but around the world (McKinlay 1996). The 1981 Education Act, although espousing a move away from medicalized categories of pupil need to a position that embraced the truly interactive social and systemic nature of learning differences, still can be seen to have adopted the language of deficit (Bines 2000; Warnock and Norwich 2010; Norwich 2019a). The subsequent tendency to label pupil needs under a single broad category ultimately led to a lack of specificity around how best to meet pupils' individual needs (Warnock and Norwich 2010; Capper 2020).

Rather disappointingly, the 1981 Education Act made it clear that no additional new funding would be put into the education system to support its implementation (Barton 1988). This has been a common theme right up to the present day (Barton 1988; Norwich 2019a; Lindsay et al. 2020).

There was no additional funding provided for teacher training either, a key component in any organizational reform on this scale (Monsen and Frederickson 2004; Monsen et al. 2014). This meant that although the ideas underpinning the 1981 Education Act were innovative and inclusive in intent, many teachers did not fully understand the concepts or how to operationalize them in their classrooms. Without such insight and the additional easy access to external specialist support, some teachers found it a challenge to create learning environments that catered for a wider range of pupil needs than they were perhaps previously used to. Some mistakenly assumed that inclusion simply meant treating everyone the same (equality) rather than each according to need (equity) (Monsen and Frederickson 2004; Monsen et al. 2014).

As a result, some teachers continued to hold on to, seemingly for them, more comprehensible medical models for understanding their pupils' differences and needs. The staged model of assessment over time evolved into a focus on pupil failure rather than success, as schools needed to evidence that the pupil had not responded to interventions they had put in place before they could apply for a statutory assessment and the promise of additional funding from the LEA (Frederickson and Cline 2015; Lindsay et al. 2020).

The first major iteration: the 1993 Education Act and the subsequent 1994 SEN Code of Practice (DfE 1994)

The 1993 Education Act signalled central government's intention to develop an SEN Code of Practice (CoP). This provided LEAs with specific guidance on what their roles, duties and responsibilities were towards children and young people with SEN, their families and schools (DfE 1994). It included sections describing identification, assessment and support, as well as what the rights of parents, carers and their children were with regard to the SEN process (DfE 1994).

For the first time the needs of the 18 per cent were explicitly acknowledged and described in a graduated five-stage model.

Stage 1 – A parent, carer, outside agency (health or social services) and/or the class teacher may have noticed that a particular pupil was finding some aspect of their learning or wider development more challenging than expected. Following joint discussions to clarify initial concerns, the pupil was placed on an SEN register and received slightly modified support in the classroom (an example being a primary-aged child who finds it difficult to get started on tasks or complete classwork to the standard expected and is acting out). They were given more directive initial verbal prompts from the teacher (the teacher checked that the demands of the task were at the child's level, task requirements were simplified and repeated) and perhaps a sand timer would be used to help the child visualize the time they had left. The teacher followed up with specific praise, rewards and informal monitoring.

Stage 2 – Following informal reviews, if insufficient progress was being made, the teacher informed the special educational needs coordinator (SENCo) and an Individual Education Plan (IEP) was drawn up. This detailed the one or two priority targets for the pupil, the approaches to be adopted, how the teacher (or others) would undertake any alternative input and how progress would be monitored more formally. Targets were framed in a SMART manner (Specific, Measurable, Achievable, Realistic and Time-bound) (Doran 1981).

Stage 3 – Following a formal review, if there was still a lack of progress the SENCo would inform the LEA and they would consult external support services (e.g. specialist teachers (STs), educational psychologist (EP), speech and language therapist (SALT) and/or occupational therapist (OT)). External practitioners, depending on need, would work with the class teacher/SENCo to establish a clearer baseline, clarify what could be contributing to the observed difficulties, and review and revise the IEP, including suggesting revised targets, strategies and approaches. Parents and carers would be involved.

Stage 4 – Following a formal review of progress, if the concerns continued, the pupil was then considered for a statutory formal assessment, which the LEA oversaw and carried out, if the evidence suggested that the child or young person might require a Statement of SEN.

Stage 5 – Following the statutory formal assessment the LEA would review the evidence collected from the various advice givers (medical, specialist teacher, educational psychologist, speech and language and occupational therapists, as required, including school and parental views and perspectives) and may as a result determine the type and degree of special educational provision the pupil required. A Statement of special educational needs was formulated detailing needs, severity and type of provision.

Table 2.1 A summary of the SEN terminology used in the 1994 (DfE), 2001 (DfES) and 2015 (DfE and DoH) Codes of Practice (adapted from Capper 2020: 30)

1994 Code of Practice (DfE 1994); Education Act 1993	2001 Code of Practice (DfES 2001); Education Act 1996 and SEN and Disability Act 2001	2015 Code of Practice (DfE and DoH 2015); Children and Families Act 2014
1 Emotional and behavioural difficulties 2 Learning difficulties Specific learning difficulties (dyslexia) 3 Medical conditions 4 Physical disabilities Sensory impairments (hearing or vision) 5 Speech and language difficulties	1 Cognition and learning behaviour 2 Communication and interaction 3 Emotional and social development 4 Sensory and/or physical Disability is officially included in the new title SEN and D	1 Cognition and learning 2 Communication and interaction 3 Sensory and/or physical 4 Social, emotional and mental health difficulties

The legislation and Code of Practice appeared around the same time as the United Nations Educational, Science and Cultural Organization (UNESCO) World Conference on Special Needs Education, referred to as the Salamanca Statement (UNESCO 1994) which the UK government fully committed to. The Salamanca Statement is arguably one of the most significant international documents that has ever appeared in the field of special educational needs (Ainscow and César 2006; Frederickson and Cline 2015; Ainscow et al. 2019; Lindsay et al. 2020). It called on all national governments to 'adopt as a matter of law or policy the principle of inclusive education, enrolling all children in regular schools, unless there are compelling reasons for doing otherwise' (UNESCO 1994: ix).

At its core the statement challenges the prevailing view that it was the pupil who needed to change to fit into a mainstream school. The focus and emphasis shifted to a critical look at the school/classroom environment and the teaching approaches used, and how these needed to alter so that pupils could fully access an appropriate curriculum for them (Armstrong et al. 2011). The 1994 CoP (DfE 1994) can be seen to reflect the spirit and intent of the Salamanca Statement.

The CoP (DfE 1994) restates the position first outlined in the Warnock Committee report (1978) that a pupil's needs arise from a complex interaction between within-person aspects (biological, cognitive, affective, behavioural) and environmental factors (early life and intervention experiences, level of home support, quality of teaching–learning). The guidance points out that some pupil needs may become more or less severe over the course of their education as a result of the quality of teaching–learning provisions made for them.

The 1994 CoP (DfE 1994) and its subsequent iterations (DfES 2001; DfE and DoH 2015) adapt the original Warnock SEN category labels to better reflect changing attitudes and expectations (see Table 2.1). Lehane (2017) states that the 1994 CoP is seen as being the most accessible of all the iterations so far produced, including the 2015 CoP (DfE and DoH 2015). Whether this subsequent lack of specificity was a deliberate strategy is hard to know. What is known is that the clear and comprehensive guidance on procedures, processes and practical recommendations did enable LEA officers, schools and practitioners to operationalize it, and know what they and others had to do, how they could go about doing it, who was responsible for what, and what outcomes were expected. This clarity has since been watered down to the present.

The 1994 CoP (DfE 1994) stressed the pre-eminent role that mainstream schools have in educating the vast majority of pupils with SEN. Although the option of segregated or separate specialist placements was seen as being part of a 'continuum of provision', it was seen as only being appropriate for those whose needs were complex, severe, multifaceted and long term (Lindsay 2003).

Another important aspect of the 1993 Education Act was the establishment of a parallel and separate Special Educational Needs and Disability Tribunal (SENDIST) (Education Act 1993; Runswick-Cole 2007), which is still in operation today. It is an independent tribunal organization that is responsible for handling appeals by parents and carers against local (education) authority decisions regarding their child's special educational needs and/or disabilities.

The only observation to be made here is that for an SEN system that aspires to be inclusive, collaborative and child centred the SENDIST has become bureaucratic, legalistic, expensive (for both parents/carers and local authorities) and adversarial, pitting parents, carers, children and young people against the local authority (LA) in the pursuit of 'justice' in a diminishing environment of support. The current Green Paper (HM Government 2022) proposes that mediation between parents, carers and the LA before a tribunal is now mandatory not optional. But no thought has been given to completely rethinking the whole basis of adopting such an adversarial legalistic model to resolve differences in perceptions around how children and young people's learning needs are met. Adapting more consensus-based models, such as the New Zealand/Aotearoa 'family group conference', might provide a refreshing alternative (Ministry for Children 2017).

The second major iteration – 2001 SEN Code of Practice

The 2001 CoP (DfES 2001) represents the second major iteration of the evolving SEN process. This time the policy made much stronger links between SEN and disability, with reference to the 2001 SEN and Disability Act (Special Educational Needs and Disability Act 2001). In popular usage increasingly the acronym SEN was changed to 'SEN and disability', but the two labels remain separate entities in the document, and not clearly defined.

The 2001 CoP (DfES 2001) further supports the philosophy of inclusive teaching practice. Children and young people with SEN were seen as having a right to be included and educated in the mainstream education system along with their typically developing peers (Lehane 2017). Conversations around inclusion as an educational strategy were not new, but the emphasis placed on changing schools' organizational cultures was (Lindsay 2003; Capper 2020). It was the school as an organization that was increasingly expected to meet the needs of all of its pupils, including those with SEN and other barriers to their learning and wider development (Bines 2000).

The ongoing challenge was seeing organizational change, with reference to SEN, as being much more than piling on additional 'special' programmes, and/or increasing one-to-one support, often delivered by teaching assistants (sometimes also referred to as learning support assistants) rather than looking fundamentally at what the teaching–learning relationship was all about in an inclusive classroom and school (Frederickson and Cline 2015; Clarke and Visser 2019; Webster and Blatchford 2019).

Yet, for what can be seen to be wider political and pragmatic reasons, even though inclusion is seen as being championed, the 2001 CoP (DfES 2001) retained the right for mainstream schools to 'refuse' a pupil with SEN if they judged their attendance to be 'incompatible with the efficient education of other children' (Department for Education and Skills 2001: 14; D. Armstrong 2005). Wording it in this way makes it almost impossible to quantify in any meaningful sense what is being said. It only served to water down the challenge inherent in the original Warnock Committee report (Warnock 1978; Warnock and Norwich 2010) and the Salamanca Statement (UNESCO 1994; Capper 2020).

Children and young people's needs were now described under four primary categories – behaviour, emotional and social development (BESD); cognition and learning; communication and interaction; and physical or sensory impairment. Although no longer seen as being necessary, many schools continued to record pupils on an SEN register for administrative and accountability purposes. The previous CoP's Stages 2 and 3 became **School-Action** and **School-Action-Plus**:

- **School-Action** – The class teacher, in consultation with the child or young person (as appropriate), parents, carers and SENCo, decided to place the pupil on this level if they were seen as not making adequate progress, and as requiring input which is additional to, or different from, that provided in a differentiated mainstream classroom/curriculum. There was the option of devising a Group IEP if a small teaching group of pupils with similar needs was identified. Again, aims were framed using SMART targets.
- **School-Action-Plus** – Following monitoring and review, the child or young person could be moved to the next level if their progress was still inadequate. The school might wish to consult with external agencies like EPs for guidance and support. Again, aims were framed using SMART targets.

The final two stages of the statutory formal assessment and Statementing process remained unchanged.

14 Inclusive Education Theory and Policy

Table 2.2 Summary of key policy initiatives leading up to the 2014 Children and Families Act and subsequent 2015 SEND Code of Practice (adapted from Capper 2020: 2)

Key documents	Warnock report (Warnock 1978) and 1981 Education Act	1993 Education Act and 1994 Code of Practice (DfE 1994)	2001 SEN and Disability Act and 2001 Code of Practice (DfES 2001)
Core features	• For the first time special educational needs (SEN) and special educational provision introduced. • An appeals process for parents and carers set up. • Annual review process set up. • Statements of SEN with legal protection introduced.	• Now a legal requirement for government to produce a 'code of practice' to guide LEAs and educational settings. • 'Tribunals' used as the formal terminology for the appeals process. • The 1994 Code recognized key SEN categories for identifying pupil need. • Implementation of a five-stage graduated approach to assessment/intervention.	• Disability policy was introduced into SEN policy. • SEN categories of need were reduced to four and SEN graduated assessment stages were reduced to 'School-Action' and 'School-Action-Plus'
Position on inclusion	• The Warnock report (Warnock 1978) adopted a position that while special schools have a place in supporting SEN, they are primarily for pupils who could not have their needs met easily in a mainstream school. • The 1981 Education Act stressed that placement in 'ordinary school' was encouraged, so long as it demonstrated the efficient use of resources and effective provision was provided.	• This policy was developed with reference to the Salamanca Statement (UNESCO 1994) which promoted mainstream over specialist placement. • The Code reports that most pupil SEN will be met in mainstream settings, with special schools again viewed as a final option of support.	• The Code espoused that it promoted stronger rights for pupils to be educated in mainstream schools and settings.

(continued)

Table 2.2 (Continued)

Key documents	Warnock report (Warnock 1978) and 1981 Education Act	1993 Education Act and 1994 Code of Practice (DfE 1994)	2001 SEN and Disability Act and 2001 Code of Practice (DfES 2001)
Parent, carer and children/ young person rights	• Parents and carers were given the right to review draft versions of Statements to ensure they were accurate, and to appeal decisions they may be unhappy with to do with the assessment process. • Pupil views or rights are not detailed or specified.	• Parents' and carers' rights remained largely consistent in the new Code and Act. • The Code was developed following the publishing of the United Nations Convention on the Rights of the Child (UNGA 1989). • The new Code detailed that in the statutory assessment, some local authorities would want to establish the views of pupils and these were placed in an appendix of the statement.	• LEAs were required to provide services to parents and carers which supported and informed them of SEN processes and dispute resolution. Schools were required to inform parents and carers when they were making SEN provision for their child. • 'Pupil participation' was given its own section. Pupils, where possible, were to be involved in decision-making processes and feel valued. All professionals should seek to ascertain pupils' views in their assessments (EPs). These views remained in the appendices.
Some reported positives	• Warnock (2005) reflected on this policy as a driver in the process of removing the labelling and stigma previously associated with SEN and disability.	• Bines (2000) recognized that this code promoted the development of whole-school SEN policy. • Lehane (2017) praised the accessible nature of the 1994 CoP which used language commonly adopted in schools, making it easy to read and follow.	• Bines (2000) suggested this Code aimed to promote greater school responsibility for supporting pupils with SEN and aimed to reduce the number of Statements of SEN produced.

(continued)

16 Inclusive Education Theory and Policy

Table 2.2 (Continued)

Key documents	Warnock report (Warnock 1978) and 1981 Education Act	1993 Education Act and 1994 Code of Practice (DfE 1994)	2001 SEN and Disability Act and 2001 Code of Practice (DfES 2001)
Some reported concerns	• Barton (1988) criticized the policy changes for coming with no additional funding to support schools to implement it. • Powell and Booker (1987) criticized the continued 'within-child' focus adopted in the policy, alongside the absence of considerations such as the pupil's home/community in the Statement of SEN, the difficulty arising in distinguishing between needs and provision, and the absence of strengths in the assessment process.	• The policy was seen to be in direct conflict with the education market forces culture of the time (MacBeath et al. 2006). • The introduction of the national curriculum directly conflicted with the Code's promotion of personalization (Armstrong 2005). • A report by the Education and Skills Committee (2007) criticized the responsibility placed on LEA SEN services regarding funding, leading to poor internal support for pupils with SEN.	• Armstrong (2005) suggested the Code's promotion of pupil voice provided a mechanism for controlling troublesome perspectives and was largely tokenistic in nature. • This assertion was supported by the Lamb Inquiry (2009) which conducted a comprehensive review of SEN practices. It found that statutory processes were notably stressful for parents and carers due to poor support and information. Statements of SEN were seen to be lacking and vague, supported by papers such as Cameron and Monsen (2005) and Warnock (2005). The enquiry also criticized the broad nature of outcomes in the statements. • Despite previous intentions to reduce the overidentification of SEN in pupils, numbers continued to rise (Norwich and Eaton 2015).

The case for further change

Table 2.2 describes the period between the Warnock Committee report (1978) and the 2015 Code of Practice (CoP) (DfE and DoH 2015) and how understandings of SEN, disability, inclusion and the rights of parents, carers and children and young people have evolved (Capper 2020). The policy changes can be seen to have aimed at supporting a more responsive and effective state-maintained system for the identification, assessment and provision of 'SEND pupils', largely but not exclusively in mainstream classrooms.

Such policy changes can be seen to have given much greater prominence to the 'rights' of parents, carers and children and young people as 'consumers', certainly at an espoused level. But never was there any discussion or balance between the mutual rights of parents and carers on the one hand, their school, and LA partners on the other and their shared obligations to each other. Such a discussion would have modelled a far more inclusive, collaborative and consensual approach.

The local education authorities (LEAs), now referred to as local authorities (LAs), were given much greater responsibility, and therefore legal accountability, to make sure SEND support happened. This effectively provided central government with an organizational buffer defending against any direct criticism or comeback from parents and carers and other lobbying groups (Capper 2020; Waters and Brighouse 2021).

With the development of the free schools and academies movement starting in 2010 (Academies Act 2010; Education Act 2011) (and later multi-academy trusts (Baxter and Floyd 2019), although technically state-funded these schools are out of the direct control of the LA, making its very important advocacy, advisory, monitory and challenge roles much more complicated and problematic to achieve. These policy changes occurred during a period of financial austerity, with significant budget cuts right across the public sector, making effective implementation and the embedding of inclusive understanding and practice very challenging (MacBeath et al. 2006; Frederickson and Cline 2015).

There had been a growing dissatisfaction with SEND policy and practice from about the second iteration period onwards around the rights of parents, carers and children and young people (Lamb 2009). Parents and carers increasingly reported that they were not aware of their rights and were confused because of the complexities of the SEN processes and procedures (Lamb 2009). These perceptions were set against the incompatible agendas of school performance league tables and the ethos of personalized and individualized teaching and learning. These factors combined, along with financial cuts, to lead to incoherent provision being offered to pupils with SEN (Bines 2000; MacBeath et al. 2006; Frederickson and Cline 2015).

There was the view that Statements of SEN were not fit for purpose and had often become a bureaucratic gatekeeping device, producing vague descriptions of pupil needs and generalized outcomes. The default top-up provision was a currency of teaching assistant hours that schools used to 'fit' the pupil identified with SEN into their existing systems (Cameron and Monsen 2005; Warnock and Norwich 2010; Capper 2020). The ambition of a holistic appraisal of a pupil's SEN needs, based on a careful multi-practitioner analysis, and leading to a clear formulation, personalized aims and targeted provision just did not really occur in practice (Cameron and Monsen 2005).

Looking back, SEND policy and practice, apart from slight changes in category names and the tweaking of procedures, largely remained unaltered between 2001 and 2014. Although there were several reviews undertaken and policies focusing on education and equality. In 2003 the then New Labour government published *Every Child Matters* (HM Treasury 2003), which emphasized that every child and young person had the right to reach their potential (though this was never clearly defined). There was an explicit commitment to improve communication with parents and carers, encourage multidisciplinary working and the sharing of information, and an acknowledgement that SEN support varied depending on where you lived in the country (Capper 2020).

The *Every Child Matters* report led to the restructuring of LAs to create children's services which would retain key support teams centrally (specialist teachers, EPs and advisors, as examples). The idea behind this was that it would encourage greater integrated working and economies of scale (HM Treasury 2003; Woods and Farrell 2006). Hodkinson and Burch (2019) expressed the view that in reality such policies were just incompatible with the wider schools standards agenda and the growing 'market' model of service delivery. (For example, a scarce specialist resource like educational psychologists were finding themselves in the situation of having to 'trade' to schools who may or may not buy them in. Such a market model reduced further the notion of ready access, impartial advocacy, monitoring and appropriate challenge to ensure that the children and young people in most need were identified equitably, and appropriate and proportionate provision made for them. We refer to this rather facetiously as the 'playing corner shops model' of public sector specialist service delivery!)

In 2011 the publication *Support and Aspiration: A New Approach to Special Educational Needs and Disability* was launched by the then Conservative–Liberal Democrat coalition government (DfE 2011). This report detailed a list of concerns around how current SEN policy and practice was being implemented. The emphasis was on its 'consumers', namely parents and carers, who were reported to find the SEN system 'bureaucratic, bewildering and adversarial' (DfE 2011: 4). Pupil needs were in some cases identified late, and SEN continued to be overidentified by schools (Warnock and Norwich 2010; Capper 2020). There is an irony here as it had been inconsistent and often incompatible central government policies that had contributed to these various dilemmas (Tomlinson 2012, 2017; Naraian 2021; Hallett 2022).

Table 2.3 A summary of the key changes made in the 2015 Code of Practice (DfE and DoH 2015) (adapted from Capper 2020: 6)

General changes

- Statutory support now covers the age range 0–25 years. This includes specific guidance relating to disabled children and young people and those with SEND.
- There is an expectation that parents, carers and children and young people should be included in strategic and individual decision-making processes.
- The need for all local authorities to develop a 'local offer' to provide clearer information for parents, carers and children and young people about what SEND provision is available in LAs across education, health and social care sectors.
- A re-emphasis of the graduated approach to identifying and supporting children and young people with SEND, using 'Assess, Plan, Do, Review' and categorizing as either 'SEN Support' or in receipt of an EHC plan (this replaces the previous 'School-Action' and 'School-Action-Plus').
- Classroom and subject teachers are given the core responsibility of identifying and supporting pupils making less than expected progress.

Changes to the statutory assessment process

- Education Health and Care plans replace Statements of SEN and promote collaboration between education, health and social care services.
- Children and young people's views and aspirations are specifically included in Section A of the EHC plan and the strengths of each pupil are included in the assessment outcomes.
- Statutory assessments and EHC plans focus on producing SMART outcomes for children and young people (specific, measurable, achievable, realistic and time-limited).
- An emphasis is placed on preparing children and young people for post-16 education and/or employment, independent living, participation in society and leading a healthy adult lifestyle.
- There is the introduction of 'personal budgets', allowing parents, carers or children and young people to secure their own provision as part of the EHC plan.
- Behaviour is no longer recognized as a SEND category. Instead it is replaced by the term 'social, emotional, mental health'.

The third major iteration – the 2014 Children and Families Act and the 2015 Code of Practice (DfE and DoH 2015)

The 2014 Children and Families Act introduced far-reaching reforms, including a focus on family justice, child welfare and safeguarding. In Section 3 of the Act a new method of describing and detailing the support that pupils with SEND would receive now included the active involvement of health and social care departments, along with education, which can still be seen to hold a first amongst equals position. This resulted in the cessation of the Statementing process and the commencement of a statutory education, health and care assessment process which may result in an Education, Health and Care (EHC) plan (DfE and DoH 2015). Table 2.3 provides a summary of the key changes and practices in the 2015 CoP.

To address the perception that there was an inequality of provision depending on where a pupil and their family lived, the Code of Practice replaced the four-stage graduated response in the previous code with just two levels of support – **SEN Support level** which is school-based, and the **EHC plan statutory assessment process** which is overseen by the LA (Hodkinson 2019).

SEN Support level

The SEN Support Level reflects the new graduated approach that all nurseries, schools and post-16 settings were required to use to structure their thinking and practice around the identification and assessment of the needs of children and young people. Under this umbrella, schools were asked to adopt a four-stage action 'cycle' of **Assess**, **Plan**, **Do** and **Review** (as we will see in Chapter 3, we advocate adding the need to **Reflect** in this cycle). At any point in the cycle schools can consult with external specialists for advice and guidance. The views of specialist teachers, EPs, SALTs and/or OTs can then be factored into the thinking about pupil needs and their management. But in an increasingly market-driven model, schools were required to buy in such support if they could procure it. Specialist staff morale, retention and recruitment were and are becoming increasing constraints.

It is important to highlight that some pupils presenting with more complex needs may require more than one cycle operating at any given time, each targeting specific areas that are seen as requiring a more detailed analysis and action (attention, concentration and focus; self-regulation of emotions and behaviour; social-communication skills; literacy). Interventions are monitored and reviewed, and adjustments made, and the cycles continue until identified issues are more under control – the aim being that such a structure will enable more focused and effective interventions to occur.

Assess – The class or subject teacher, in consultation with parents, carers and pupil (as appropriate), and the SENCo, clarifies the pupil's presenting priority need(s) and establishes a baseline unique to that individual so that their progress can be clearly measured. This reflects elements of person-centred planning as progress over time is not measured against external normative scores but that individual's progress against clear functional criteria. (For example, baseline assessment established that Ruby's reading self-correction rate and comprehension was zero. For more social-emotional concerns proxy indicators can be used. Ahmed, a 15-year-old male, has been a school refuser due to anxiety issues. The school set up a phased return programme using teacher and peer mentoring, and used percentage attendance at targeted lessons as an indicator of success, along with self-report.)

Plan – Following clarification of priority needs and baseline assessment, a working **provision plan** of additional support is mapped out for the pupil. This is formally recorded, and parents, carers and pupil (where relevant) are actively involved. The plan details what the school, parents, carers and pupil agree is reasonable progress, given the pupil's needs and baseline assessment starting point. These are again framed as SMART outcomes and a review date provided (e.g. by Week 8 Ruby will be able to self-correct a third of all her reading errors and be able to correctly answer 50 per cent of comprehension questions about what she has read, on material which is at her current level).

Do – This is the action stage, when the intervention plan is put into practice. The detail of who does what, when, how and why are recorded. The class or subject teacher and SENCo are responsible for making sure things occur. Given Ruby's literacy needs it was decided that during the first eight-week cycle of intervention, using the Pause, Prompt and Praise Programme (i.e. Wheldall et al. 1987) daily for ten minutes, the goal would be to achieve a self-correction rate of one in three words and 50 per cent comprehension accuracy level. Ruby's regular class literacy programme would aim to support generalization of new skills.

Review – The 2015 Code of Practice (DfE and DoH 2015) is rather vague as to specific guidance on the frequency of formal reviews. The CoP does say that parents and carers should be consulted *at least three times per year*, so a termly formal review does not seem unreasonable. Clearly, the school will be holding more informal monitoring reviews to make sure intervention plans are progressing as intended and problem-solving any issues that arise.

The expectation would be that a school would actively seek the advice and guidance of external specialists, like EPs, when a pupil has made little or no progress despite several intervention cycles, and/or their functional core learning skills are significantly below that of other typically developing peers. Such support would usually involve a fine-tuned analysis of the pupil's needs and a reframing of expectations, demands and approaches. Progress is defined with reference to the pupil themselves, not to their peers. Some pupils may never reach age-appropriate levels of literacy, for example. But they can reach a level that enables them to function as independently as they can (learning to recognize 'signs' so they can travel on public transport unaided, following a simple coloured route map after practice).

Request for an EHC plan statutory assessment

Following a number of SEN Level Support cycles, school staff, with parent/carer involvement, may conclude that the current level of provision and the services that are normally available in mainstream schools are not sufficient to enable a pupil to access an appropriate curriculum for them. At such a point the school and/or parents/carers can request from the LA an EHC needs assessment, to find out whether an EHC plan is indeed required.

The request will include evidence of the cycles of graduated responses experienced and will provide evidence (aims, goals, baseline, measures of progress and outcomes) detailing the support that was put in place (provision plan) which is seen as not being powerful enough. There might be an indication of the additional components that people feel are now required.

A formal diagnosis or any other health or social care need will not necessarily mean that an EHC assessment or EHC plan is actually required. A request for an EHC needs assessment is relevant when a pupil's needs are *significantly* impacting on their ability to access an appropriate education (for them) despite the support being delivered by the setting or school's SEN Support level.

The 2015 CoP (DfE and DoH 2015) introduced for the first time a code that clarifies a SEND need with reference to what is required, as well as what is available. Assessment in its broadest sense is based on an appraisal of a pupil's strengths, interests, hobbies, and what they like as well as their special and additional needs. This can be seen as a symbolic, but perhaps not a meaningful, way of placing the child or young person at the centre of a bureaucratic process (Hellawell 2018).

In the 2015 CoP (DfE and DoH 2015) there is an explicit expectation that all of those involved will work fully with parents, carers, children and young people as partners in the decision-making processes (both at the individual and strategic levels: emphasizing the 'co-production' model, which is not clearly defined nor operationalized – does it mean collaboration, and if so for what and how?). For the first time there is an explicit commitment that children and young people must be formally involved in the statutory assessment process, with their views (framed as 'aspirations') being seen as central and the starting point of the subsequent assessment process.

An ongoing paradox is that the way the EHC assessment process is construed still assumes within-person models of difference and disability, not the supposed holistic appraisal promised (Hodkinson and Burch 2019).

For the first time there is clear reference to the important role that health and social care can or could play to enable a truly holistic appraisal of a pupil's needs, and in working as partners with education in coordinating targeted, appropriate and proportionate responses and provision.

The 2015 CoP (DfE and DoH 2015) can be viewed as being a far more technical document than any of the previous iterations. There is though a lack of specificity and practical guidance unlike earlier iterations (Norwich and Eaton 2015; Lehane 2017; Capper 2020). There may well have been a rationale for this, but it is not clear. The language of inclusion is far more limited and constrained. There is much greater prominence given to the status of specialist provision including units and special schools as being legitimate and equal placement options for some pupils with SEND, than was seen in earlier CoP iterations.

One of the main findings of a 2019 review of the EHC plan process was that parents and carers *still* perceived that they were poorly informed about their children's needs (House of Commons Education Committee 2019). In some cases, this lack of confidence and understanding led some parents and carers to obtain private educational psychology, speech and language and/or occupational therapist's assessment reports in the mistaken belief that this would somehow support their case, either for starting a formal EHC assessment or as part of one. This obviously fails to comprehend that such assessments would be provided where appropriate as part of the multi-practitioner EHC assessment process, and is a free service provided by the LA (Lamb 2009; House of Commons Education Committee 2019).

Lady Warnock herself raised concerns that the evolving SEN iterations since the 1981 Education Act and the development of new categories have not removed the stigma attached to such terms (Warnock and Norwich 2010). Hodkinson and Burch (2019) put forward the view that while SEND labels have altered over time this has not led to a widely held embrace of diversity and inclusion in the state-maintained school system (or beyond).

There is a phenomenon that the more complex a policy is the less likely it is to be understood by those it was intended for, and thus less likely to be implemented effectively (see Chapter 4, where we look at further reasons for this, utilizing Robinson (2018) bypass model). Lehane (2017) observes that the 2015 CoP (DfE and DoH 2015) is both very conceptually complex and technical in its focus on procedures and processes and compliance with implementation timescales. Robinson et al. (2018) point out that the document is rather vague, and though it talks about general practices and principles is not framed in ways that make it easily actionable by those that need to implement its intentions. That is, it is not framed in a way that can easily inform and be converted into decision-making actions by school leaders, SENCos and classroom and subject teachers (Argyris and Schön 1974; Argyris 1999).

This lack of detailed, practically focused content, when compared to previous CoP iterations, has intentionally or not resulted in LAs having to waste lots of time and energy 'reinventing the wheel', each making different interpretations. For example, there is no standardized or uniform EHC plan template, leading to wordy and at times impenetrable documents (Lehane 2017). Although the language of individual aspirations is there, the logical and coherent link between pupil aspirations, strengths, needs, severity, provision and outcomes is not. The EHC plan's job is to identify what are the unique aspirations, strengths and needs of the pupil, clarify these and conclude with broad priority outcomes or expectations of where that pupil will be at the end of a key stage and/or other major transition point – not a detailed IEP (this is the 'tip of the iceberg' model). A school should be trusted to be able to then translate the general 'big picture' document into more specific and time-limited actionable plans in the Assess, Plan, Do, Review (and Reflect, our addition) cycle. But such an approach is not trusted by some parents and carers as they worry that their child will not get what they are entitled to, often framed as more one-to-one TA support. The LA therefore feels obliged to be overly prescriptive as a way of guaranteeing that a school follows the plan. Thus a vicious cycle develops (Blandford 2013; Capper 2020).

The counterargument could well be made that such a situation is exactly what is meant by personalized and individualized planning, but this does sound rather disingenuous. This is especially so given that the rhetoric and vision detailed in the CoP (Department for Education and Department of Health and Social Care 2015) is actually in stark contrast with wider central government agendas during a time of great and ongoing financial austerity – the 2008 financial crisis, Brexit, the Covid-19 pandemic, the war in Ukraine, and rising inflation and falling living standards (Save the Children 2011; Lehane 2017; EEF 2018). Many LAs have struggled greatly against high parental and carer expectations to fully implement its recommendations because the money and resources, material and staff are just not there. This has led to inconsistent and inequitable provision, one of the very things that the CoP aimed to address (Pinney 2002).

The legislation aimed to address the increasing concerns about the overidentification of children and young people with SEN (Warnock and Norwich 2010; Tomlinson 2012). But the very nature of the legislation unintentionally incentivized schools to identify children and young people with needs so they could access additional funding from the LA and to paradoxically revert to and further embrace diagnoses (autism, attention deficit hyperactivity disorder and similar).

Recent official numbers show that there were 473,255 children and young people with EHC plans as at June 2022 (National Statistics 2022). This has increased each year since 2010. There were 62,180 new EHC plans made during 2022 (as at June 2022). The number of new EHC plans has increased each year since their introduction in 2014.

This increase may be linked to the decreasing support available for pupils without an EHC plan. State-maintained school budgets are constrained, and with a market model operating, often they cannot afford to 'buy in' much needed external support, such as EPs, SALTs or OTs. Indeed the House of Commons Education Committee (2019) identified a vicious cycle with low levels of funding to schools meaning pupils without EHC plans being 'neglected' (House of Commons Education Committee 2019: 15), leading to increased parental anxiety and thus increased requests for statutory assessment. The lack of standardization in the EHC plan process across LAs, and the inconsistent input from health and social care practitioners in the process were identified for criticism.

2023 SEND Green Paper: *Right Support, Right Place, Right Time*

On 29 March 2022 the government issued its long-awaited SEND Green Paper for public consultation (HM Government 2022). Following an extended period of consultation and feedback, on 2 March 2023 the final revised SEND Green Paper was issued (HM Government 2023).

The paper aims to address three main challenges facing the current SEND system:

1 The outcomes for children and young people presenting with learning and other needs and those in alternative provision (AP) – a large proportion of children and young people in such 'settings' present with SEND needs – are seen as being inadequate.
2 Parents, carers and families (and indeed practitioners) find navigating the SEND system and alternative provision arrangements complex, bureaucratic, inconsistent and frustrating.
3 Despite the government's view that 'unprecedented investment' has been put into the SEND system, it is seen as not delivering value for money for children and young people and their families – or indeed for schools, LAs and the public purse.

The revised SEND Green Paper can be seen to be offering a fine-tuning and refocusing of existing legislation and practice. An implicit goal is to work towards much greater national consistency. As such it does not represent a radical departure from previous legislation, certainly conceptually or in the underlying assumptions being made.

Overall, the emphasis is on:

- Greater **clarity, consistency and confidence**: (introducing an evidence-based national standards framework to enable the early identification of pupil needs and the provision of appropriate and proportionate interventions (whole class, small group and individual, as well as an expanded role for 'special schools'), along with clear expectations on the range and type of support that should be 'ordinarily available' in mainstream settings. This builds on and makes much more explicit what Quality First Teaching and targeted support actually looks like).
- Increased **accountability**: (holding settings and schools far more accountable for the early identification and timely intervention for SEN pupils; changing the culture and practice in mainstream schools to be more inclusive through early intervention and improved targeted support; a reformed role of AP as part of an integrated three-tier continuum that is an integral part of the local SEND approach; new national standards across education, health and care for a higher performing and more coherent SEND system; a requirement to introduce local inclusion plans bringing together system partners ('who is responsible for what and when, and who pays') to drive better outcomes).
- Developing **workplace skills and competences**: (the introduction of a new leadership SENCo national professional qualification; increasing the number of staff with an accredited Level 3 qualification in Early Years settings; increasing the numbers of EPs to focus on supporting settings/schools at SEN Support level and reviewing teacher training).

The revised Green Paper talks about a 'National Change Programme' to coordinate systems-wide change that will be consistent, enabling and cost-effective across the country. As we see in Chapter 4, it will be interesting if the points made by Robinson (2018) are actually reflected in this systems-wide programme of change – or will a subsequent government return yet again to another SEND review?

SEND legislation and guidance within a wider socio-political context

Central government policy, legislation and guidance can sometimes appear contradictory and inconsistent, even when it emanates from the same department. When critically reviewing some of the SEND reforms in England since the Warnock Committee report (Warnock 1978) it is clear that an increasingly separate shadow special education system operating within the wider state-maintained school sector has evolved (Norwich 2019a; Capper 2020). The state-maintained system is heavily target-driven, academically focused and less inclusive (Hodkinson and Burch 2019). The next section selectively highlights some of the constraints which have impacted on SEND policy development, legislation, guidance and practice in England.

What exactly does 'inclusive education' mean?

The terms 'integration' and 'inclusion' have often been used as if they referred to the same thing, especially when looking at mainstream school practices in England (Avramidis and Norwich 2002; Lindsay 2003; Education and Skills Committee 2007). The concept of integration was formally referenced by the Warnock Committee report (Warnock 1978) when it was trying to structure how learning could take place for pupils with learning difficulties. They came up with three tiers:

Tier 1: Locational integration is where special schools or classes are established within the grounds of, or near to, mainstream primary and secondary schools.
Tier 2: Social integration is where pupils with SEN have dedicated time to interact with their same-aged, typically developing peers outside of the classroom.
Tier 3: Functional integration is where pupils with SEN are educated alongside and with their typically developing, same-aged peers.

This simple tiered framework has had an enormous influence on English education and acknowledges the very real lived experiences of children and young people taught in parallel to their typically developing peers and those who are fully included (Booth 1996; Waters and Brighouse 2021). Yet despite this there was never a single definition of inclusion adopted across the country. The common element appears to be an emphasis on increasing the active and meaningful participation of pupils with SEND in mainstream schools and classrooms (Frederickson and Cline 2015).

The Salamanca Statement (UNESCO 1994) demanded that policymakers, parents/carers and educationalists work actively towards a situation where **all** children and young people with SEND were educated in their local community schools. Their unique learning needs would be recognized by the provision of individual and personalized curriculums and experiences (Hodkinson 2010).

In acknowledging the lack of clarity around definitions of inclusion, Lauchlan and Greig (2015) and Ravet (2011) suggested that there were two main conceptual positions. First, the 'needs-based' view uses the continuum of provision idea to see a viable place for separate special schools in their model of inclusion, and secondly the 'rights-based' view sees separate special schools as fundamentally undermining the concept of full inclusion. This position sees inclusion in a much broader sense, going beyond just a focus on 'SEND' and including the demand to be mindful of other differences and their equal place within a wider pluralistic society (ethnicity, gender and gender identity, sexual orientation, religious beliefs and so on).

This absence of any consensus within educational policy and practice on exactly what is meant by inclusion, let alone actionable guidance on what best educational practice looks like in schools and classrooms, highlights real conceptual and practical problems. For example, in a large, inner-city, mainstream primary classroom of 35 pupils, of which three have 'complex' SEN (EHC plans), what does inclusive practice actually look like on a day-to-day basis? As a result some teaching staff and schools continue to adopt what can be seen to be a simpler and more comprehensible within-child understandings to locate issues and needs rather than critically looking at the school and classroom learning environment (ethos, structure, curriculum, pedagogy, resources and relationships) (Monsen and Frederickson 2004; Monsen et al. 2014). The provision of TAs is then seen as being sufficient to enable inclusion to occur and to not significantly disrupt the learning of others (Education and Skills Committee 2007; Frederickson and Cline 2015; Lindsay et al. 2020).

The national curriculum

The national curriculum was introduced across England in 1988 (Education Reform Act 1988) and occurred during a time when the integration/inclusion of pupils with SEN in mainstream settings was being emphasized in central government policy. Yet a policy of integration/inclusion on the one hand and a national curriculum on the other were fundamentally incompatible in terms of their aims, scope and impact. The national curriculum was set up to deliver a uniform education for all pupils attending state-maintained schools – the assumption being that such an approach would raise pupil attainment and equalize disparities between schools, geographical areas and different socio-economic and ethnic groups.

D. Armstrong (2005) discusses the view that an unintended consequence of this policy was that for pupils with SEN there was a narrowing rather than a more individualized and personal educational experience offered. In a real sense we see the development of a two-tiered education system: the mainstream core for typically developing pupils, with its emphasis on academic attainment, and an increasingly perfunctory parallel add-on system with pupils with SEN being located physically in classrooms but expected to access essentially the same experience, to fit in and keep up. Therefore the language of 'the gap between Luci and her classmates is increasing and I don't know how she will keep up with her peers at GCSE' becomes a more pronounced narrative between teachers and parents and carers. Clearly, this goes against the spirit of person-centred approaches which compare the pupil against themselves over time. Such narratives graphically reflect the growing disconnect between mainstream and SEN understanding and provision in some state-maintained schools (Frederickson and Cline 2015).

Warnock and Norwich (2010) felt that many educators and policymakers had fundamentally misunderstood the 1978 Committee's statement (Warnock 1978), particularly around what integration/inclusion meant in mainstream settings. This confusion led to some schools believing that they needed to provide the same education for all pupils and treat them all alike, rather than seeing their role as meeting individual needs through different and varied educational experiences and opportunities (Daniels et al. 2019).

Along with the adoption of a national curriculum came standardized assessment methods and the ability for schools to band pupils into different attainment groupings (streaming and setting). Such organizational arrangements undermined core notions around inclusion and led to segregated classrooms, which were in effect very similar to the old special classes or units – locational and perhaps at best representing some social integration (MacBeath et al. 2006).

So the wider and more dominant educational policy directly challenged the development of more individual and personalized learning plans in the SEN strategies of the time (Pinney 2002). The notion of personalized learning for pupils with SEN was not consistent with the aims of the national curriculum and school performance measures.

The ongoing legacy of marketization

The national curriculum was brought in during a period when there was a growing 'market forces' culture driven by the ideology of neoliberalism, which was and is having a disproportionate impact on educational policy, thinking and practice. Neoliberalism is a philosophy that assumes that the free market is neutral, emphasizes deregulation, stresses competition, and works to reduce central government spending and limit the role of the state in people's lives. It advocates individual freedom and the exercising of volition and choice (Mccafferty 2010; Baltodano 2012; Souto-Otero 2013; Lucal 2015; Stevenson 2015; Ball 2016; Monbiot 2016; Bamberger et al. 2019; Roberts-Holmes and Moss 2021; Waters and Brighouse 2021).

The 1988 Education Reform Act, also called the 'Baker Act' (Education Reform Act 1988) can be seen as the formal beginning of this phase. Published league tables were established with the explicit goal of setting up competition between schools. This was often framed within a rhetoric of 'parental choice' and 'raising standards' as it was assumed this would enable parents and carers to make informed choices about what schools to send their children to. Parents and carers morphed into being 'consumers' and 'purchasers'. Those schools with subsequent falling rolls would be pressurized to 'up their game', amalgamate with better performing schools or to close. Thus, the market had spoken. But in many cases the reality of choice for parents and carers was very limited and illusory, guided by wealth, geographical location and agency (Bines 2000; MacBeath et al. 2006).

It is assumed that by positioning relationships in such a way rewards merit and diminishes inefficiency. Notions of developing an inclusive classroom or school, let alone a community or society, are in this model seen as counterproductive as the market will reward wealth generation, and any surplus will 'trickle down', ultimately benefiting everyone. The market thus makes sure everyone 'gets what they deserve' – but this has not in fact ever been the case (Giroux 2005; Monbiot 2016).

State-maintained education and the pedagogy it was underpinned by began to be systematically and progressively deconstructed from a semi-autonomous and respected problem-solving profession, driven by the interests of pupils, to the technical role of deliverers of a standard national curriculum under explicit centralized state control (Stevenson 2015).

The ongoing policy tension between raising academic attainment and inclusion is seen right up to the 2015 CoP (DfE and DoH 2015) and to the present day (HM Government 2023). The decision by central government to locate the overall responsibility for SEN provision (read additional funding) on the LA resulted in more not less co-dependency by schools – indeed, in some cases almost a loss of memory of the last 40 years of educational thinking and good teaching practice. Some schools increasingly looked to the LA for additional financial support rather than embrace a critical review of the things that they had control over and power to act on – such as their internal policies, educational practices and procedures, how they delivered the curriculum, support staff development and relationships to meet the needs of all pupils, including those with learning and other needs – let alone joining with their local community and other schools (Bines 2000; Pinney 2002).

The inclusion of diverse learners in mainstream classrooms increasingly became a de facto policy of 'within-class separation'. To enable this shadow system to operate, schools increasingly relied on teaching assistants, often working in isolation to contain the 'different pupil' so they did not disrupt the learning of others (MacBeath et al. 2006). Inclusion is seen in terms of one-to-one and some small-group work following an essentially watered-down version of the mainstream curriculum. The TA's job is to help the pupil with SEN to 'keep up' (Pinney 2002; Lauchlan and Greig 2015; Norwich and Eaton 2015; Webster and Blatchford 2019).

Conclusions

Since the Warnock Committee report (1978) right up to the present day it can be seen that a journey away from deficit and medicalized models of understanding difference and disability in educational contexts has occurred. There has been the growing acknowledgement that learning needs can arise because of complex interactions between internal person, external environmental and sociocultural factors.

One of the key changes illustrated in the Warnock Committee report (1978) was the introduction of the notion of integrative or inclusive education. Implicit in this view was that most children and young people presenting with learning and other differences could actually receive their education along with their peers in mainstream settings and schools.

The development of a common core set of educational goals for all children and young people, including those with SEN and other barriers to their learning and development, was introduced – independence, enjoyment and understanding. In our selective review the overwhelming impression is that the Warnock Committee report (1978) made an enormous contribution to how we think about special educational needs, mainstream education and the teaching and learning relationship. Implicit in its vision is the challenge that schools needed to change, not the pupils presenting with learning differences. It acknowledged the fact that at any one time in an education system about 20 per cent of pupils will require different approaches to be adopted as part of regular classroom practice. This will often involve the teacher undertaking closer monitoring or offering tailored prompts and micro-interventions during the course of regular daily teaching practice. It might involve the teacher operating a small-group cycle where they move around giving direct input to the various groups, and within such a cyclical model making time for some one-to-one input and consolidation as well.

The core objective of all SEND policy has always been the same: to legally protect a focus on *individual* identification and assessment of needs and the provision provided to them (Norwich 1995). The Warnock Committee report (1978) in its reconceptualization of learning and developmental differences was very aware of a fundamental dilemma, but at the time did not tackle it and it is still not addressed to this very day (Norwich 1995). On the one hand you remove stigmatizing categories of educational difference (applying medicalized labels outside of their usual domain), so that these children and young people can be 'label-free' and treated like all other learners. Yet at the same time a 'new' SEND label is applied pragmatically so that scarce resources can be protected for a marginalized minority group (Warnock 1978; Warnock and Norwich 2010).

The crux of the dilemma is: do you identify and risk further stigmatizing by labelling, or do you not identify and lose often hard-won protected provision (Norwich 2008)? There are a number of ways of understanding this identification dilemma. One view offered by Norwich (2019b) sees that the different educational approaches and placements for pupils with SEN reflect that their provision is both *integral* to general education, and a *distinct* aspect of education (Norwich 1995).

Norwich's (2019b) view contrasts with the perspective that sees SEN provision as being *additional and different from ordinary education*. This view positions SEN as a specialist area with its own identity, culture, language, training and workforce. The history of English legislation since 1978 would reflect this position very clearly.

Another view sees 'SEN' largely arising from pedagogical rigidity and the failure of mainstream schools/classrooms to fully embrace the philosophy of inclusion and meeting the needs of all its learners. In this view diversity in all its forms should be embraced so that difference does not mean discrimination and the need for arbitrary and stigmatizing labels (Cigman 2007). Such a view underpins the Inclusion Index and focuses pragmatically on the unique set of functional skills and needs that a child or young person presents with. This tailored functional analysis then feeds into a targeted intervention (Norwich 1995, 2019b; Booth and Ainscow 2011; Hornby 2015).

Therefore, the conclusion that we have come to is that it is the classroom and school level that we need to refocus on in teacher pre-training and continuing professional development: in other words, the purpose, content and quality of pedagogy. We argue that *all* teachers need to be knowledgeable and competent practitioners able to meet the needs of *all* their learners, irrespective of learning differences.

This we believe will contribute to the reprofessionalizing of teaching based not only on subject content expertise, but embracing what some see as specialized and rarefied knowledge around the history and philosophy of teaching–learning, child and adolescent development (physical, cognitive, affective, behaviour, language, psychosocial, social-emotional, mental health/well-being and so on), evidence-based or informed teaching approaches and strategies (covering the full range of learners), the management and organization of an inclusive classroom and school, and the roles and responsibilities of others (parents, carers, external specialists).

We therefore conclude that it is now way overdue to stop using the SEN and disability and indeed other labels altogether, certainly in educational contexts, and instead embrace and celebrate all learners and their differences as individuals on their own unique learning journeys.

3 Classroom-Level Inclusive Educational Practice: Quality First Teaching for All Learners

Introduction

Chapter 2 concluded that an English state education system that truly embraces inclusion for all learners needs to abandon the use of terms like special educational needs and disabilities (SEND) and the SEN pupil, certainly in educational contexts. The SEND label has become by default yet another in a long line of terms that marginalize and stigmatize different types of learners (Lauchlan and Boyle 2007; Billington et al. 2022; Sahli Lozano et al. 2022).

Although the medical model is highly appropriate within its domain of influence and can provide useful background and contextual information, when it comes to finding real-world solutions for learning and other related needs we must draw on educational, pedagogical and psychological frameworks, strategies and approaches.

Chapter 2 argued that educators needed to refocus their efforts at the level of the learner, through evidence-based Quality First Teaching and targeted support which is applicable to a broad range of pupil needs in the mainstream classroom.

Such a change will necessitate a critical relook at the following:

- the efficacy of current teacher training routes (their focus, depth, breadth and preparedness; Maynard et al. 2022)
- questioning why core services like educational psychologists (EPs) have to be 'traded' in a 'neoliberal learning market'
- looking creatively at the potential role of reformed local *education* authorities.

A new role in bridging and coordinating central government, communities, schools and parents/carers' perspectives, let alone health and social care partners.

This chapter begins by examining the conceptual shift from medicalized to more eco-systemic and interactional understandings of how children and young people's learning and other needs can be met in educational contexts. It then reconnects with key educational theorists who put forward a range of pedagogical strategies and approaches that have become integral to contemporary understandings of what effective teaching–learning is. Initially, 21 educational thinkers were researched, of which 4 were women[1] and 17 were men, but because this chapter adopts a social historical perspective only three were finally chosen due to their significant historical and contemporary impact on educational thinking and practice around the world. We recognize that the female voice is excluded from this final number, but on balance we felt that due to the historical and cultural context, Dewey, Vygotsky and Bruner offered the most profound insights into the areas we most wanted to focus on. Next the chapter details the work of Hattie (Hattie 2009, 2012; Hattie and Zierer 2018; Hattie and Clarke 2019; Hattie and Larsen 2020), who has empirically confirmed the efficacy of many of the approaches shared by the three theorists. The discussion then highlights that we have known for some time what works for children and young people from a teaching and learning perspective. The issues are not so much *where* pupils will be taught, or *what* pupils will be taught, but *how* they will be taught and by *whom* (Weselby 2014; Frederickson and Cline 2015).

A paradigm shift in thinking in education – from within-child to eco-systemic and interactional understandings of learning and other needs

Since the Warnock Committee report (Warnock 1978) there has been a growing movement amongst educationalists and educational and child psychologists to better understand pupil development, learning differences and disabilities within more eco-systemic and interactional frameworks (Bronfenbrenner 1986, 1996; Tudge et al. 2021; Woodland et al. 2021; Navarro and Tudge 2022; Scarpa and Trickett 2022). The view is that individual differences reflect a complex interaction between within-child characteristics (be they biological and/or physical, cognitive, affective and behavioural), the home and teaching–learning environments they inhabit.

The eco-systemic interactionist perspective contrasts with the still persuasive and powerful medicalized or within-person model of understanding learning differences outside the medical context (Frederickson and Cline 2015; Bogart et al. 2019). The latter position views learning differences and disability as being present when there is a cognitive and/or physical 'constraint' which limits the child or young person's ability to fully take part in 'normal' (what most children or young people of their age would be expected to be doing) developmental tasks and activities (Frederickson and Cline 2015).

This view compares the child or young person's skills and abilities against those of their typically developing peers. As a result, we get the well-worn tropes of 'Jan is significantly behind his peers', 'The gap is increasing between Maria and her peers' and 'I worry about the transition to secondary school as Shira is so far behind. They could cope at primary but secondary will be a different story.'

---

[1] Margaret McMillan, Maria Montessori, Susan Isaacs and Margaret Donaldson.

The response to managing such needs is largely directed at the provision of 'specialist' programmes. Yet not being able to carry out 'normal' tasks and activities will be greatly influenced by not only the degree of individual cognitive and/or physical 'constraint' but by the *environment* the child or young person inhabits and how well attuned it is to them. An example might be a secondary-aged pupil who uses a wheelchair. The school has a rolling programme of installing lifts which has enabled the pupil to participate fully in all lessons, including those conducted on the second floor, just like their peers.

Another example is where a parent/carer obtains a private EP or specialist teacher assessment to clarify why their child is not making sufficient progress with their reading. The 'diagnosis' obtained states that the child presents with 'severe developmental dyslexia'. Yet such a diagnostic label tells us absolutely nothing about the individual child and their unique set of needs – what reading strategies or cues they currently use and to what level of proficiency, what their progress has been, their wider history and background, including health (any glue-ear), teaching and learning, the current level of curriculum demands, or the teaching methods and approaches adopted, their frequency and duration.

The implicit assumption is that the diagnostic label alone tells us all we need to know about that pupil: that the child is 'dyslexic'. It is therefore self-evident what the teacher needs to do with 'The Dyslexic Child'. As a result, it is likely that generic, off-the-peg strategies will be applied, to what is in effect a very heterogeneous group of literacy learners. The label will inadvertently rarefy the child's needs so that those around them might feel disempowered. This can lead them to seek 'specialist' input rather than looking at the important role played by Quality First classroom teaching practices and structured small-group work using evidence-based approaches such as reciprocal or precision teaching, and Pause, Prompt and Praise (Hattie 2009, 2012).

In contrast, the eco-systemic interactionist frame sees the degree of an individual's level of learning difference and disability as reflecting a far more complex interaction between *both* pupil-centred *and* environmental factors. An individual's ability to positively engage in their home, classroom, school and wider community is dependent not only on their cognitive, physical and/or other differences, but also on central government policy (protections under the law, level of social care and public health), material (including socioeconomic factors, parental income, housing), social (including class, gender, sexuality-based factors), ethnic, cultural (including religious belief systems and languages) and attitudinal differences, and the physical spaces within which they operate. An individual's degree of relative difference reflects how the wider community and society views and reacts to their uniqueness and how committed it is to embracing and including those individuals (Oliver 1990; Swain et al. 2014; Frederickson and Cline 2015).

One of the overarching goals of education is to work with all learners to carefully, systematically and positively enable them to extend their life choices, whatever the functional starting point or baseline. This position resonates well with the English SEND 2015 Code of Practice (DfE and DoH 2015) (see Chapter 2) and its focus on individualized personal life aspirations and outcomes. What it does not say is that learning how to learn and the skills of independence need to be crucial elements in an education system.

In Chapter 2 most of the focus around suitable provision for pupils with learning differences, disabilities and wider needs focused on *where* such children and young people were educated – mainstream, units or special schools (the continuum of provision model). If we move away from a reliance on 'diagnostic labels' to a more pedagogically sophisticated analysis of a pupil's unique needs, then due consideration must be given to classroom-based factors (teacher attitude, classroom ethos and climate, grouping and organizational systems, curriculum content, level of task demands, teaching approaches and strategies, level of pupil involvement, engagement, level of material support, level of parental and wider community involvement), monitoring how the pupil has responded over time to various micro-interventions and whether a differential and more individualized approach is required (Monsen and Frederickson 2004; Monsen et al. 2014; Frederickson and Cline 2015).

It is now almost 45 years since the Warnock Committee report (1978), and it is really time to refocus our energies back to the classroom level, to core pedagogy and look at *how* pupils are taught (Frederickson and Cline 2015; Waters and Brighouse 2021; Thomas and Loxley 2022).

A refocusing on the 'how': reconnecting with core pedagogical foundations

This section highlights three seminal educational theorists and their contributions to our understanding of aspects of the teaching and learning relationship. Often overlooked today, their individual and combined influence on the practice of teaching and learning has been enormous. These are John Dewey, Lev Vygotsky and Jerome Bruner (in birth order rather than degree of importance).

John Dewey (1859–1952)

> The most important attitude that can be formed is that of desire to go on learning.
>
> (Dewey 1998: 49)

Based on Dewey's extensive naturalistic observations, research and reflections on how children and young people went about problem-solving and learning (largely at the University of Chicago Laboratory School) he concluded that education at its core needed to be child-centred, active, interactive and connected with the pupil's social reality. In Dewey's thinking the importance of **experiential learning** and the social relationship between teachers and their pupils learning together was central (Gray and MacBlain 2015a).

For Dewey (1998) learning involves **learning how to think**, and is far more than just completing a specific task or activity and getting the right answer, then ticking a box and moving on. The process of learning requires **active reflection** and then learning from this over time while applying new understandings in different contexts. Such mental activity is aimed, in Dewey's terms, towards attaining a state of equilibrium, enabling a learner to solve problems and preparing them for further more challenging active inquiry.

Dewey's view was that sustained lifelong learning could only occur if:

1. The pupil plays an active role in the teaching–learning relationship and process.
2. The pupil utilizes as many senses or modalities as possible (I see, I hear, I touch/feel, I write/draw/construct, I do, and I understand).
3. The task or activity is meaningful, relevant and pitched at the pupil's developmental and conceptual level.
4. Pupils have lots of opportunities (concrete, material and imagined) to critically reflect on the experiences or information presented to them (living it, drawing on and linking with past experiences and learning, and integrating it so they are prepared for their next challenge). This is why the Early Years curriculum, and its workforce, is so important as it provides the foundations of learning (Soan and Hutton 2021).

Teachers adopting such experiential approaches play a central role in the learner's development. The teacher is seen as being a facilitator, partner, enabler and a co-learner. For example, the teacher gets to know their children's prior experiences first before launching into an activity or unit of study (prior knowledge); plans teaching inputs that encourage active participation with the material; over the course of a module they draw on as many senses as possible; teaches, models and utilizes reflective thinking (there are links here to meta-cognition and multisensory approaches, repetition and active practice; Hattie 2009, 2012); and creates a space where pupils can organize their own learning with teachers providing external structure, support and encouragement (links here with personalized and individualized learning and Bruner's scaffolding notion; Hattie 2009, 2012; MacBlain 2014). Such things highlight the importance of teachers reflecting on what they and their pupils have achieved and revising next steps on the basis of this insight.

Dewey viewed each learner as bringing a collection of individual differences to the learning space. Part of this, he argued, was a function of genetics, personality and temperament, but was also derived experientially (meaningfully and directly interacting with both the material and social worlds). As a result, each learner interacts with the curriculum presented to them in subtly and qualitatively different ways. Therefore, the curriculum needs to be sufficiently robust and flexible to acknowledge this reality and embrace such differences (links again with personalized and individualized learning; Hattie 2009, 2012).

A major theme implicit in Dewey's writing on education and teaching and learning is that schools have a much wider social mission. The learning journey is preparing pupils to be able to function and contribute positively in their own communities and the wider society for the benefit of not only themselves but others.

In Dewey's framework, while teachers still require subject-specific content knowledge, they also need to get to know their pupils' cultural and personal backgrounds before fully working with them. Learning involves the pupil building up their own ongoing knowledge base. Such teachers adjust the curriculum to fit pupils' prior knowledge as fully as possible. In this way, real-life 'problems' derived from the life experiences of their pupils can be creatively woven into lessons (Hattie 2009, 2012; Seifert and Sutton 2009; Hildebrand 2018).

For Dewey the distinction between mainstream and special education was artificial and arbitrary, failing to consider what he saw as the true purpose of education and the development of self and community. All children and young people, even those with learning differences and needs, *should* be educated together as part of a community of learners for the betterment of themselves, others and the community – a true foretaste of inclusive thinking.

In Chapter 2 we saw that such considerations were largely lost, and special education in England evolved as a separate shadow system under the umbrella of difference, disability and othering. Dewey's enduring legacy, and indeed challenge for educators today, is for us to refocus back on all learners and their unique set of strengths and areas to develop, and use the classroom learning environment to support their growth through **experiential pupil-centred teaching** (Thomas and Loxley 2022).

Lev Vygotsky (1896–1934)

> What a child can do with assistance today [they] will be able to do by [them] self tomorrow.
>
> (Vygotsky 1978: 87)

For Vygotsky the importance of the child's social world, and in particular meaningful interactions with peers and adults, was central to the development of cognitive and wider skills. Vygotsky's view was that all children are pre-wired with a range of unlearnt cognitive functions – such as attention, concentration, focus, visual, tactile, auditory, working memory and processing speed – that facilitate their active engagement with the world around them and underpin adaptive learning (Vygotsky 1978).

In terms of cognitive development Vygotsky described three main concepts:

1. Culture is key to learning (culture in this context being defined as the attitudes, beliefs and values of the community surrounding the pupil at any given historical time, which are maintained by customs, rituals, routines, systems, procedures and practices).
2. Language is at the heart of culture (language is used to communicate and maintain acceptable attitudes and behaviour at any given historical period).
3. Individuals learn and develop within their wider community (home, school and neighbourhood, which develops over time in response to specific sociocultural and environmental events; Arikan 2009).

Vygotsky offered us many ideas, but one key concept which has influenced thinking around teaching–learning and applied practice right up to the present is his notion of a **Zone of Proximal Development (ZPD)**. This concept can be best understood as describing what a child can do with the support of a more able other (an adult or peer).

In Vygotsky's social-cultural model, formal tests can be seen to sample what a child can do on their own at a particular point in time. But the outcomes do not reflect what the pupil's potential next level of performance could be in a collaborative relationship. Vygotsky's position is that there can be for some learners, especially those with added complexities, a significant gap between what they can do without help and what they can do with guided assistance. This is especially so for skills that the pupil is initially learning and for those they find consistently difficult to do on their own and require targeted support and guidance from others.

The ZPD achievement or attainment gap has lower and upper limits which change over time in response to teaching, learning and maturation. Through careful naturalistic observations teachers can identify a pupil's current developmental level (tasks they can solve or complete on their own, however small or large) as well as make predictions about what the next upper limits might be (problems or tasks for which the pupil will need adult guidance: Vygotsky 1978; see also task and functional analysis: Hattie 2009, 2012).

Vygotsky conceptualizes the ZPD within a four-stage process. The pupil is observed using:

1 little structure or strategies and shows limited understanding of the task or key concepts involved – referred to as the *Vague Syncretic Stage*
2 some strategies independently but not consistently or effectively enough – referred to as the *Complex Stage*
3 more systematic approaches but there is still a tendency to focus on only one aspect of the problem or task at a time – referred to as the *Potential Concept Stage*
4 systematic approaches independently and successfully, with evidence of clear concepts being formed – referred to as the *Mature Concept Stage*.

For Vygotsky a learner's growing skill development is co-constructed through formal and informal **social** and **cultural interactions**. Such interactions include those with parents/carers, family members, teachers and peers. Interaction and engagement involve fantasy play, imagining, books, toys and wider cultural practices that occur in school, the classroom, at home and in the community. This social and cultural construction of knowledge, awareness and skills development is mediated by words, language, signs and symbols.

In the ZPD framework the quality of a learner's skill development is enhanced if they can have access to a skilful and knowledgeable teacher, other adult or peer. Vygotsky saw the central role of the teacher in the ZPD model as that of facilitator and enabler. To do this the teacher draws on a wide range of strategies such as modelling, using concrete materials, using metaphor and analogy, and prompts to facilitate a learner's accessing ideas and concepts which are slightly *above* their current skill and knowledge level. The approaches adopted and the level of intensity and frequency will vary depending on the learner's starting point and the degree of complexity (see differentiation and personalized and individualized curriculum: Brown et al. 1989; Rogoff 1990; Lave and Wenger 1991; Greeno and Middle School Mathematics through Applications Project Group 1998; Hattie 2009, 2012; Reusser and Pauli 2015).

For our purposes one of the enduring legacies of Vygotsky's work is the need for educators to monitor pupils carefully (naturalistic observations), identifying what they can do on their own and what they can do with support, and to then set up a series of responses (micro-interventions) to move them forward at their own pace and in their own time. It is important to note that Vygotsky was talking about work with individual children not groups.

Jerome Bruner (1915–2016)

> We begin with the hypothesis that any subject can be taught effectively in some intellectually honest form to any child at any stage of development
> (Bruner 1977: 33)

Bruner, like Dewey and Vygotsky, views learning as being an active, inquiry-based process. For those working with children and young people Bruner would say that their chief focus is on understanding the cognitive processes which underpin and direct pupil actions, derived through careful observation and getting to know their children. Bruner was fascinated by identifying the strategies that pupils use when they are learning and problem-solving and the experiences that support and form lasting concepts.

Bruner focused on how learners used symbols and words to form mental concepts and how these representations can be generalized and linked up with other ideas. Structuring learning in this way, Bruner saw the inferences that learners make through their mental constructions and manipulation of symbols and words as being central to learning and cognitive development (symbolic mode).

The big idea in Bruner's theory is that individuals construct an internal mental representation of the world that they experience around them, and they learn through three '**modes**'. The **enactive mode** is concerned with actions, the **iconic mode** with images and pictures, and the **symbolic mode**, which is the more complex, is concerned with words, symbols and language. These inter-linked modalities can be used to describe a pupil's ways of structuring their learning and as a basis for 'scaffolding' adult responses and micro-interventions in the classroom. A pupil may connect with all or any one of them in the course of their learning.

Bruner offered us many powerful strategies with which to support pupil learning. For the purposes of this section, instructional scaffolding will be highlighted.

Table 3.1 Summary of the theoretical approach and key principles of Dewey's, Vygotsky's and Bruner's theories of learning

Theorist	Theoretical approaches	Key principles of the theory
John DEWEY 1859–1952	Social, experiential, reflective, enquiry-based and cross-curriculum learning	• Learning is pupil-centred, active and interactive, and it should involve the child's social world and their community. • Pupils need to interact cooperatively with their peers and adults, and also have time to work alone. • Education should reflect the pupils' interests and backgrounds and that their social and cultural worlds are important. • Dewey viewed learning as a lifelong process and that educators need to not only teach academic skills and knowledge but also help learners to live and exist positively within their communities.
Lev VYGOTSKY 1896–1934	Constructivism, social interaction, language, self-initiated discovery and collaborative dialogue	• Social interaction (shared experiences) between learners, peers and adults is fundamental to the development of thinking (cognitive) skills. • Within these social interactions there is an important role for the More Knowledgeable Other (MKO). This refers to anyone who has a better understanding than the learner (peer, parent/carer, teacher) of a given task or activity. • The Zone of Proximal Development (ZPD) is the gap between a learner's current ability to perform a given task with adult and/or with peer collaboration, and their ability to manage the task on their own. According to Vygotsky, learning occurs within this zone as the learner internalizes 'tools' (culture, language, speech, writing) to more effectively mediate their developing thinking.
Jerome BRUNER 1915–2016	Active discovery-based learning, play, spiral curriculum and instructional scaffolding	• Learning is an active process in which learners construct new ideas or concepts based on their current and prior knowledge to make sense of their world and culture. • Pupils construct a mental representation of the world they experience, and they learn through three 'modes': the enactive mode, concerned with physical actions, the iconic mode in which one thing stands for another through images and pictures, and the more complex symbolic mode, concerned with the representation of experience through words, symbols and language. • Pupils need to actively explore and manipulate objects; wrestle with problems, questions and controversies; and perform mini-experiments.

Instructional scaffolding

The teacher uses strategies (social, environmental, material) to support, or 'scaffold', learning tasks for the learner. These scaffolds are gradually modified, changed and removed depending on the learner's progress. The idea is that the learner will internalize the strategies (scaffolds) as they develop at their own rate.

Although scaffolding offers the pupil varying degrees of external structure to help guide learning, it is not rigid. Take, for example, the primary-aged child whose teacher is demonstrating on the whiteboard how to multiply fractions together. The teacher explains, models (using concrete materials as required) and talks through what they are doing themselves (external self-talk). The child has a mini-whiteboard device in front of them and slowly mirrors what the teacher is doing as they apply the new strategies for solving the fraction problem. Sometimes they may use concrete materials such as Cuisenaire blocks alongside the whiteboard to physically see, manipulate and experience what the notations are standing in for in the real world. For some learners one cycle is sufficient, and they can progress on to new novel examples and practice on their own (links with repetition, practice and consolidation). For other learners the teacher might need to break down the child's learning into smaller, more manageable and meaningful 'chunks', demonstrate again with concrete materials (first understanding the child's worldview, then working at helping them make the link between real-world materials and the language and symbols that are used to represent them – as an example the relationship between colour and length when using Cuisenaire rods can confuse some children) and allow the child more time and space to practise steps with prompting and specific praise. Such scaffolding allows the child to extend their knowledge, skills and understanding at their own pace (links with task and functional analysis).

Pupils' level of interest or motivation for a particular task is one of the best starting points for engaged, focused and purposeful learning. The teacher's role is to have the freedom to be creative and innovative, using many different approaches which create an ethos in the classroom that encourages learners to become actively curious and involved in their own learning, with a clear purpose (intrinsically rather than extrinsically motivated: Bernaus and Gardner 2008; Nugent 2009; Henry and Thorsen 2018). Learners of all abilities become engaged because they choose to, because by doing so they experience profound and long-lasting personal feelings of satisfaction, pride and achievement, no matter what their level (Gray and MacBlain 2015b).

Summary

In all of Dewey's, Vygotsky's and Bruner's models the central place of the pupil's culture and prior experiences, environment and active participation in their own learning are core to the teaching–learning process and relationship (see Table 3.1). This table summarizes all three people's views. The teacher's role is that of facilitator and enabler, skilfully using questioning (open, closed, hints and leading questions), feedback, prompts and modelling. Such approaches provide a great deal of support to all pupils and especially those with learning differences and needs or other barriers to their development. With such pupils it is not so much using different approaches or strategies but a matter of level of regularity, intensity and duration. As the pupil progresses, such supports are gradually modified and more responsibility is transferred to the pupil when they are ready for this (Slavin and Madden 2006).

In an inclusive classroom the need for an emphasis on personalized and individualized approaches and active pupil preparation becomes of paramount importance. Unless such considerations are managed (creative use of small-group and paired working), pupils with learning needs may become overwhelmed in a complex and difficult learning environment which has little relevance in their lives.

What are the most effective evidence-based teaching strategies and approaches?

Some would respond to the previous section by saying 'Isn't that just good teaching practice?' This indicates how the strategies and approaches highlighted have become so embedded in contemporary thinking around teaching and learning practice, to a greater or lesser extent, even if their origins and rationale have been long forgotten.

The gratifying thing is that more recently people like John Hattie (2009, 2012) have empirically supported many of these important teaching–learning strategies and approaches. Hattie (2009, 2012; Hattie and Zierer 2018; Hattie and Larsen 2020) has had an enormous global impact on the development of the research aspects involved in the reflective scientist-practitioner role (or data-based teacher development: Borg 1998). It is important to stress that Hattie's research provides some of the *content knowledge* or the 'what' a teacher requires to inform their wider problem-solving and reflection on the unique classroom issues they need to manage, and how best to work with a range of diverse learners.

Sometimes Hattie's work has been constructed as checklists of best practice and then used to judge or evaluate teachers' performance. Hattie's work is far more nuanced than this. What he is offering to the reflective teacher is ideas based on a careful synthesis of published research around what approaches and strategies work under certain conditions and with certain pupils. The teacher who is the problem-owner and solver can draw on these ideas alongside their own practice knowledge to inform their active problem-solving, reflection and subsequent micro-'experiments' in their classrooms. They can then see what impact they have, or variations of them have had, within the Plan, Do, Review, *Reflect* cycle. We have added 'reflection' as we feel that to support their own learning teachers need to not only review the impact of interventions on pupils but also what they have learnt, what works and under what conditions, and what they would do differently next time.

Hattie and his team examined over 800 meta-analyses and identified sets of the most effective evidence-based teaching approaches or strategies that can be used at the classroom level. Many of these approaches and strategies are either directly or indirectly linked back to the ideas offered by Dewey, Vygotsky and Bruner. Hattie and his team worked out the effect size for each intervention, approach and/or strategy. Effect size refers to how much an intervention contributes to improving pupil learning, which plays an important role in interpreting the effectiveness of teaching strategies adopted by the classroom teacher.

An effect size of 1.0 would improve the rate of learning by 50 per cent and would mean that, on average, pupils receiving that approach or intervention would exceed 84 per cent of those not receiving that approach or intervention. At least half of all pupils can and do achieve an effect size of 0.4 in a given year (the so-called 'hinge point'), so anything with an effect size of over 0.4 is likely to be having a visible effect or impact.

For the purposes of illustration, we highlight three of the most effective evidence-based teaching strategies that Hattie identified (2009, 2012):

1 *Explicit teaching*

   Explicit teaching involves showing pupils what tasks they need to complete, and *how* they should complete them. Teachers need to give pupils direct instructions, making the success criteria and learning goals clear to them to reduce the chance of misunderstanding. When a teacher models what the pupils have to do, they need to probe for understanding and monitor each pupil's progress towards meeting each goal. The aim of explicit teaching is to teach pupils new concepts in a meaningful way and to avoid rote learning. In explicit teaching, each pupil's progress towards the learning goals is monitored. Hattie (2009) found that explicit teaching had an effect size of 0.57.

2 *Oral feedback*

   Oral feedback has been found to benefit both pupils and teachers. Feedback tells the pupil and the teacher about what areas may be confusing and misunderstood, what areas they have mastered and what is still yet to learn to achieve the learning goal. This information can be used to monitor pupil performance and to measure how they perform against set learning goals. When feedback is used appropriately, it can offer advice to pupils on how they can improve their performance. Feedback therefore enables pupils to refocus and work towards achieving the learning goals. Feedback benefits teachers by informing them about what strategies work well in the classroom and how to guide their future practice. Hattie (2009) found that delivering focused oral feedback had an effect size of 0.73 on pupil learning.

3 *Differentiated teaching*

   Differentiated teaching refers to the methods that teachers use to support pupil learning by using individually tailored intervention approaches and strategies. A differentiated approach involves teachers recognizing that all pupils have varied abilities, skills and aptitudes identified via summative assessment and regular monitoring. Teachers are able to use evidence-based interventions to improve each pupil's performance, based on differences in learning, readiness and interest. Targeted interventions are then tailored and applied to provide differentiated teaching input. When differentiated teaching is implemented effectively, information from formative assessments (verbal feedback) is used to tell teachers which interventions work best and when the pupil is ready for the next step. Hattie (2012) found the Response to Intervention approach had an effect size of 1.07 on pupil learning.

Current teaching and learning approaches: Quality First Teaching in a waves of intervention model

In the English state-maintained education system a number of frameworks have been developed to help focus the 'what' of school- and classroom-level practice. Most notable of these is the term Quality First Teaching, which fits within a graduated approach to level of support and its intensity (universal, targeted and specialist – see Figure 3.1) (Warnes et al. 2021).

The term Quality First Teaching was developed by the Department for Children, Schools and Families, and referred to in a policy document called *Personalised Learning – A Practical Guide* (DCSF 2008).

The rationale for its development links very well with the thinking we saw in the previous sections, and sees the regular social interactions between teacher and pupil in the mainstream classroom as underpinning quality teaching and learning. Quality First Teaching engages and supports the learning of all children and young people, including those with more complex needs. It provides opportunities for more personalized approaches to be adopted for certain pupils. Again, conceptually it can be seen to link with the thinking of Dewey, Vygotsky and Bruner in stressing that learning builds on a pupil's prior learning and experience.

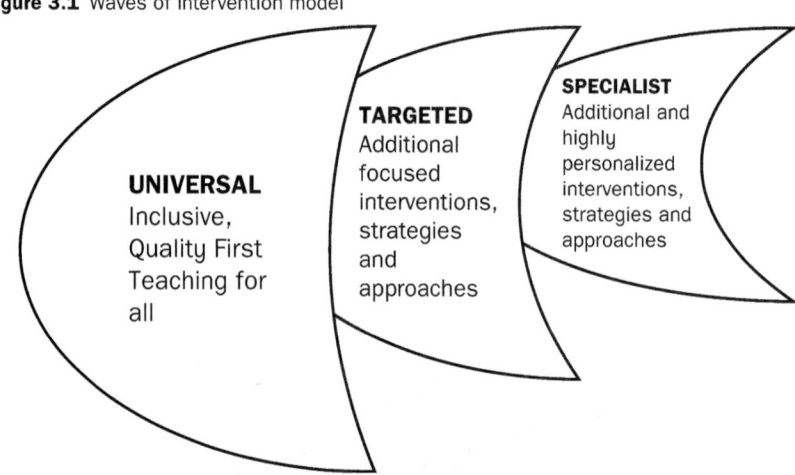

Figure 3.1 Waves of intervention model

UNIVERSAL
Inclusive, Quality First Teaching for all

TARGETED
Additional focused interventions, strategies and approaches

SPECIALIST
Additional and highly personalized interventions, strategies and approaches

Explicit in the model is the view that all teachers can work to meet the needs of the vast majority of learners in their classrooms. This is done by getting to know their pupils, their life experiences and backgrounds, what their strengths are and what areas need to be developed (not just academic attainment but wider social-emotional, behavioural, self-regulation, including social skills, resiliency, well-being and mental health). The vehicle for achieving this is a refocusing back to teaching practice and planning – that the classroom learning environment is a powerful intervention in itself (knowledge of child development, content knowledge, organized and varied lessons, structure, boundaries, using mixed approaches – whole class, small group and one-to-ones; Hattie's work can greatly inform teachers' thinking around these aspects of practice).

In an attempt to be more inclusive, current teaching approaches in mainstream classrooms have tended to emphasize differentiation by looking at the level of support a pupil requires to access a meaningful curriculum for them. This can be achieved by providing open tasks (setting mixed-ability activities that stretch the learner whatever level they may be at), by consolidation (time to practise and overlearn skills), and extension and enrichment activities (inquiry-based individual or group work) for particular pupils and groups. At the planning stage thought is given to what reasonable adjustments need to be made for certain individuals or groups of learners (Warnes et al. 2021). The national frameworks provide clear guidance on progression and on developing approaches to assessing pupils' progress (APP) over time.

The key components of Quality First Teaching

1. The careful design of focused and structured lesson and unit plans with clear learning aims and outcomes.
2. Building into lessons and unit plans a range of opportunities that actively involve and engage pupils in doing, talking and reflection. Actively connecting with their environmental and lived cultural experiences along with the flexibility of 'catching those teachable moments' – the changing of the seasons, rain, snow, heatwaves – and organizing appropriate linked activities to these in a creative way.
3. Adult (and wherever possible peer) modelling, self-talk, questioning, providing oral feedback, and explaining to develop higher-order critical thinking skills (such as critical analysis, synthesis and inference).
4. Stressing pupils' personal responsibility for their own learning and working independently.

The DfE Code of Practice (DfE and DoH 2015: 25, para 1.24) states that 'High quality teaching that is differentiated and personalized will meet the individual needs of the majority of children and young people. Some children and young people need educational provision that is additional to or different from this.'

The Waves of Intervention model

The Waves of Intervention model, within which Quality First Teaching sits, details a three-layered progression that teachers can use to structure their teaching and provide a graduated approach which is accessible and inclusive.

Wave 1: Universal offer

This is the bedrock of contemporary mainstream classroom practice, its organization, planning and delivery based on Quality First Teaching principles. In Wave 1 teachers plan for the whole class and its various subgroupings in a systematic manner. Each lesson/unit of work has clear learning objectives, goals and varied input (whole-class 'chalk and talk', small groups, paired work and some individually focused time) alongside consolidation activities and other teaching–learning choices.

Wave 2: Targeted – additional interventions

Wave 2 support can be used by the teacher alongside Wave 1 to provide additional, usually relatively short-term input to pupils who are not meeting age-related expectations. Wave 2 involves clearly identifying these pupils (formative and baseline assessments and observation) and putting in place a more tailored and personalized learning programme for a specific period of time. The aim is to work to reduce the need for Wave 2 input. Additional support is delivered in the classroom as part of normal teaching–learning practice. Wave 2 is where more differentiated activities, tasks and approaches are used.

Wave 3: Specialist – personalized interventions

Wave 3 focuses the teacher's attention on the need – following monitoring and review of the efficacy of Wave 2 support – for planning a much more personalized learning programme for pupils who are still not meeting age-related expectations. Wave 3 is often the point when school staff involve external specialists like EPs, speech and language therapists (SALTs) and occupational therapists (OTs). Wave 3 provision can be in place for a much longer period dependent on pupil progress and needs (Almond 2021).

A key constraint to the effective implementation of inclusive classroom practice: misunderstanding differentiation, differentiated instruction and use of teaching assistants

Our discussion thus far has shown that we know very well what works for children and young people, from a teaching and learning perspective. The three core educational theorists put forward approaches and strategies that have become integral to contemporary understandings of what is effective teaching and learning. Indeed, as we have shown, many of the approaches and strategies have subsequently been empirically validated by Hattie and colleagues.

So the issues are not so much *where* pupils will be taught, or *what* pupils will be taught but *how* they will be taught and by *whom*. One of the key frameworks teachers refer to when talking about 'meeting the needs of SEND pupils' is *differentiation* (and within this the use of teaching assistants (TAs) to enable it). The lack of clarity as to what is meant by differentiation and the equally confused position on the use of TAs has limited the ability of some mainstream schools and teachers to fully embrace and deliver an inclusive learning experience (Gunner 2014; Weselby 2014; Humphreys and Jimenez 2018; Webster 2018).

Differentiation has been misunderstood and misapplied by some teachers as they try to meet the needs of an increasingly diverse group of learners. This is set against an increasingly financially constrained environment where ready access to external specialists like EPs, SALTs and OTs is not that easy as it often involves additional costs.

A focus on the use of TAs as one of the main strategies to facilitate differentiated instruction may reflect a lack of training as well as lack of easy access to external support. With the added pressures of the national curriculum with its focus on academic attainment, it is not surprising that some teachers find it a challenge to look more critically and systemically at their important role and how to utilize TAs to best effect.

Differentiation stresses the need for all teachers to use the best available evidence-based approaches (see the three theorists and Hattie's iterations research) to support each individual learner to progress at their own pace, comparing their development against their own baselines over time.

Some teachers understand differentiation as operating different ability groupings (e.g. the Lions, the Elephants and the Giraffes groups, yet everyone knows that the Lions are the 'better' group and get all of the teacher's time!) and using TAs either with a named child (via additional resources as a result of an EHC plan) or with small groups funded from the school's own budget. This can result in some classes having three or more TAs working alongside the teacher. Currently TAs do most of the structural work with children and young people with additional learning needs and keep the current system afloat (Webster and Blatchford 2017).

Webster and Blatchford (2017) identified that the majority of TAs were not trained for this role. Equally many classroom teachers felt ill-prepared for the complexities of managing and effectively deploying other adults in their classroom. The paradox is that the least able learners actually experience less educational input from teachers than more able peers. What concerned the researchers was that classroom teachers had a tendency to group learners by ability and then allocate TAs to the lower ability groups. By so doing the less able learners get direction from the least qualified and least pedagogically trained staff in school, instead of additional targeted support consolidating the direct input of the teacher.

The Making a Statement (MAST) study (Webster and Blatchford 2013) found when looking at Year 5 pupils with learning needs that 27 per cent of their interactions with the teacher and/or TA took place out of class (compared with 0 per cent of regular attaining pupils); 22 per cent of interactions were with the teacher as part of class (compared with 35 per cent of regular attaining pupils); 27 per cent of interactions were with the TA (compared with 2 per cent of regular attaining pupils); 19 per cent of interactions with the TA were on a one-to-one basis (compared with 1 per cent of regular attaining pupils); and finally 18 per cent of interactions were with peer(s) (compared with 32 per cent of regular attaining pupils).

The Deployment and Impact of Support Staff (Blatchford et al. 2009) project was set up to describe the characteristics and deployment of support staff in schools and to address their impact on teachers, teaching and pupils. One of the main conclusions was that children who received the most support from TAs made significantly *less* progress than similar pupils who received less support (Blatchford et al. 2012).

The researchers concluded that using a disproportionate amount of TA support as the main vehicle to enable differentiation comes at a cost to meaningful social interactions with teachers and peers. As identified earlier in this chapter, all of the key educational theorists that we reviewed highlighted that learning at its core is a social and collaborative activity centred around relationships.

Webster and Blatchford (2017) do though helpfully stop us from 'throwing the baby out with the bathwater' in stressing that there can be an important role for TAs as part of *supporting* the teaching and learning process for all learners. Again referencing the three educational theorists and the centrality of language and meaningful interaction, TAs can be trained to open up pupil talk rather than closing down dialogue: knowing when not to talk themselves and allowing pupils time to process, formulate and respond; adopting a stance with pupils of exploring and understanding an activity rather than just completing a task correctly; and adopting varied questioning formats that enable the pupil to develop independence (Radford et al. 2015; Bosanquet and Radford 2019).

The paradox is that teachers spent a disproportionate amount of their time with the more academically able pupils rather than those with learning needs. Webster and Blatchford (2019) found that the overuse of TAs was associated with a negative impact on the learning of pupils presenting with the highest level of need. The researchers concluded that the systematic use of TAs in English schools merely blurred and confused the lack of adequate teacher training, task planning and preparation, and efforts to make the teaching–learning process more inclusive.

Webster and Blatchford (2017) also looked at the experiences of pupils in mainstream secondary schools who had Statements of special educational needs (SEN). The project followed on the earlier MAST study.

The SEN in Secondary Education (SENSE) (Webster and Blatchford 2017) and the Making a Statement (MAST) (Webster and Blatchford 2013) projects' outcomes revealed that the educational experiences of pupils with Statements/EHC plans are largely characterized by a form of streaming – some may say segregation. Schools tended to handle SEND provision via the wider organization of teaching by ability and by allocating TAs to classes with higher numbers of pupils in need rather than concentrating on improving the quality and accessibility of the teaching–learning processes.

The Education Endowment Foundation guidance report, *Making Best Use of Teaching Assistants* (2018), offers a range of evidence-based recommendations aimed at enabling TAs to make much more of an impact. School leaders need to ensure that TAs are:

- not deployed in classrooms merely as an informal teaching resource solely for low achieving pupils
- deployed so that they add value to what the classroom teacher is already doing
- deployed to assist pupils in learning greater independence and encourage them to take on increasing responsibility for their own learning
- fully trained and supported for their role in the classroom
- trained and supervised so they can deliver evidence-based, one-to-one and small-group structured interventions
- supported to help pupils make connections between classroom teaching and structured interventions.

It has been argued that we need to reframe differentiation as creating a learning environment that 'teaches-up' (Tomlinson 2012, 2017, 2021; TES 2021; Tomlinson and Hewitt 2021). By this Tomlinson means, in a mainstream classroom, looking holistically at the curriculum and initially planning for the most advanced learners (the overall plan or road map analogy which we will use as a metaphor in this section) and then looking creatively at the range of strategies which can be used to enable other learners to access the learning via differing degrees of differentiation (building in time and space for some learners to take side roads, excursions, and spend more time at service stations or wayside stops, consolidating their skills).

Differentiation can be understood as adopting a 'pupil-first' stance, both in terms of overall planning (road map) and in terms of the micro daily decisions teachers make with their pupils (TES 2021; Tomlinson 2021). This puts learners first and content material, though important, second within a person-centred relationship. In such a forward-focusing curriculum there are three central learning goals (TES 2021; Tomlinson 2021):

1 What knowledge do the learners need to have?
2 What understandings do the learners require?
3 What skills do learners need?

The curriculum is embedded within adult–pupil and pupil–pupil relationships, and emphasizes critical understanding, problem-solving, adaptability, resilience, personal responsibility (or agency) and life skills (transition to adulthood) rather than merely recall and retention of content information.

Once the teacher is clear about these fundamentals they can strategically use formative assessment to make sure they know exactly where their pupils are in relation to the curriculum. In this way they can identify what is working, what might be less effective and what additional strategies might be explored. Clearly the classroom teacher cannot do any of these things unless they have organized a clear and structured learning environment where pupils feel safe and secure. Classroom management, organization and routines provide the bedrock for inclusive practice and flexible differentiation to occur effectively (Robinson 2018; TES 2021; Tomlinson 2021).

The difficulty with such a conceptualization of differentiation is that it can be counter to the view that some teachers hold intuitively about what teaching–learning is. Using Tomlinson's (2021) road map analogy again, the curriculum can be seen to be one long straight motorway, which you start on day one of term and stop on the last day when you say 'now we have all covered the curriculum'. But as we have identified, differentiation involves the teacher making micro-decisions about when, where and for how long to deviate from the motorway for some pupils, some of the time. The challenge for teachers and schools is the need to question implicit, often comfortable and taken-for-granted assumptions about pupils and their teaching and learning needs.

As we have seen, differentiation is a framework to guide instruction which asks teachers to put their pupils at the centre of decision-making, not the curriculum or tests/examinations. Differentiation involves the creative and skilful orchestration of the teaching strategies detailed earlier with the explicit goal of supporting learners in different ways so that they can grow and develop at their own pace and to their own level – 'each according to need'.

The teacher can be viewed as being the host and facilitator of the classroom learning environment, who thinks about and plans for what everyone must do in common, then thinks carefully about points where some learners may experience challenges or may require additional support (using the road map analogy again – changing the type of vehicle, adding a trailer, setting up exit ramps, rest and service areas, re-entry points and B-road alternatives). The question posed here is: does the current structure of initial teacher training provide the necessary knowledge, understanding and experiences to develop what is a complex undertaking?

Paradoxically, teachers' and schools' pragmatic responses to the Covid-19 pandemic, and the need during the various lockdowns for virtual teaching–learning, has actually reinvigorated and refocused what it means to differentiate. The challenge of working remotely really forced some schools and teachers to alter their approaches, as just talking for any length of time online simply does not work. Moving forward, the Covid-19 legacy of creative and diverse solutions to meet pupil need during lockdowns will continue. Things with regard to differentiation will never be the same again – a monumental shift has occurred in how schools and teachers understand how they flexibly deliver differentiation (Tomlinson 2021).

In addition, as schools are forced to cut the use of TAs because of budgetary constraints then the sustainability of the current model of inclusion which is so dependent on them will be brought into much starker relief. Webster and Blatchford (2017) caution with reference to the DfE's own people projections that indicate a 15 per cent increase in the number of children and young people requiring some form of specialist education by 2025. They conclude that mainstream schools and classrooms will be forced, whether they like it or not, to enact a much more coherent and evidence-based approach to meeting the needs of all of their learners.

Tomlinson (2021) describes a teacher working remotely with a class of primary-aged pupils. First, they got all the class together and presented visually and with prompt words what they were required to work on (the tasks, with clear session objectives), then they outlined four possible ways to achieve common outcomes. The pupils could work in an *open workroom* with their microphones on so they could chat with their peers about the task and explore ideas and possibilities; or they could work in a *quiet room* with their microphones off, but the chat box open so they could collaborate when they wanted to; or they could work in an *independent room* because they did not want to get distracted; and finally if anyone wanted to get additional support from the teacher they could go to the *teacher support room* at set times, where the teacher could assist one or several pupils. The teacher of course would be rotating between the different rooms offering views, guidance, questions, feedback, challenge and checking on progress.

Conclusion

In England many teachers have found the concept of inclusion and differentiation difficult to both understand and to implement in practice. In those schools where levels of appropriate training and support were high and there was a positive whole-school ethos, inclusive practice was found to be more effective (Ainscow et al. 2000; de Boer et al. 2011; Humphrey and Symes 2013; Navarro-Mateu et al. 2019).

The key challenge for personalization in the classroom is how to cater simultaneously for all the different needs in one class. The priority is to support pupils so that they can keep up with the pace of learning and make good rates of progress. In the past it could be argued that teachers differentiated by task or expectation, and accepted different levels of success. While realistic in some instances and with some pupils, this approach ran the risk of lowering expectations. Today effective teachers expect everyone to succeed by offering higher levels of support or extra challenge for those who need it, so that all pupils can access the learning and gain a personal sense of success.

As we have seen since the adoption in both central government policy and applied practice of inclusive education, there are at times polarized debates on where and how children and young people with learning and related needs should be educated. As we saw in Chapter 2, the Warnock Committee report (Warnock 1978) offered the view that as many as 20 per cent of pupils at some point in their education present with additional learning needs, with 2 per cent of this group presenting with needs which are more complex and long term. Assuming such figures and the assumptions underpinning them are valid, and certainly by default the educational system has not disputed them, then this heterogeneous cohort of learners form a sizeable grouping within any mainstream school or classroom. We argue that such a state of affairs demands that *all* teachers need to be able to work effectively with this broad range of learners.

Successive governments have, whether inadvertently or not, deprofessionalized teaching–learning with slimmed down training routes and introduced a neoliberal market model into education, resulting in access to external specialists like EPs being dependent on ability to pay, not on need.

For many teachers, learners with more complex needs prove to represent an ongoing challenge and, in some cases, a structural 'nuisance' as they are quietly moved to the periphery of the classroom and school community with little or no public or media challenge or indeed concern. For many of these pupils such an uneasy positioning within mainstream schools may negatively impact on their self-acceptance, leading to more limited learning and general disaffection with school (Rose and Howley 2007).

We reconnected with three now somewhat overlooked but enormously influential educational thinkers, Dewey, Vygotsky and Bruner. The challenge is for all teachers to reconnect as scientist-reflective-practitioners to core pedagogical principles (Kelly and Perkins 2012). Such an approach emphasizes for all learners the whole pupil, their culture, background, lived experiences and the need for more personalized and individualized approaches in an inclusive classroom. It was gratifying to review some of the Hattie research, which we argue can be used to inform teacher problem-solving and practice, and find that many of Dewey's, Vygotsky's and Bruner's approaches and strategies or their logical descendants have empirical credibility.

In the next chapter we explore why successive educational reforms have largely failed, and advocate for a refocusing on policymakers and school leaders leading on demonstrable improvement rather than merely change (Robinson 2018).

4 'Too Much Educational Change': Leading Educational Improvement through Theory Engagement between School Leaders and Teachers

Introduction

Since the Warnock Committee report (Warnock 1978), over 40 years of educational reform and organizational change have significantly impacted on English state-maintained schools (government-driven change via legislation, policy, guidance, programmes and interventions, particularly in the area of special educational needs and disabilities; see Chapter 2). There is little research evidence to show that many of these initiatives have actually worked – worked in the sense of leading to sustained institutional change at the school and classroom level, resulting in raised pupil attainment equitably across the country. See the evaluations of the National Literacy and Numeracy Strategies discussed more fully later in this chapter and the more recent debate around the teaching of systematic synthetic phonics (SSP) versus analytic phonics (AP) (Wyse and Bradbury 2022).

The Centre for Social Justice (2007) was one of the first to clearly point out a disturbing quandary in the English state-maintained education system: that despite a 50 per cent increase in central government direct spending on education since 1997, there continued to be a significant educational failure in the most disadvantaged and marginalized groups in society (those with learning or other barriers to their development, those from lower socioeconomic backgrounds, and those in public care, the 'looked-after children'). Indeed, the United Kingdom as a whole has the highest level of educational inequality in the Western world (Centre for Social Justice 2007; Magadi and Middleton 2007; UNICEF 2007; National Equity Panel 2010; Save the Children 2011; Edmond 2017; EEF 2018).

A more recent report (Blundell et al. 2021) clearly demonstrated the large socioeconomic discrepancies in the daily number of hours of education children and young people received during the first national lockdown in England due to the Covid-19 pandemic (March/Spring 2020). During the March/Spring 2020 national lockdown, 74 per cent of pupils attending private schools accessed a 'normal' virtual school day, while the figure for pupils in state-maintained schools was only 38 per cent. A further 25 per cent of pupils attending state-maintained schools did not access any formal schooling and/or tutoring (Andrew et al. 2020; Benzeval et al. 2020; Elliot Major et al. 2020).

Rather reluctantly, politicians, policymakers, researchers, school leaders and teachers alike have come to the conclusion that the sustained impact of many change and reform initiatives on children and young people, in terms of, for example, academic attainments, has been largely marginal (Fullan and Earl 2002; Fullan 2010, 2013; Robinson 2018). Moreover, such a position has emerged despite significantly increased expenditure on education: on developing its school leaders, its staffing, on its infrastructure, on lowering class sizes, and on new polices, curricula and programmes, on an unprecedented scale and scope (Fullan 2010; Waltmann et al. 2020; Bolton 2021; Farquharson et al. 2021).

In this chapter, we emphasize the need for school leaders to focus on the leadership of improvement rather than change. To elaborate on this position, this chapter draws on the pioneering thinking and work of Professor Viviane Robinson (1993, 2018). We hope that by doing so we will raise a timely and much-needed debate in England amongst those involved in starting change initiatives in our schools, to reflect and do things differently.

Educational change and the effectiveness of school reforms: the example of the National Literacy and Numeracy Strategies in England (1997–2002)

In this section, we will explore aspects of the National Literacy and Numeracy Strategies and some of the assumptions they were based on. We then highlight the critical issue that system-wide change often does not lead to sustained educational improvement for children and young people.

In England, before 1998 there are few examples of significant systematic attempts by central government to lead on the *'raising school standards agenda'* by focusing on how core subjects could be developed, constructed and delivered in state-maintained schools.

The National Literacy Strategy, followed by the National Numeracy Strategy, can be seen to be the first examples of such a systematic approach being adopted by central government. These initiatives were followed by the Key Stage 3 Strategy (for 11- to 14-year-olds) and the Early Years Foundation Stage. Such developments ultimately resulted in the National Strategies encompassing all core subject areas (Early Years, Key stages 3 and 4, behaviour and attendance, the School Improvement Partner Programme and special educational needs and disabilities) (DfE 2011, 2016; DfE and Morgan 2016).

Fullan and Earl (2002) provided one rationale for why such large-scale, system-wide educational reforms were needed in the first place. They argue that the 1990s in England and elsewhere saw a distinct conceptual shift in focus by politicians and policymakers towards the notion that some of society's most perplexing issues (child poverty, inequitable pupil achievement, youth disengagement from learning, youth drug and alcohol abuse and violence) did have examples of possible 'solutions' that were working somewhere, however small and obscure.

The assumption seemed to be that many interventions or programme ideas would spread serendipitously in an unplanned manner by articulating a set of guiding principles. The worldwide spread of Alcoholics Anonymous is a good example of this. Sometimes such organic 'learning networks' connect people and places trying to deal with similar dilemmas and who share overlapping goals. The challenge is how to replicate those very local-level solutions everywhere, identifying their key critical components and how their impact is measured. They became known as 'going to scale' initiatives (Bradach 1998; Taylor et al. 2004).

Cyclical faux unease by politicians about the effectiveness of state-maintained schools motivated people to look at how the overall school system could be improved and changed. Alongside the notion of 'going to scale' was the concept of 'sustainable' change. Neither of these concepts was ever clearly defined in operational terms, nor was the underlying theory of systems change being adopted articulated (Hargreaves and Fink 2000).

The National Literacy and Numeracy Strategies can be seen to come from central government taking a directive position (top-down approach), setting and putting in place transparent accountability processes and procedures, and building school capacity. The government's implicit assumption was that by applying organizational *pressure* alongside school- and classroom-level material and pedagogical support, they could achieve substantial system-wide change over a relatively short period of time – in this case, just 5 years. These system-wide initiatives involved all 19,000 primary schools in England at the time. They were and are some of the largest educational change programmes seen anywhere globally.

Fullan et al. (2005: 3–4) stated:

> They established base-line achievement figures (in 1996, 57% of all 11 year olds in the country were achieving at the proficient level in literacy; the mathematics figure was 54%). They set targets for 2002 of 80% for literacy and 75% for numeracy.

The initial outcomes of these large-scale school reforms appeared on the surface to be successful. Fullan and Earl (2002: 3–4) considered that:

> By and large, with some reservations, the English initiative has been an impressive success. In quantitative terms, the 2001 achievement level for literacy is 75% (compared to the 57% starting point); for mathematics it is 71% (versus 54%). It remains to be seen whether the 2002 targets are met.

Later results can be found in *The National Strategies 1997 to 2011* (DfE 2011).

It was Fullan et al.'s (2005) initial view, as the commissioned researchers of the initiatives, that most schools and local authorities at the time were in favour of the reforms. Indeed, who could possibly disagree with the stated intention of 'raising standards for all pupils'? Fullan et al. (2005) were nonetheless cautious. Though the outcomes were initially 'real and impressive', they were seen as being only the first phase in raising literacy and numeracy attainment levels across English state-maintained schools.

The next phase needed to focus much more on developing pupils' 'higher-order thinking' and 'deeper understanding' rather than just core mechanical literacy and numeracy skills, though these are obviously important and provide a foundation for the development of subsequent higher-level skills. The change was directed centrally by government for the first 4 years. At a local school and classroom level, considerable investment in the capacity building was seen, but the overall ownership and conceptual direction were prescribed by the centre (predetermined targets, goals, aims, objectives, scripted lessons, assessment, monitoring and evaluation processes and proformas). This was justified by Fullan et al. (2005) as a necessary prerequisite in any large-scale, system-wide educational reform on such a scale:

- ***Phase 1*** – Top-down initiative designed, directed and led by central government, followed by
- ***Phase 2*** – School system and classroom-level capacity building, followed by
- ***Phase 3*** – Active encouragement to support school leader and teacher reflection, review, creativity and networking with other schools.

The assumption was that the wider school system and classroom would be fundamentally changed forever, leaving behind high-quality programmes for literacy and numeracy that would be sustainable over time (Fullan and Earl 2002).

In a later, more critical review of the evidence, Fullan et al. (2005) were much less effusive. They found that school and classroom environments and the support systems around them had not improved sufficiently to impact on teacher recruitment and retention, that it had negatively affected teacher morale and perceptions of professionalism, and, most starkly, had not resulted in more effective schools and leadership. They found that the school infrastructure (perceptions of professionalism, ownership, agency and ethos) had weakened, and they concluded rather soberly that sustainable large-scale educational change is not possible.

There is little research evidence to support many other key central government policy initiatives which have had equally high public profiles. These include providing schools with more resources, reducing class sizes, streaming groups within classes and teaching of phonics (Allingham 2021). The reality is that much of the guidance sent out to schools by the Department for Education (DfE) have not in fact benefited from high-quality systematic research reviews of available evidence. They have also not actively involved specialist academics and informed practitioners from across the educational community, including teachers and educational psychologists (EPs), nor included the recipients of the planned approaches. Equally, there is an apparent lack of any articulated systemic model of change that leads to improvement and, importantly, takes as its starting point a critical understanding of existing processes and practices rather than imposing external solutions (Robinson 2018; Allingham 2021). School leaders and local authorities have been expected to implement these initiatives even when they have had reservations (see the debates around the teaching of systematic synthetic phonics versus analytic phonics; Wyse and Bradbury 2022).

The remainder of this chapter focuses on sharing some of the pioneering ideas and perspectives developed by Professor Viviane Robinson (1993, 2018) to help us understand the challenges inherent in leading school improvement. Unfortunately, it is beyond our scope here to present her thinking and work in its entirety (please see Robinson 1993, 2011, 2018; Robinson and Lai 2006; Robinson et al. 2008). For our purposes, we will highlight and discuss in *Part 1* some of the key conceptual and definitional distinctions that Robinson makes and about which we need to be clear. In *Part 2*, some of the key elements in understanding the challenge of system-wide school improvement and the importance of engaging with school leaders and teachers' theories of practice will be discussed. In this way, we hope that policymakers and school leaders will be motivated to follow up on Robinson's work in more detail. In so doing they will then be encouraged to review and understand their current approaches critically and look at how they could engage with teachers (and other relevant participants) to focus more on improvement than change.

Part 1: selective key conceptual and definitional distinctions

As we have highlighted already, education is renowned for continual change and reorganization depending on the current central government's ideological orientation, and its perception of wider public opinion and societal trends. But, as we have seen so often, much of this 'change' has resulted in either no improvement or in some cases a regression and increasing inequalities between learners (Fullan et al. 2005).

Making a distinction between leading on change and leading on improvement

Robinson (2018) argued that educational policymakers and school leaders need to distinguish between leading on *change* and leading on *improvement*. Often these two positions are seen as essentially meaning the same thing. But Robinson (2018) argued that this lack of conceptual clarity is why we have 'too much change' and not enough 'sustained improvement' over time in our schools.

The narrative that educational change is somehow inherently good is enshrined in populist discussions around educational policy, reform and concerns about pupil attainment. Settings or schools that have not changed recently can sometimes be dismissed and perceived rather critically. The explicit demand of school leaders is that they should be the 'agents of change', and they are the ones by virtue of their positional management role (and training) to naturally 'lead on such change'. Teachers and other associated staff who do not share such a worldview may be perceived as 'resistant to change' and are either ignored or in extreme cases marginalized in the school system. Their perspectives and voices are not listened to or heard, yet they will still be required to implement 'the change' decided for them whether they understand it, or whether they agree with it. Such an approach merely leads to further confusion, resistance and an increased likelihood that the planned top-down change initiatives will not be fully implemented or embedded in applied educational practice (Robinson 2018).

With time, it is highly likely that any superficial 'change' will merely dissipate, waiting for the next review – and thus the cycle starts again. This is clearly and sadly seen in the government's SEND Green Paper (HM Government 2023) and the very real explicit criticism of its own system-wide programme of supposed 'radical reform', namely the 2014 Children and Families Act.

Equally, parents and carers can be directly and indirectly encouraged to seek out the 'innovative setting or school' in their area or the latest educational approach or 'fad' – good, bad or indifferent as it might be. Such encouragement may be underpinned by an assumption that any innovation or change is inherently better, even when evidence for its positive impact can be merely anecdotal and impressionistic. Central government and local authority politicians and senior officers readily showcase the latest 'innovative setting or school' and/or approach as unequivocally providing evidence of the efficacy of the latest organizational reform or instructional programme (Robinson 2018).

So, in practice, *change* and *innovation* are often interpreted as being synonymous with *progress* and *improvement*. Robinson saw these two concepts as being very different. She contended that to:

> 'lead change is to exercise influence on the ways that move a team, organisation, or system from one state to another. The second state could be better, worse, or the same as the first. To lead improvement is to exercise influence in ways that leave the team, organisation, or system in a *better* state than before.'
> (Robinson 2018: 2, emphasis added)

She stressed that if we make such a functional distinction, we direct policymakers and school leaders to actively and explicitly distinguish between change and improvement. By doing so, they then necessarily need to engage in more critical and reflective conversations with *all* those involved *before* implementing any significant educational reforms – either at an educational system, school or classroom level.

A direct consequence of such an explicit repositioning is an increased accountability for educational policymakers and school leaders to both formulate and communicate the underlying rationale of exactly how a 'proposed change *will* produce the intended improvement' they advocate so vigorously

(Robinson 2018: 3, emphasis added). But such a transparent narrative is very rare in discussion and practice around educational reform and change. The usual approach at central, local and school-level governance is for people to be told to make changes. The objectives of change are often framed in vague terms and in language that is sometimes hard to dispute (for example, teachers will be asked 'to differentiate the curriculum to increase inclusion of SEN pupils and reduce exclusions'; see Chapters 2 and 3). What is missing is any guidance on what these terms mean in the actual classroom (in actionable terms), where they came from and why (what are they a solution to, and what is their evidence base?), how these approaches will impact positively on pupil learning, and how we will know this.

In the following sections, we primarily focus on specific legislation related to SEND (the 2014 Children and Families Act shared in Chapter 2). As we have seen, this legislation emphasized the centrality of families and children and young people as 'co-partners' and at the centre of the SEND process. In addition, the rhetoric focused on concepts such as co-production, aspirations and outcomes, and a fit-for-purpose streamlined process. But as we saw in Chapter 2, this has not been the case, and the numbers of children and young people being put forward for Education, Health and Care assessments has increased (National Statistics 2022), as has dissatisfaction with what has arguably become a more expensive, complex (Sales and Vincent 2018; Pearlman and Michaels 2019), misunderstood, and at times adversarial and overly bureaucratic system (HM Government 2023).

The critical question to ask ourselves is what would have happened if more thought had been given by the central government (Department for Education policymakers) to clearly articulating exactly *how* the proposed changes in the legislation (Children and Families Act 2014) and subsequent *SEND Code of Practice: 0 to 25 Years* (DfE and DoH 2015) would be *more* successful than the then status quo (the previous Statementing process; see Chapter 2). Such a deceptively simple question provides a basis for further critical thinking around identifying the factors that would need to be in place for the proposed change to actually deliver the stated improvements.

Such a position seems sensible and ethical, as change can enormously impact ordinary people's lives, both personally and professionally. In addition, the upheaval of change can be costly in terms of money, resources and human capital, let alone staff morale and mental health. Unless managed well, growing cynicism and distrust can develop, which paradoxically can further undermine implementation.

The following example illustrates this point well. The Children and Families Act required all local authorities to convert their existing Statements of special educational need into a new EHC plan. No standard nationally agreed template was provided, and the EHC plan approach was conceptually significantly more complex than the old Statement format, with the added introduction of 'aspirations' and 'outcomes'. This demand occurred as the austerity cuts across the public sector severely impacted local authorities and resulted in insufficient trained staff, including not enough special educational needs caseworkers or EPs. Some of the unintended consequences of this probably political decision were that the quality of transfers was variable, with some local authorities having to outsource this work to expensive and at times inconsistent private companies and locum agencies. The decision, whether intentionally or not, further consolidated the marketization of education. Private providers proliferated (such as locum EPs and SEN case officers, consultants on short-term contracts and not part of any organizational headcount; see Chapter 2), paid for by scarce public resources that could have potentially been better used and to better effect elsewhere.

In hindsight, and perhaps rather naively, central government could have phased in the transition from Statements to EHC plans and simply directed local authorities to honour Statements up to the age of 19 years old and then review. Those requiring ongoing support would then follow the new EHC plan pathway, as would all new requests from a specific date. Such an approach would have significantly reduced the amount of organizational and personal pressure, and some of the expenditure would have been unnecessary.

What does improvement mean?

Robinson (2018) advocated that the measure of success of any educational change or reform initiative must be the direct impact on learners (academic attainment and wider social-emotional development or similar indices). This goes back to the core purpose of education, which Robinson (2018: 6) summarized as working 'to enable all children and young people to succeed at intellectually engaging and enriching tasks and in so doing to become confident and connected lifelong learners'.

Such overarching statements of the purpose of education are often reflected in school mission and vision statements, policies and development plans; far less so as guiding principles in school leaders' day-to-day decision-making. There is an inherent challenge in using impact as a measure of improvement. Who decides and on what basis which interventions, approaches and strategies will have the most significant impact on pupil learning? Recently education has benefited, as we saw in Chapter 3, from large-scale meta-analysis studies distilling what approaches work and under what conditions (see Hattie 2009). Hattie's work, along with others, provides an increasingly robust evidence base, freely available online to school leaders and teachers to draw on to inform their thinking and practice. But as Hattie (2009) has cautioned, such material is only one aspect of a wider decision-making matrix that needs to reference local context and conditions, including attending to those who will be expected to implement any change – the teachers, and their current practices and pragmatic solutions. There is a place for the full range of quantitative and qualitative approaches.

Research provides school leaders and teachers with the ability to select interventions, approaches and strategies that increase the likelihood of achieving positive improvement. But school leaders and teachers need to undertake their ongoing inquiries into the outcomes the changes are making in their own unique context. At key stages in implementation school leaders need to ask, 'Is the change likely to or actually delivering improvement?' In this way, everyone involved can learn the specific conditions required in their unique context to make interventions work and last (Robinson 2018); see the implementation science literature (Kelly and Perkins 2012).

School leaders do make a difference

Since the introduction of the national curriculum, there has been an increasing focus on comparative data on pupils' educational and related outcomes in schools (Education Reform Act 1988). There is now national and international comparative subject-based data on pupil attainment across regions, countries and educational systems.

Whole-system or school-level change aimed at improving the educational outcomes for pupils focuses largely on developing the attitudes, values, beliefs, skills and competencies of school leaders to lead on the change initiatives. The research evidence is clear that leadership in schools is an important component *after* the quality of classroom teaching and learning practice – often referred to, as we saw in Chapters 2 and 3, as Quality First Teaching (Leithwood et al. 2008; Palardy and Rumberger 2008; Brown et al. 2010).

Quality First Teaching displays the following key characteristics: highly focused lesson design with concrete and clear learning objectives; high demands of pupil involvement and engagement with their learning; high levels of interaction for all pupils; appropriate use of teacher oral feedback, questioning, modelling and explaining; an emphasis on learning through dialogue, with regular opportunities for pupils to talk both individually and in groups; an expectation that pupils will accept responsibility for their learning and work independently; regular use of encouragement and specific praise to engage and motivate pupils (see Chapter 3).

The effective school leader draws on systemic thinking to coordinate those factors that are required to facilitate improvement in their unique context, informed by research (providing a clear vision, order and structure; developing policies; clarity of roles, purposes and responsibilities; developing teacher skill, knowledge, confidence and competence; drawing on the active involvement of children and young people, parents/carers and the wider community).

Robinson (2011) undertook a systematic quantitative literature review of published research focused on the relationship between types of school leadership and associated pupil outcomes. The main conclusion she reached was that school leaders do make an impact by effectively orchestrating five different dimensions. She argued that effect size (see Chapter 3 for a definition) alone does not determine the relative importance of each dimension. It is instead the collective impact of all five of these dimensions on how school leaders can make a difference on pupil outcomes that is relevant.

Robinson (2011, 2018) highlighted the following dimensions:

- Collaborative and rational working relationships with others to set and agree whole-school goals based on the demands of the teaching–learning curriculum, wider community priorities and the data they have about their own unique set of pupils and their learning needs (**Dimension 1**, effect size 0.42).

- Strategic, open and accountable allocation of money, resources and staffing to directly support whole-school goals (**Dimension 2**, effect size 0.31).
- Actively championing, supporting and developing the quality of classroom teaching and learning practice (**Dimension 3**, effect size 0.42).
- Open and realistic orientation about what they and their colleagues need to learn to achieve their collective priority goals (**Dimension 4**, effect size 0.84).

Robinson (2018) further emphasized that the impact of Dimensions 1 to 4 are not on their own likely to support improvement unless school leaders and teachers jointly create an orderly, safe, secure and positive teaching and learning environment for all learners, including those with learning and other barriers (**Dimension 5**, effect size 0.27).

The key takeaway message from Robinson's (2011) meta-analysis is that the more school leaders focus on their professional identity, role, relationships, daily work patterns and learning about the core business of teaching and learning, the greater their impact on pupil outcomes.

Part 2: key elements in understanding the challenge of improvement

Robinson (2018) advocated that in any planned change initiative, whether at a national, school or classroom level, it is a vital first step for school leaders to spend dedicated time really understanding the current practices, strategies and approaches that they wish to alter. The rationale offered is that the most challenging part of the change process is not the planning phases but the implementation (see implementation science initiatives and models; Kelly and Perkins 2012). This is because there is always uncertainty associated with the processes required to integrate and calibrate new practices with existing behaviour patterns.

The following worked example illustrates some of the points being made. Based on a recent central government-led research synthesis and a school-wide review, a head teacher has become increasingly concerned about the teaching of early literacy in their primary school, especially with those who were apparently struggling at the very early stages. As a result, they decide to introduce a new approach to the teaching of early literacy. The change involves teachers being required to adopt and use an integrated whole language approach to the teaching of early literacy skills. The plan is to embed the current grapho-phonic (phonological processing or phonic elements) within meaningful text reading instruction in small, teacher-led instructional groups, rather than separated out as was done before (relying on small-group teaching of phonic rules and patterns in isolation, with follow-up practice worksheets). For a significant majority of teachers, adhering to this 'new' teaching model requires them to alter their classroom practices and related values, attitudes and beliefs around the best way to teach early literacy, and more particularly phonic skills, especially to those who struggle. This creates a dilemma, with some teachers continuing to believe in the need to directly teach phonics as a separate component before introducing structured text reading.

Understanding teachers' theories-of-action

Robinson (2018), building on the earlier work of Argyris (1993, 1999) as well as Argyris and Schön (1974, 1992), argued that an essential part of leading on improvement is understanding a teacher's current thinking and reasoning about their role and practices. Often the gap between the intentions for change, the reality of implementation and the lack of impact partly exists because this thinking and reasoning (the practitioner's 'set of governing variables' or their 'theory-of-action') is not engaged with or understood but is in fact bypassed (Robinson 1993, 2018; Kennedy and Monsen 2016).

Theories-of-action take two forms: **espoused theory** (what teachers *say* they do, termed 'talk theories') and **theory-in-use** (what teachers *actually* do, termed 'walk theories') (Argyris and Schön 1974, 1992; Argyris 1999; Robinson 2018). Identifying theories-in-use is vital in identifying the impact of teacher thinking and reasoning on their actual classroom practice. Theories-of-action have three components: (1) the actions (or outward teacher behaviours), (2) the beliefs, attitudes and values assumed to have produced those actions and (3) the intended and unintended consequences of those beliefs, attitudes and actions.

The example shared earlier around the teaching of early literacy and phonics shows that the practices that the head teacher has unilaterally identified as needing to change are the outward indication of underlying and tacit teacher theories around how they achieve their goals (in this case 'How do I teach children to read?' 'How do I teach struggling early readers to read?' and the belief that teaching phonics as a separate, distinctive component is a defensible teaching strategy).

Uncovering theories-of-action is not easy, and is made even more complicated by (1) the differences between espoused theory-of-action and theories-in-use, (2) the observation that most people are unaware of the discrepancies between the two and (3) the prevalence in organizations such as schools of single- as opposed to double-loop learning processes (Argyris 1999) (see Figure 4.1).

'Double-loop learning' occurs when the mismatch between a teacher's espoused and in-use theory-of-action (i.e. the mismatch between *what I say I do* and *what I actually do*) is made explicit and an effort made to correct the

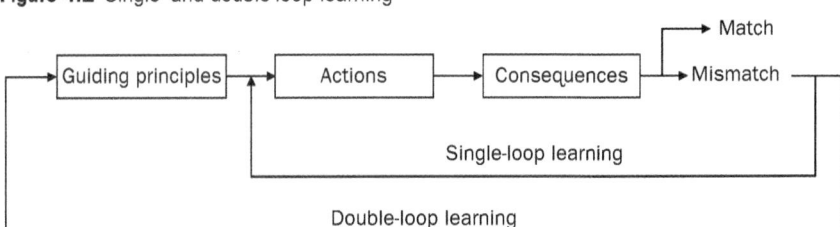

Figure 4.1 Single- and double-loop learning

Source: Adapted from Robinson (2018): Figure 2.4.

discrepancies by examining the governing variables underpinning those actions. Engaging with double-loop learning processes is more likely to increase teacher and, therefore, implementation effectiveness, as it leads to changes in the underlying principles governing teacher actions (classroom organization and teaching practices). This has an increased likelihood of ensuring that any change will be long-lasting (Argyris 1993; Robinson 1993).

'Single-loop learning' leads to superficial changes in teacher behaviour and practice. This type of change may deal with problem situations. However, because the core principles governing teacher actions are not changed, the issues manifest themselves elsewhere, or the change is never embedded in practice and therefore not sustained.

An approach like Robinson's (2018) provides policymakers and school leaders with a framework for uncovering espoused and in-use theories-of-action, but it also provides a structured process to support the implementation of change that leads to improvement.

Building on the earlier literacy example, Table 4.1 presents the theory-of-action for Elissa, who teaches a Reception class (5- and 6-year-old children at varying stages in the literacy process, from emergent to independent). Though her classroom is well managed and orderly, she is struggling to cater for the literacy needs of all of her pupils – in particular, those who are emergent and who she has concluded probably have special educational needs. Class attainment data demonstrates a pattern of a small but significant grouping of children across the Reception classes who are still at the emergent stage, even after a term of structured small-group phonics input. The head teacher is not convinced that they therefore must all have SEN.

Although we are focusing on one teacher for illustrative purposes, it is important to stress that theories-of-action can cover a group, and organizational and wider levels of analysis as well. If Elissa's head teacher could ascertain her theory-of-action, they would then be in a much better position to understand the causal relationships between what she currently does (in terms of her classroom approach to the teaching of early literacy skills, particularly with those children who struggle with getting past the phonic screener hurdle) and why she does it (the core value she places on the importance of the direct instruction of phonics in small groups), and the consequences of those beliefs, attitudes and actions for her pupils' level of attainment in early literacy skills.

When the head teacher fully understands Elissa's theory-of-action (thinking and reasoning), they will appreciate the basis of her current practice and what may be involved in trying to change or alter it. The challenges of change are proportional to the degree of 'tension between theories-of-action in current practice and the theories-of-action required by the proposed new practice' (Robinson 2018: 17).

Such an understanding supports school leaders in foreseeing teacher responses to their proposed changes more accurately. If Elissa's head teacher accurately understands her current theory-of-action, they will be in a better position to identify the specific areas of difference between her theory and the theory they are advocating. Elissa may take from the head teacher's proposals a direct personal criticism of her view of the centrality of directly teaching phonic rules and patterns. This may lead to defensiveness and disengagement. Unless managed well, the head teacher's plan may in fact be seen as undermining both Elissa's view on phonics and her teaching practice.

Table 4.1 A comparison between Elissa's current and possible future theory-of-action for teaching early literacy (adapted from Robinson 2018: 16)

Elissa's current theory-of-action for teaching early literacy skills	Head teacher's preferred theory-of-action for Elissa's teaching
Key beliefs, attitudes and values • My job is to run a well-managed and orderly classroom. • My job is to teach children how to read. • I believe that children need to know their phonics, which is critical to reading, and these need to be taught first and separately. • I believe that only when the children have passed their phonics screener test can they be introduced to real books.	Key beliefs, attitudes and values • My job is to teach children how to read. • Although phonological processing (grapho-phonics) is an important component, semantic (meaning), syntax (structure) cues and oral language are equally relevant. • With support and training I can learn how to integrate grapho-phonic skills by exposing children to actual meaningful text reading (enabling children to cross-check between the three main cue systems as they learn to become independent readers).
Current actions	**Proposed actions**
• All pupils who do not know their phonics are taught these skills and patterns in a structured small group. • Follow-up worksheets are used for practice and consolidation. • Once they have passed a phonic screening test then they move on to real books (some emergent pupils have been in the direct instruction phonic group for over a term).	• Using running record analysis, all children are provided with texts that are at their level. • Using a grouping system the teacher provides direct small-group support to all pupils, encouraging the development of the three main cues and reinforcing their use with a focus on accuracy and comprehension. • Self-correction rate (derived from running record analysis) is used as a measure of progress over time. • There is a strong emphasis on rich oral language, word study and storytelling in the class. • Follow-up worksheets are used as consolidation practice only.

Table 4.1 (Continued)

Actual consequences	Future consequences
• Children are taught phonics through direct instruction in a small group. • Once they pass a phonics screener they then move on to real books. • There is a small group of emergent children who have not progressed even after a term of input. • Labels such as 'SEN pupil' are being applied to them. • Teacher not sure what to do to raise their attainment and feels they need formal assessment by an EP.	• All children have had a screening assessment (using running record analysis not a phonics screener) and are provided with appropriate real books. • Children's progress is monitored regularly using self-correction rate as an indication of progress. • The children are all reading books and making progress against their baseline levels.

The takeaway point here is that school leaders who spend time actively inquiring into their teachers' theories-of-action are in a far better position both to understand what might be at stake for them and to have access to potential pathways to facilitate positive change. In Elissa's situation, those pathways might include:

- learning opportunities that share both the latest content knowledge around the teaching of early literacy and why (evidence-based insights delivered by their link EP, specialist teacher, school advisor or similar with the school lead on literacy)
- opportunities to shadow or observe other teachers that build on her current skills and introduce the required new teaching approaches and acknowledge that grapho-phonic skills *are* important but need to be embedded within actual text reading at the child's level.

School leaders leading on improvement – to engage or to bypass?

Figure 4.2 presents the bypass and engage pathways that school leaders need to be aware of if they are to 'reduce change and increase improvement'. Within each pathway, a school leader actively and passionately advocates their proposals for change, either at the school or classroom level. Sometimes the perceived necessity for change is generated by the head teacher (as in the literacy example), and at other times by directives from central or local government. The beginning phase of each pathway is exactly the same; the head teacher wants change to occur in their school.

In Figure 4.2, change can be seen to involve two theories-of-action. In the literacy example, the head teacher wanted Elissa and her colleagues to alter aspects of their current approach to the teaching of early literacy, in particular phonics and meeting the needs of all learners, some of whom were finding the initial stages challenging. The head teacher's stated position is an espoused

Figure 4.2 The bypass and engage approaches to leading improvement

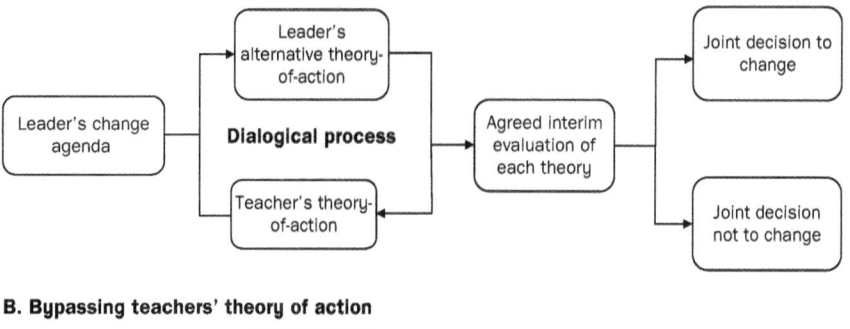

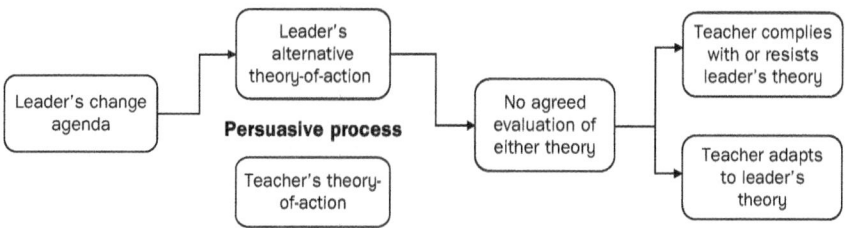

A. Engaging teachers' theory-of-action

```
Leader's change agenda → Dialogical process:
  • Leader's alternative theory-of-action
  • Teacher's theory-of-action
→ Agreed interim evaluation of each theory →
  • Joint decision to change
  • Joint decision not to change
```

B. Bypassing teachers' theory of action

```
Leader's change agenda → Persuasive process:
  • Leader's alternative theory-of-action
  • Teacher's theory-of-action
→ No agreed evaluation of either theory →
  • Teacher complies with or resists leader's theory
  • Teacher adapts to leader's theory
```

Source: Robinson et al. (2009).

theory, and highlights that they are concerned about the variable levels of literacy attainment in their school at the Reception level, particularly in a group of emergent readers. Their belief is that this situation can be improved by changing how early literacy lessons (and phonics in particular) are structured and delivered by teachers. The theory-of-action of the other participants, Elissa and her colleagues, makes sense of what they are currently doing regarding the teaching of early literacy skills, particularly phonics (and is a theory-in-use).

Robinson (2018) stressed that the key difference between the two pathways (bypass and engage) is the degree to which the head teacher, at an early stage in the proposed change process, critically engages and explores the tacit theories that underlie, maintain and make sense of current teacher classroom practice. In this way there is an increased likelihood that a constructive dialogue can occur between the two theories-of-action.

It is vital at the early stages of any change project to spend time understanding the current situation and jointly checking out assumptions and attributions before deciding to move forward. This key phase is largely left out of the majority of change projects, where at best, a rather superficial 'consulting with key stakeholders' time-bounded exercise is undertaken. This can lead to cynicism and disengagement, where people feel 'done unto' and that 'hidden agendas' may be operating. Such consultation activities may elicit feedback on the proposed change plan, but they do not enable anything meaningful to be said or factored into thinking about current practice, what maintains it, what its impacts are and what aspects actually require revision, or indeed if they actually do.

The outcome of the first phase of shared inquiry is a clear understanding of the theories underpinning current practices agreed on by all of those involved. The strengths and limitations of current practice can then be compared with a school leader's proposals. Remember, the measure of the success of any educational change project is the stated positive impact it will have on pupil achievement: this focus needs to be at the forefront of all inquiry, discussion and analysis.

Figure 4.2 talks about an 'agreed interim evaluation of each theory'. This is framed in this manner to reflect the very real uncertainty at this stage that the proposals will actually make a positive difference to emergent pupil literacy attainment data, for children who at an early age are beginning to be labelled 'SEN'. If we look at the engagement pathway, a key outcome is both a shared understanding and an agreement that, overall, the current teaching of literacy (phonics and meeting the needs of those pupils who are struggling) is not as effective as it could be. As such, trying out a new approach is therefore justifiable, given the effort both personally and professionally and in terms of the resources required. In this systematic process, it is equally valid for there to be consensus that actually change is not currently required, or is not possible at this time due to clearly agreed constraints (Robinson 2018).

If we now turn to the bypass pathway, some head teachers (and school leaders) appear to operate as if they do not realize that the teaching practices and approaches they are so keen to change are merely the outward signs of underlying tacit theories-of-action. While head teachers may have a clear view on such practices, and may indeed judge them negatively, there is in fact no shared evaluation of the underpinning theories, because the values, attitudes and beliefs that help us understand those actions remain largely hidden and not open to scrutiny (Robinson 2018).

Head teachers going down a bypass route ultimately end up in one of two places. The first is that teachers implement their proposals because improvement can be achieved with single- rather than double-loop changes. This recognizes the fact that teachers can integrate new approaches and strategies into their existing classroom practices as long as they fit within their existing teaching repertoire and do not significantly challenge their equilibrium. The second is that their proposals are either complied with or resisted by teachers due to positional power, entitlement and influence issues over them (Robinson 2018).

Some limitations of adopting the bypass pathway

Double-loop learning is less likely to occur – In situations where change proposals are largely in conflict with teachers' values, attitudes and beliefs and double-loop changes are needed, adopting a bypass pathway is likely to be ineffective. If the areas of disagreement between the current and alternative theories-of-action are not openly dealt with and resolved, teachers may be resistant to changing their current behaviour as they cannot see how the new proposals address their core values, attitudes and beliefs. To implement improvement requires the discipline of spending time jointly identifying and then resolving areas of disagreement in a systematic manner. As one can imagine, this work is not easy and may well put people off attempting it in the first place. In the bypass pathway, this task is left to teachers to work through by default. As an unintended consequence, there are often large gaps between change vision, designs, proposals, implementation and ultimate impact. This is often expressed through delays, resistance, inadequate budgets and the polarization of positions by both the leaders of the change and those expected to put their ideas into practice. Robinson (2018) suggests that a lack of a detailed conceptual understanding of the theories underpinning the practices they wish to influence will deny change leaders opportunities to be aware of what their proposals actually mean in the real-world context, including both an appreciation of the factors that will enable and distort implementation (Robinson 2018).

A lack of rigour in scrutinizing the alternative theory – The bypass pathway may be ineffective because those involved – both those leading and driving the change and the participants who are expected to put it into practice – fail to spend sufficient time fully understanding what the change means and its intended and unintended consequences. Whatever the proposed change is, be it a new educational policy or reform, a new intervention or teaching approach is based on the presumption that it is better than current custom and practice. This is an empirical question and demands objective inquiry exploring both the strengths and weaknesses of the existing and proposed theories-of-action. Without such critical scrutiny, errors in reasoning and misunderstandings about a shared agreed definition of what the starting problem or need is in the first place ('What is the problem that this proposal is a solution to?' and 'Is it actually a problem and for whom?') will not be voiced. As a result, opportunities to revise project designs and implementation protocols are largely lost (Robinson 2018).

Mutual mistrust may develop – Adopting the bypass strategy can unintentionally increase the likelihood of mutual mistrust developing between the leaders of change and those that will be expected to implement their vision in the real world. Teacher mistrust may develop if those leading on change have articulated limited knowledge or interest in trying to understand the differences between current practice and the changes they advocate. Often discussions focus on generalized statements around what is perceived as being wrong with current practice and/or rarefied statements such as 'we need to move to a situation where we meet the needs of all children and young people by hearing their voices'. But what does this statement actually mean? Have teachers not been listening to pupils for many years? Is there a new way of listening that will do what, and is it better? The evidence base, and certainly the reasoning behind some of these assertions, is often hard to track down.

Teachers may therefore, rightly or wrongly, interpret a presumed lack of knowledge and interest, and recourse to platitudes as signalling that those leading on change have little real regard for what it is that they are requiring of them. Change leaders may equally become frustrated and not trust teachers (or similar participants), interpreting their behaviour (questions, concerns, worries, anxieties, slowness) as indicating that they are stuck and do not want to change, and are by association 'a problem'.

Those serious about wanting to lead successful educational improvement need to sincerely believe in the power of building and sustaining strong working coalitions between themselves and teachers. Such coalitions are the foundations that support the development of trust and shared understandings. They are central to well thought through, coherent and coordinated change initiatives. Adopting the bypass pathway, either deliberately or by default, is unlikely to engender the interpersonal and intellectual trust required to forge such coalitions.

It is beyond the scope of this chapter to detail the precise phases, processes and methodologies that facilitate such theory engagement. What we can do by way of a summary is to highlight the 'four phases of theory engagement' described by Robinson and Timperley (2013; Robinson 2018):

Phase 1 – Agree on the problem to be solved and clearly define it.
Phase 2 – Inquire into the relevant current theory-of-action.
Phase 3 – Evaluate the relative merit of the current and alternative theories-of-action.
Phase 4 – Implement and monitor a new, sufficiently shared theory-of-action.

The methodological approaches used at each phase to sample and scrutinize perceptions can involve: the sharing and critical interpretation of data (pupil attainment data, research on the efficacy of various teaching strategies and interventions); observation of practice, individual and group interviews, where skilful questioning is vital (using accessible dialogue frameworks to explore assumptions, attributions and theories (Monsen et al. 2021); and engaging in authentic exploration of real-world situations (see Robinson 1993, 2018)).

Conclusion

The crucial takeaway message from Robinson's (2018) thinking and work is that it is the quality of both interpersonal and intellectual relationships that is key. Leading on improvement always involves working skilfully through others. It is the skilfulness of those leading on such improvement initiatives in forming coalitions that is core. This theme percolates throughout the process from the initial stages of gaining a detailed 'appreciation' of the theories that give meaning and purpose to the practices of people that others want to change.

Robinson (2018) carefully used the words 'respect' and 'curiosity' as key attributes if policymakers and school leaders want to understand the day-to-day impact of their proposals fully. For some school leaders and policymakers, such a position necessitates an enormous personal, professional and cultural shift from a stance of advocating their views and opinions from a position of power and entitlement towards much more of a collaborative-focused inquiry.

Such an inquiry identifies, checks out and evaluates the relative standings (assumptions, attributions) of current and proposed alternative theories-of-action. This then is what Robinson terms leading improvement through theory engagement, which we feel needs much wider dissemination, exploration and development by policymakers and school leaders (Robinson and Timperley 2013; Robinson 2018).

5 Time for a Revisioning of the State School System: Acknowledging What Is Not Working and Creating an Educational Pedagogy that Reflects a Nation's Values and Aspirations

Introduction

In this chapter it is argued that the English state education system is long overdue for an in-depth and thorough review, to enable quality pedagogical reform to be enacted which reflects the aspirations and values of its citizens. As Fullan et al. (2020: 22) say in their report:

> Across the globe, there is a growing recognition at the policy level, of the need to revamp national systems relative to goals, curriculum, pedagogy, assessment, and the roles of teachers, students, and just about everyone who works with students. Put another way, there is a radical convergence that something is fundamentally wrong with education – a disquiet that is felt at both the policy and local level (which is not to say that there will be agreement about the solution).

Such a reimagining will and should be influenced and directed by all in society, and despite human nature a democratic consensus is, we believe, achievable if all are engaged in the conversation. The UNESCO Report *Reimaging our Futures Together* (2021: 13) says:

> As a shared societal endeavour, education builds common purposes and enables individuals and communities to flourish together. A new social contract

for education must not only ensure adequate and sustained public funding for education, but also include a society-wide commitment to including everyone in public discussions about education. This emphasis on participation is what strengthens education as a common good – a form of shared well-being that is chosen and achieved together.

In order to participate in this discussion, it is vital that citizens are explicitly told about how over the past couple of decades governments have tried to convince them (or the populous?) that their political and economic reforms help develop both an inclusive education system and an inclusive society. It is therefore our intention in this chapter to provide several key examples of how educational policy, and specifically special educational needs (SEN) legislation and required guidance, have been deliberately constructed through a neoliberal, marketization lens, resulting in direct conflict with the vision and aspirations of inclusive education, and impacting significantly on the curriculum, the role of teachers, the well-being of our pupils, and on the state-run education system itself.

Inclusion and inclusive practice – is this actually possible in our current system?

Our answer to this question is a definite and loud 'no', despite the fact that we believe the majority of state schools and academies in England mention in their mission or vision statements or policies that they are 'an inclusive school'. We suggest that, if asked, the vast majority of educators (qualified teachers) would wholeheartedly agree with the principle of inclusion and inclusive practice (Schâringer 2022). But when asked how possible it is to implement it as a continual process in English classrooms, the percentage agreeing would fall significantly. As already discussed (see Chapter 2), the lack of a national definition provided in legislation, detailed in policy and applied to classroom practice (Chapter 4) means that a coherent approach is unachievable. This results in the inconsistent and disparate application of policy into schools, particularly impacting on equity of provision and resources for our most vulnerable children and young people across England.

Unsurprisingly, such an unwillingness to tackle this issue by successive governments across the decades has meant that other key educational changes such as the introduction of the radical, but arguably necessary national curriculum in 1988 (see Chapter 2) and the reliance on examination-only qualifications more recently, while aimed at raising standards, cannot be deemed to be positive for disadvantaged pupils or teachers. When reviewing the impact of the national curriculum, Oates (2011: 130) wrote that:

> In line with research on high quality pedagogy (Stigler and Stevenson, 1999), contextualisation of this content [of the national curriculum] should be left to teachers and schools, since the careful and subtle contextualisation of fundamental concepts is the key to deep learning and to unlocking the motivation of individual learners, and of different groups of learners
> (Stigler and Stevenson, 1999; Black et al., 2003)

The requirement of teachers to evidence 'pace and continual progress', we would argue, has continued to hinder this vital aspect of the teaching of the national curriculum. Politicians and society need to trust teachers as professionals skilled in their craft rather than just as deliverers of the national curriculum. With regard to the latter earlier point, Burgess and Thomson's recent study (2019: 4) relating to the 2017 GCSE reforms found that:

> The overall result is clear: we find a statistically well determined effect, small but going in the direction of further disadvantaging the disadvantaged, in all of these areas across the nation. So far at least, and although it could be argued that positive effects may take longer to come through, the GCSE reforms have widened the attainment gap as young people move into the labour market or on to further study.

These two examples, written almost a decade apart, show how changes to the curriculum and assessment can easily impede inclusive practice and increase inequality. Such pressures can cause professional tensions, parental dissatisfaction and anxiety for many pupils who are considered disadvantaged, such as having a special educational need.

Generic curriculum changes were made to meet what was deemed necessary to increase standards and provide a suitably skilled workforce for economic growth. Such an aim cannot be faulted, but by following a neoliberal economic philosophy, the wider implications were neglected. As time has demonstrated, such an approach has had a negative impact on the professional identity and experiences of teachers, on the well-being of pupils (especially the most vulnerable) and on the wider employability of young people for the benefit and efficiency of society. Due to the national curriculum teachers were less able to teach in a manner most appropriate for their context and for the needs of the individual pupils. It tended to ignore the 'softer' but essential social and emotional needs of the pupils which, as professionals, teachers would recognize through their acquired theoretical knowledge. We remember the many subject files produced when the national curriculum was introduced, and later the rigid objectives and time frames for lessons with the National Literacy and Numeracy Strategies. As Earl et al. (2001: 36) say, 'There is, at best, uneven evidence that such practices can be counted on to "produce" numeracy and literacy gains.' Fortunately, the precise teaching of lessons inherent in the National Strategies has loosened, but the stresses and strains of league tables, expected levels of attainment and a knowledge-based curriculum remain (Oates 2011).

It is in this manner, we argue, that as stated previously (Chapter 2) a teacher's role began to be seen by governments (and perhaps by wider society, as discussed in Chapter 6) as a technical para-professional, one where knowledge is 'delivered' to pupils, who learn it (Stevenson 2015). Thus began, either consciously or subconsciously, what we would describe as the deprofessionalizing of teachers and the decline in the quality of pedagogy and teacher development (NASUWT n.d.). We are certainly not disputing that a national curriculum was positive and necessary, and as Dewey, Vygotsky and Bruner (explored in Chapter 3) all emphasize, teachers do need to have good subject or content knowledge, but they also argue that the curriculum should be flexible enough for them to be creative and innovative (Gray and MacBlain 2015).

Of course, the financial and organizational 'cost' of inclusion cannot be ignored. This is an influential reason why in the past few decades only 'adjustments' have been made to the various special educational needs Codes of Practice and other policies trying to meet the needs of vulnerable pupils, rather than undertaking the total remodelling of the whole system, and preferably in our view doing away completely with the SEND 'shadow' school system, as has even recently been 'celebrated' (HM Government 2023: 3). Dramatic and costly certainly, but is there a different way if politicians, policymakers and society as a whole decide they want to continue with the process of educational and societal inclusion?

In the next section of this chapter, we look at a selection of actions which have disrupted and stalled the progress of educational inclusion and brought greater inequalities for those pupils labelled as having a special educational need or disability.

A selective overview of the recent past and current inequity in the state education SEND system: a perfect storm in waiting?

The state education system, especially since the 1944 Education Act, has seen considerable change in the management, funding and running of schools, its curricula, pedagogy, teacher education, assessment and inspection systems and societal expectations of schools (West 2022). These various changes in national policy have frequently been actioned due to the election of new governments or education ministers, and have required school staff to be unquestioning in response to the timescales for implementation of new legislation. What has become clearer is the lack of a cohesive, progressive school education plan which can evolve and develop alongside the 4 or 5-yearly change of governments and cabinets. Visions have been written but then quietly disappear if another political agenda is introduced, causing confusion and disruption to local authorities, school leaders, teachers and parents/carers (Smith et al. 2018).

The inclusion and special educational needs agendas have been particularly vulnerable to such changes, and clearly illustrate the complexities of providing for all pupils' needs. All English governments since the signing of the Salamanca Statement (UNESCO 1994) have stated that they wish to see the development of inclusive practice in education and society but have neglected to provide a clear definition of how they interpret 'inclusion and inclusive practice' for those implementing policy into practice at the local level, and indeed individual school and classroom levels. With such a lack of conceptual clarity it is not surprising that the interpretation of policies, and thus the implementation processes, vary between regions or local authorities. Often perceived as unfair or inequitable by educators, parents, carers and pupils, with their own understanding of inclusion, the various application processes for additional 'special educational need' and/or disability support (as described in the SEND Code of Practice; DfE and DoH 2015) can be interpreted as inflexible, process-driven and dependent on how well forms are completed instead of on the actual needs of the child or young person. Further, as discussed in Chapter 2, the SEND 'shadow' or silo system (Hodkinson and Burch 2019) frequently operates in opposition with the wider school system agendas, which are attainment- and target-driven.

In an attempt to ensure their school(s) achieve positive inspection grades and high academic targets, some head teachers can feel that they have no option but to redirect and 'ignore' their inclusive principles in favour of achieving these nationally set attainment goals, due to financial and resource scarcity. An example of this conflict for school leaders and Year 6 teachers can and does occur when they are preparing pupils for their statutory assessment tests (SATs) in Year 6 (age 10–11) (Schâringer 2022). Year 6 is the final year of primary school education, when pupils are prepared to move on to secondary school. The results from the SATs will travel with them to their new school and influence decisions made about the classes they are placed in and access to curriculum subjects. Therefore they are considered important by both parents and carers and pupils. Additionally, the results from these tests are recorded nationally in league tables, and schools (and thus teachers) are judged on how many of their pupils meet or exceed the 'expected'[2] level of attainment. This in turn can have a negative or positive influence on inspection outcomes, and thus on teachers' and especially head teachers' roles or careers. With such 'high stakes', some head teachers decide to direct teachers to focus on providing additional support for pupils who will be able to achieve this requirement with a little additional short-term tuition. In order to do this, time, resources and much-needed support has to be 'taken away' from those with additional/special educational needs. Faced with such consequences, it is not surprising that some choose to follow this route.

To us, the whole foundation of this thinking is lacking sense, and in conflict with what we know about child development. Even having an 'expected' or 'average' attainment is problematic. At times pupils need to be allowed to be slow in understanding and embedding new skills or information. The real reasonable

---

[2] Such practice and testing does not recognize pupils as individuals with many different qualities and speeds of development and progress.

and sensible (and measurable) question needs to be 'Is the pupil making progress against their own baseline, albeit slow?' Being slower than others does not mean that a pupil needs to be supported or 'taught' by a TA or even attend a special school. We need to look at each pupil's learning and social needs in comparison to themselves and in relation to how their curriculum needs are being met. Such conflicting policies, we suggest, lead without doubt to an inequitable education system where inclusive practice is put aside in favour of reaching national targets, failing pupils and excluding them from opportunities to gain functional needs, and to feel valued and safe. Not only is this harmful to pupils' social-emotional development and their ongoing education, but it can cause teachers to become disillusioned and question their worth. They may have a personal and professional belief in inclusive teaching, but being instructed to act in an exclusionary manner for the benefit of the school's reputation can be devastating, leading them in some extreme circumstances to leave the profession altogether, or just accept that they are there merely to deliver the curriculum (DfE 2018). This was evidenced in a Department for Education (DfE) 2018 report which stated that:

> Teachers spoke of feeling demoralised for not having their own professional judgement trusted and their experience/teaching skills undermined, and that the restrictive curriculum and teaching methods took the 'excitement' and pleasure out of teaching.
>
> (DfE 2018: 25)

In conclusion, this report stated that:

> A number of teachers reported that increasing respect for the profession would support retention. Although there were no suggestions as to how this could be achieved, it was clear that teachers feeling more respected and valued would have gone somewhere to retaining them in the sector. With this there appeared to be a need for more trust and autonomy for teachers, with less scrutiny to allow them the flexibility to teach how they feel would best suit their pupils.
>
> (DfE 2018: 52)

It is suspected that emphasis on pupils achieving an 'artificially' proclaimed expected level can also encourage some teachers to identify pupils who might be developing a little more slowly for a specific period of time, with a special educational need, instead of supporting them appropriately without a label, giving them the required experiences to move forward physically, socially, emotionally and cognitively. In this way they can feel there is an identifiable reason outside of their immediate control for the lack of pupil progress (Daniels et al. 2019).

This may be one of the reasons why the rise in the number of pupils identified as having a special educational need, either at the SEN Support level or requiring an EHC plan, has risen year on year since the introduction of the revised SEND Code of Practice in 2015 (DfE and DoH 2015). National Statistics (2022) clearly demonstrate that the demand for pupils to be recognized as requiring additional support at either SEN Support or EHC plan level has grown considerably. For example, as of January 2022 the number of pupils with an EHC plan has increased to 473,255 from 430,697 (+9.9 per cent) in 2021, and by 50 per cent (4 per cent of all pupils) (54 per cent if Statements of special educational needs are included) since 2016. In the same time period pupils requiring SEN Support has increased by 14 per cent (12.6 per cent of all pupils), resulting in a total of 1.5 million, or 16.5 per cent of all pupils, in England regarded as have special educational needs (January 2022) (DfE and DoH 2015).

Although the manner in which the statistics have been presented from the Office of National Statistics does not allow for each year group's figures to be examined separately, the data clearly state that SEN is most prevalent at age 10, reaching a peak of 20 per cent, just when SATS are being held. In this way the 'new' SEND system appears to have replicated the identification increase caused by the previous version of the Code of Practice (DfES 2001), which reached a level of 21.1 per cent in 2010 instead of 'playing a vital role in underpinning the major reform programme' (DfE and DoH 2015: 11). Although a SEN Review had already been commissioned by the then New Labour government, some local authorities, suffering immense financial pressures, encouraged or told schools to remove pupils who were on the SEN register requiring 'School-Action' (as required under the SEN Code of Practice; DfES 2001), as these pupils should be able to be appropriately included in school without further external support.[3] This caused a huge conundrum for many school leaders, and especially SENCos, who, perhaps only a few weeks after telling parents/carers that their child was being placed on the SEN register, had to inform them that this was no longer necessary – such actions adding to parental dissatisfaction with the educational system.

Parental engagement in the SEND system

Of course, there are many other factors involved in such a complex matter which encompass the vast majority of justice concerns across society. As has already been demonstrated (Chapter 2), for example, the SEND Code of Practice (DfE and DoH 2015) purports to galvanize the involvement of parents, carers and the pupils themselves in all decisions regarding their special educational needs. Another important element of recent SEND policy is the promotion of professionals working with parents and carers in designing the interventions and provisions for their children with additional needs. Using a business, marketization approach and language such as collaboration, co-production and cooperation, parents/carers can and do believe they are valued partners whose voices are listened to regarding their child's needs. In this way the SEND Code

---

[3] This was subsequently continued and responded to by the succeeding Coalition (Conservative and Liberal Democrat) government, resulting in what became the revised SEND Code of Practice in 2015.

of Practice (DfE and DoH 2015) has without question created false hopes and expectations around what and how parents/carers can really influence the EHC assessment and plan processes. When reviewing the required processes for an EHC plan it is clear that parents/carers can little influence the procedures, and with ever-increasing pressures on specialist school places and funds local authorities have available, it is not surprising that parents/carers are frequently disillusioned and disappointed (Boddison and Soan 2021).

Statistics collected by the government demonstrate that parents/carers did feel more confident to either request or support schools in seeking an EHC assessment/plan since the implementation of the revised SEND Code of Practice (DfE and DoH 2015; DfE 2022). Since 2016 the number of pupils with an EHC plan has increased by 50 per cent across the age range (including it must be said the extended age groups 0–5 and 16–25), rising by 9 per cent between 2021 and 2022 alone. This means that 24 per cent of all pupils with SEN had an EHC plan in January 2022. Even the percentage of pupils receiving SEN Support, which prior to 2016 had stayed relatively stable, had grown from 12.2 per cent to 12.6 per cent. During the period 2020–1 there was a further rise of 77,000 to just under 1.5 million pupils identified and labelled as having special educational needs, out of a school population of 9 million (including independent schools) (DfE 2022). Of course, it must be said this was an exceptional year due to the nascent stages of recovery from the global Covid-19 pandemic, but this still represents a staggering 16.5 per cent of all pupils.

This could suggest that parents, carers and teachers felt more confident that their 'voices' would be heard. It could also indicate that parents/carers were worried their child was not getting the support they needed, and that teachers and schools were not getting the funding they required to provide such additional support. Whichever is true, it is still the case that with such massive rises in applications local authorities have to somehow provide additional administration to cope with them. This includes commissioning educational psychologists (EPs) and others to undertake assessments despite significant shortages of such personnel, in part due to the lack of a coordinated national specialist workforce development plan. Additionally, extra funding is probably most frequently requested by schools and parents/carers through the 'High Needs' (DfE and DoH 2015) process to be able to provide a pupil with additional teaching assistant time. This additional cost is unsustainable for local authorities (LAs)/local education authorities (LEAs) and causes parental/carer and educators' dissatisfaction and distrust in the system. We need to ask ourselves, is this a way of providing additional resource in an attempt to allay parental fears that their child is not getting the help they need without extra one-to-one adult attention in schools, or even an expectation that this additional support might help them become 'average'? Is it a lack of trust in teachers' skills and knowledge or even a fear that society will consider their child not as 'good' as they should be if they do not reach 'expected' levels of attainment? How often though do pupils dislike being 'othered' and refuse this support? Would not having other options such as smaller class sizes, trust in teachers and an approach that measured each pupil against their own baseline be a more positive and motivating approach for pupils? Every child in a class knows who is the cleverest, the kindest and the cheekiest, despite adults' attempts to disguise these facts. Would not it be a greater, holistic positive approach to give each child the motivation, resilience and praise to demonstrate their own progress at whatever speed and level they can achieve?

Although the Children and Families Act 2014 and SEND Code of Practice 2015 (DfE and DoH 2015) were intended to boost parental confidence in the SEND system following the previous code of practice's difficulties (as described earlier), as a result of failing to fully fund and resource the system parents/carers have once again become disillusioned and even disengaged with the education their children receive.

Equally destructive, we suggest, is the division this policy has in many cases orchestrated between parents, carers, local authorities and professionals when resources and provision are proven to be unavailable even though they might be cited as part of the local offer (DfE and DoH 2015: 59–77). It was always stated that an intention of the new SEND Code of Practice was to, through its collaborative intentions, resolve the need for expensive and time-consuming SEND Tribunals for EHC plans through early intervention, collaborative working and mediation. Indeed, one of the components expressed in the March 2015 DfE Document (DfE 2015: 4) to be used in order to demonstrate the new SEND system was successful included: 'engagement and participation of young people and families so that they have greater choice, feel that they are in control and are being listened to and their concerns are resolved swiftly'. Some might argue that the rise in appeals to the SEND Tribunal, from 3,863 in 2016 to 9,184 in 2021 (DfE 2022: 15) actually means that the intention of the government is working. We would refute this however, because parents/carers appeal if, for example, the local authority has refused to assess their child's needs for an EHC plan or they are unhappy with the actual contents of a plan. Also, the increase in numbers of cases actually reaching Tribunal in 2020–1 shows that parents/carers were not being listened to swiftly and that local authorities were trying to limit their choices. This is further evidenced by the fact that 96 per cent (4651) of the Tribunal decisions were in favour of the appellant. Undoubtedly this process would have likely caused families distress and financial hardship and could have destroyed parent/carer, school and local authority relationships. Even more worrying though is that the quarterly SEND Tribunal statistics (January to March 2022) show a 38 per cent increase in Tribunal receipts based on the same period in 2021 (DfE 2022).

We suggest that using such a marketization-driven SEND policy, promoting parents/carers as clients or customers (Boddison and Soan 2021), has resulted in the opposite being achieved to what was intended. This can be demonstrated in different avenues of education. With academization continuing to be driven forward by the Conservative government the power, influence and resources provided by government to local authorities decreases, yet they are still held responsible for academies' performance. They also act as a buffer between the Department for Education when parents/carers take their concerns out via the Tribunal system (DfE and DoH 2015), breaking down another layer of trust. Parents and carers believe, because of the way the national policies are written and promoted, that they have the 'right' and 'power' to ask for provision they feel their children needs, but again on many occasions face frustration and the realization that this is not the case. This can then lead to the fear that their children will experience rejection, anger and exclusion as they progress through their school years.

Labelling

Although the Warnock Committee (Warnock 1978) thought their actions would help remove the medical 'labelling' of children due to their requirement to receive additional learning provision, 'labelling' has continued to this day. The three versions of the Codes of Practice for special educational needs (and disabilities) have endeavoured to nudge people's thinking towards inclusive practice, to remind them that it is schools which need to change, not pupils (see Chapter 2). As a separate 'shadow system' (Hodkinson and Burch 2019) operating alongside, but also within the wider neoliberal and marketization-focused state system, labels have become the way to describe the pupils needing additional or different support and the costs of funding these.

Of course, the SEND system has required a massive bureaucracy to grow with it nationally and in local authorities, resulting in some developing funding processes which have since been described as perverse. In one example of this, SEN staff were encouraged to put forward as many pupils as they felt could be said to meet the criteria because more pupils identified on the SEN register meant increased levels of funding for the school (personal reflection from a SENCo in 1996). It became seen as a way to afford the teaching assistants needed to help teachers support pupils being included in mainstream schools and classrooms. Of course, well-trained and supported teaching assistants are valuable members of any school, but there is currently still the danger that they are asked to fulfil roles such as teaching for sustained periods of time and providing the main teaching input for those with the greatest level of need.

So once again, the connection of education with business approaches working in a silo resulted in unpredicted and exclusionary actions, giving evidence to voices that said 'inclusion does not work'. Hence 'labelling' difference can still be considered negatively, becoming detrimental to the promotion of an inclusive system. Now mostly extinct we are pleased to say, teachers used to use language such as 'those SEN pupils', 'what do you expect, they are SEN' or 'that one with Down syndrome' to describe why perhaps a pupil was not achieving as much as others, or that they were not trained to teach SEN. Unfortunately, the Teaching Standards policy (DfE 2011, updated 2021: 12), although clear that every teacher is a teacher of *all* pupils, still finds the need to specifically add that this includes those pupils which might be considered outside the 'norm'!

> Teachers will 'have a clear understanding of the needs of all pupils, including those with special educational needs; those of high ability; those with English as an additional language; those with disabilities; and be able to use and evaluate distinctive teaching approaches to engage and support them'
> (DfE 2011, updated 2021)

In countries such as Sweden and Finland, teachers and schools are not asked to label pupil need, and as such this labelling data is not collected. Schools are considered suitable for all children and young people (Takala et al. 2009).

Professional teachers – an essential or only desired?

Teachers are often seen as the people responsible for transferring knowledge to children and young people, for 'socializing' them and teaching them the skills society requires at any given point in time (Dolton et al. 2018). As an applied profession it is still considered by some to be a 'stop-gap' career (Monsen et al. 2021) and one that parents in the UK do not wholeheartedly encourage their children to enter (TeacherToolkit 2018). This view was perpetuated in practice (if not by intention) by programmes such as 'Teach First', introduced in June 2002, and as its name suggests, it asked for applicants to give at least 2 years to teaching before moving on to other sector careers – or 'teach first, then get a better job' (Simon 2014). While quite popular with growing numbers of applicants, the retention rates for Teach First as of 2012 (Allen et al. 2016) were lower than other routes into teaching, with only 40 per cent remaining in teaching 5 years after training, compared to between 62 per cent and 70 per cent through Postgraduate Certificate in Education (PGCE) and Graduate Teacher Programme (GTP) courses. Although teachers and teaching are explored in much greater detail in Chapter 6 it is pertinent to mention here that although the pandemic years saw retention stability the longer-term issue remains, with only 87.5 per cent of teachers qualified in 2020 remaining in teaching after 1 year and only 59.7 per cent of teachers qualified ten years ago still teaching (Gov.uk 2022b).

As well as financial and other reasons for teaching remaining unattractive to the workforce, there is other more abstract evidence which perpetuates a feeling of teachers being undervalued. For example, evidencing the lack of value for teachers as professionals, the most recent SEND Code of Practice (DfE and DoH 2015) was published initially in July 2014 (with further updates in early 2015) with an expectation that it would be implemented in local authorities and schools as fully as possible from September 2014. As schools are closed for the summer break during August this illustrates how the government disregarded the teaching population and particularly those leading special educational needs and inclusion. This was the time when significant subject curriculum changes were also being made, again evidencing the lack of a cohesive whole-school system plan between government departments (Gov.uk 2014). With pay and workload issues, such actions may provide additional influence towards teaching becoming a less favourable career. With an ageing workforce demoralized by teaching over time and being deconstructed to a technical para-professional role delivering a standard curriculum (Rice O'Toole and Soan 2021), a real staffing crisis is looming (Worth and Faulkner-Ellis 2022).

Recognizing the limited number of young people wishing to join the teaching profession, the last few decades have seen a decline in the initial and continuing professional development required to gain qualified teacher status (QTS). Learning to teach 'on the job' is now established and 1-year (or three terms) postgraduate programmes currently form the majority of routes into teaching. Once again, institutions such as academies and free schools do not have to follow the same standards as state-run schools, who have to provide new to career teachers with a 2-year programme of support. Further, head teachers or executives/principals are not required to be qualified teachers and the Masters-level National Award for SEN Co-ordination qualification for SENCos is going to be replaced by a mandatory Leadership SENCo national professional qualification (NPQ Level 5) (HM Government 2023: 58) despite calls to maintain the current Masters-level National Award for SENCos (NASENCo) (HM Government 2023: 57). The government says that this change 'sends an important message about the role of the SENCo and the need for it to be "whole-school, senior and strategic"' (HM Government 2023: 57).

The exploration of these few policies highlights two significant issues with our current state education system. The first is the level of accountability caused by the policies implemented to bring around education improvement. Mick Waters says: 'But reforms that helped to bring improvement have been poisoned by over-emphasis on autonomy and a devil-take-the-hindmost approach. Accountability has gone too far and become punitive' (Millar 2022). The other influential area of the education system because of our belief in social justice is the constantly growing financial cost to the nation of a special educational needs system focusing on those who are deemed unable to meet the attainment levels sought by the government. Of course, as Terzi (2010: 1) states, 'Educational equality is a fundamental principle of social justice', and as such every child is entitled to education and to be included in education and society. How sustainable, though, is this in the system's current form for not only the national economy, but also the well-being and opportunity of all pupils to be able to participate in society as equals. With this in mind we ask the question, have recent 'add-on' but quite dramatic policy changes tried to address or alter the way the English education system is run and perceived?'

Academies, academies, academies

The New Labour and Conservative governments during this century decided to develop a policy where single academies and multi-academy trusts run, or build and run, schools with government funding, using a business model approach avoiding the involvement of local authorities in the daily running of provision (Gov.uk n.d.).

On 14 October 2021, the Department of Education released a blog which stated that:

> We want every school in the country to be part of a family of schools in a strong multi academy trust.
>
> The academies programme gives individual schools greater freedoms compared to local authority control. Being an academy gives schools the power to decide on the best curriculum for their pupils, determine how they spend their budgets, and much more.
>
> (Gov.uk 2021)

So, what are academies and free schools and how do they differ from council-run state schools? Academies are funded directly from the government and are non-fee paying. They are run by academy trusts, which are not-for-profit companies. These trusts have trustees who are responsible for the performance of the academy (or academies in multi-academy trusts). They might also have sponsors (businesses, universities, faith groups or voluntary groups) who work with them to improve their trust school(s)' performance. They can employ their own academy staff on their own terms (e.g. salaries) and have more control over how they do things than community state-funded schools. For example, they do not have to follow the national curriculum or the state school hours or term times. However they are inspected by Ofsted (Office for Standards in Education, Children's Services and Skills), follow the same examination system, and have the same rules on admissions, exclusions and special educational needs as council-run (community) state schools. The DfE does have educational and financial oversight of all academy trusts via the Education and Skills Funding Agency and the National and Regional Schools Commissioners. The Education Hub (https://educationhub.blog.gov.uk/) states that there are three types of academies:

- Converters – formerly council-run schools that chose to become academies;
- Sponsored – previously underperforming council-run schools in need of support, and/or judged 'Inadequate' by Ofsted, where the law requires them to become academies; or
- Free schools – brand new schools established to meet a need for good school places in area.

(Gov.uk 2021)

The National Foundation for Educational Research (NfER) does not include free schools in the academy group (Gee et al. 2015). Over half of all pupils are already educated in academies.

The DfE promoted this approach as they thought this was a way of improving standards and meeting the needs of business for appropriately skilled workers, through their direct input. But was it because of, or part of, recognizing the need to shed ever-growing financial demands from the sector? Was it in order to try to continue funding the reconstruction, running and resourcing of ageing schools within a reasonable budget? Evidence of their success is as yet undeterminable (Angel Solutions 2022), but importantly it was the diversification from a state community system requiring all schools to meet the same standards to a more varied one which has created an unequal system (academies are excluded from many requirements put onto state-run schools, as stated in the Early Career Teachers (ECT) Induction programme) and thus inequitable opportunities for pupils (DfE 2021a). It will be interesting to see how they will resolve such differences as the recent Schools White Paper states that 'councils will be allowed to set up their own multi-academy trusts (MATs), which recognizes the important role of councils as partners in education improvement' (HM Government 2022).

The purpose of a state school education system in twenty-first-century England

Of course, at the core of school education is its purpose and role in a twenty-first-century society. As Vygotsky advocated (see Chapter 2), the role of the teacher (and thus a school) is central not only to the development of cognitive skills but to wider areas as well. Therefore, a teacher not only needs to have sound subject content knowledge, but a robust understanding of how to facilitate experiential pupil-centred teaching (Dewey 1929). In a world where knowledge can be obtained within seconds, delivering information from a standard curriculum becomes obsolete, and teachers need to focus on the skills which will be essential in future work roles and satisfactory relationships, such as problem-solving, higher-order critical thinking, review, reflection and collaborative working. Like inclusion, 'knowing' is not a product, but a process (Bruner 1966; see Chapter 3).

But what is the purpose of a state education system in this century? In beginning to attempt to answer this question we have reflected on how over the past decade schools have become the 'place' where the roles of others have been redirected, and replaced by staff in schools; to enable parents/carers to start and finish work earlier and later, schools have provided breakfast and after-school clubs, where children learn how to eat socially, and have their hygiene (teeth cleaning) and other health needs met. As well as becoming the first-line workers for social behaviours, teachers have been given the responsibility of providing the first line of support for mental health and well-being concerns (DfE 2021b), releasing other underfunded, understaffed service professionals from this early-stage work.

While we fully acknowledge that schools are for the majority of times safe places where children and young people are cared for and feel secure, are schools enabling changes in society which some will consider might deskill parents, carers and their children, weakening the bonds of family, cultural and social structures of communities and radically changing the key purpose of their role? By doing this, government is clearly able to subtly alter the overall purpose of schools and education, and thus teachers, making the institutions more economically viable as a result. They have redirected health and social care professional roles and responsibilities to be fulfilled within an education practitioner role. We are not by any means saying that early identification and provision for pupils' mental health needs is not essential, but is it really the role of teachers to carry out what is undoubtedly complex and crucial work? This action is clearly an effort to lower mental health care waiting lists, but teachers do not have the comprehensive and ongoing training to ensure each pupil gets the right support at the most appropriate time, let alone being provided with clinical supervision to protect their mental health and professional well-being (Gov.uk 2023). Undoubtedly, schools are now seen as a service where children can be safely left from breakfast through to beyond teatime, with the state providing the workforce with an affordable childcare option where a growing number of children are provided with free meals and out-of-class activities alongside a more formal education. Schools we have personally worked in provide shoes and suits (for interviews) out of their education budgets. Is this the role of schools or social care? Such provision is not new, and was justly put in place in the 1990s to support the less financially well off in society. But of course all can now access these services if required, which alters their original purpose and resultant impact. One of the authors remembers how angry they were when it was suggested their children should go to breakfast club. They felt that the state was taking over their parental role to prepare their children for the day, to ensure they were okay, have time to talk to them (if only while cleaning teeth, etc.). While it is acknowledged that there were no financial barriers to feeding the children or getting them to school or themselves to work, it was the contact time, and their responsibility for the children's welfare, that they did not want to let go of. As said, they had the luxury to be able to afford this, but should this not be what a responsible democratic society and government strive to enable for all their citizens, rather than replacing this family time, or accepting it can only be for those who can afford it?

Since the ending of the pandemic lockdowns, it is highly suspected that more pupils are being 'schooled' at home or refuse to return to schools (Long and Danechi 2022). There is now a concerted effort by the government (Long and Danechi 2022) to make a list of every pupil around the nation who is in this position, but it does not seem to be so much from a learning perspective, but from a concern that parents are not contributing to the economy (or the taxation system) by returning to work (Gov.uk 2022a).

We live in all types of families, and we would say a family environment is what we would wish for all our children in England. So why does our society support policies which deconstruct the role of all families, rather than support them by changing employment legislation? More flexible working patterns for all parents and carers, childcare facilities at workplaces and better affordable, connected transport links we would suggest could still achieve the same level of economic success, but with a more content and family/community-orientated society (UNESCO 2021). This could, and most likely would, encourage better family relationships and feelings of belonging essential for social and emotional growth. There will, unfortunately, always be children who need an alternative family or home to their birth family, due to many reasons, but would not the reliance of the many on the state be less with such a community-driven policy, enabling more to be given to those that are in greatest need of society's support? By situating all of this help in schools, we are already seeing what happens when they close for holidays. Many families feel unable to cope and feel abandoned, resulting in additional reactive provision having to be initiated by charities, local authorities and government (Sky Sports 2021). An example of this occurred during the pandemic lockdowns when the majority of pupils were unable to access school meals. Government was put under pressure to provide additional funding directly to parents/carers through an increase in Universal Credit payments and food vouchers (Gov.uk 2020; Mackley 2021). Such long-term policies have undoubtedly added to the difficulties of making substantial and long-term changes to the state school system. With funding having to be directed to providing basic human needs such as food and care, how can the changes needed for school infrastructure, the curriculum and professional education be focused on further developing the inclusion agenda?

We therefore raise the possibility that the 'state' will not be able to continue to fund the current school system for all across the age range of 0–25 for special educational needs and 5–16 for all pupils, and that in attempting to help it balance its books it might be 'nudging' society (Halpern and Sanders 2016), and particularly parents/carers, to take action and begin to reconstruct the shape of future school education in England (Terzi 2010), depending on private funding and not taxpayers' money. Is such a change in England going to be acceptable to its citizens when growth and wealth remain the main focus of government policy? Or will citizens decide that growth and wealth are only worthwhile if they (and especially the young) are mentally and physically well, are able to successfully undertake fulfilling working roles and contribute socially and culturally to their community/society – requiring the establishment and maintenance of an equitable, inclusive and professionally run education system, accessible to all and not just the few?

Figure 5.1 illustrates the possible reasons why state-run schools are finding it difficult to ensure pupils, and particularly vulnerable pupils such as those described as having 'special educational needs', achieve healthy, productive and fulfilled lives through the current curriculum and ill-resourced system.

Of course, the deconstruction of an established school system brings risks and fears as it requires great reflection into other areas of society and state-run services as well. Such innovative work would require deep soul-searching around long-maintained institutions and working practices and how they need to be reimagined to fit the requirements of twenty-first-century English society. Is the perpetuation of ancient and highly valued institutions and subjects, for example, following the habits and rituals of past generations, worthwhile and valuable in the twenty-first century? Does every child need to have access to a holistic curriculum where practical, creative, artistic and academic skills and preferences are all valued as equal contributions to the running and welfare of a society? Such questions are currently being asked throughout the Western world. UNESCO states very clearly that 'education does more than respond to a changing world. Education transforms the world' (UNESCO 2019). And Fullan et al. (2020: 22) fully support this, writing that 'The interwoven learning, well-being and equity agenda, and the corresponding system changes that will be required to enact it, is about the future of humanity itself. It is crucial that we act now!' Finally, the Director of Skills for the Organisation for Economic Co-operation and Development (OECD), Andreas Schleicher, seemed to begin to address the issue of states being able to maintain current education systems saying, 'Over the past decade, there has been virtually no improvement in the learning outcomes of students in the Western world, even though expenditures on schooling rose by almost 20% during this period' Schleicher (2018: 11).

88 Inclusive Education Theory and Policy

Figure 5.1 Some current disruptions to the further evolution of inclusion in current English state-run schools

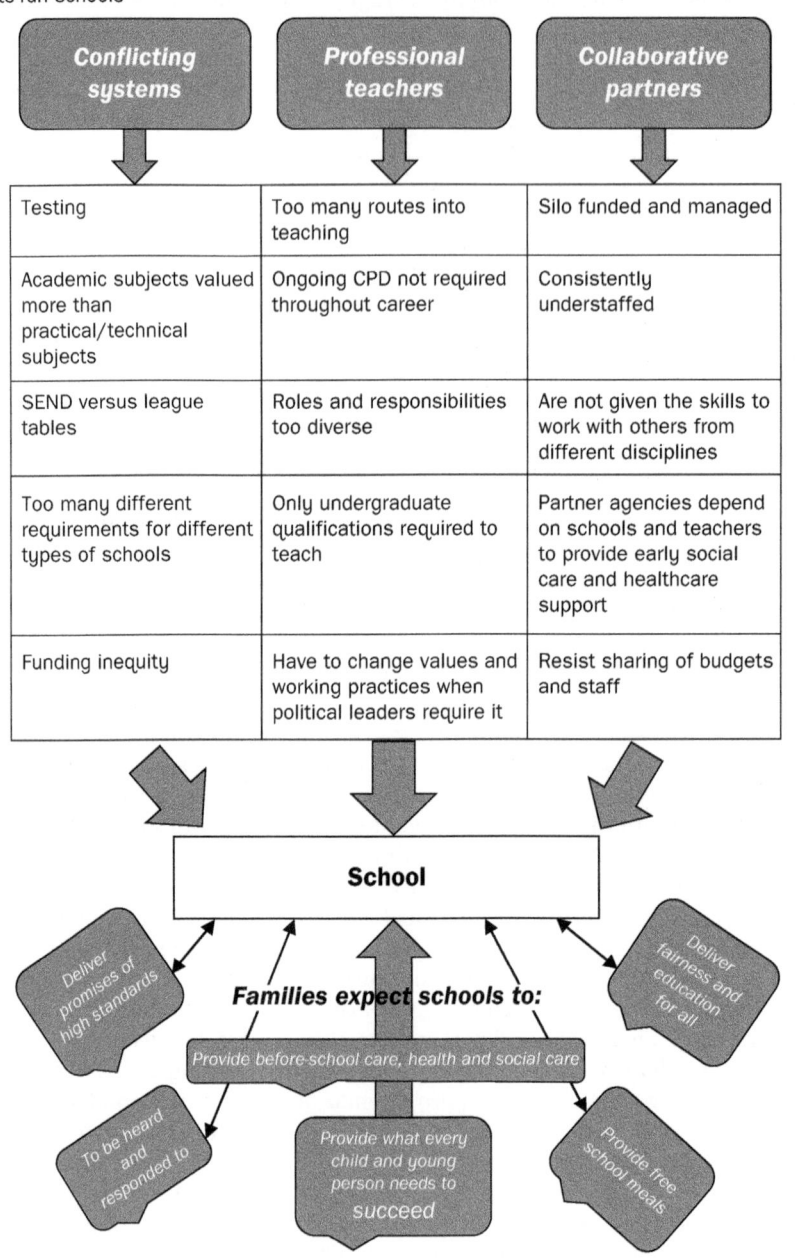

Conflicting systems	Professional teachers	Collaborative partners
Testing	Too many routes into teaching	Silo funded and managed
Academic subjects valued more than practical/technical subjects	Ongoing CPD not required throughout career	Consistently understaffed
SEND versus league tables	Roles and responsibilities too diverse	Are not given the skills to work with others from different disciplines
Too many different requirements for different types of schools	Only undergraduate qualifications required to teach	Partner agencies depend on schools and teachers to provide early social care and healthcare support
Funding inequity	Have to change values and working practices when political leaders require it	Resist sharing of budgets and staff

School

Families expect schools to:

- Deliver promises of high standards
- Deliver fairness and education for all
- To be heard and responded to
- Provide free school meals
- Provide before-school care, health and social care
- Provide what every child and young person needs to succeed

Conclusion

In this chapter we have tried to address some of the reasons why we believe England is failing to achieve an inclusive and professionally run education system (and other state systems) for all children and young people. There are undoubtedly many more reasons that we have not been able to discuss here, but the continual covering over of the cracks which keep appearing are now at a point where the fissures are too broad and deep, and a repair will not fix the problem. A replacement is required. Schools and teachers are being bombarded from so many different directions (Figure 5.1) to meet targets and objectives from government, parents/carers and other service agencies that the rigour and daily 'knowing' the pupils and their learning, physical, social and emotional needs become lost. It is time to review, reflect and reinvigorate the system so that all pupils can 'lead happy and fulfilled lives' (DfE and DoH 2015: 11).

In Chapter 6 we work towards the final chapter by providing an in-depth exploration of the teacher and their role, and why it is not as attractive a career as it should be.

6 Why Become a Teacher: Why Not?

Introduction

In this chapter we deconstruct the government and society's view of a teacher in England in the twenty-first century, the training required to become and continue as a teacher, the pressures and benefits of the occupation, as well as the roles of others in an educational setting.

So often when discussing the future of education in England we talk about the needs of pupils and families, inclusion, practical and financial resources, and the curriculum. How often though do we as a society reflect on the people that actually make the system work on a daily basis? Do we see teachers as essential and skilled or as glorified 'childminders' and the purveyors of information, preparing our children for the world of work? Having been members of this community of educators for four decades we would say that at the personal level pupils and parents/carers mostly do appreciate and have regard for teachers and other educators. When thinking about politicians, policymakers, legislation, regulations and the great machinery which is focused on accountability and end products, then we sincerely regret to say that, despite the rhetoric, the respect for teachers' skills is 'absent in action' for the majority of the time. Over recent decades what is said to be a Bernard Shaw adage, 'those who can, do; those who can't, teach', remains a popular cultural saying.

We want to challenge this folk cultural perception of teachers in this chapter. Indeed, we would like to start changing the way society values and thinks about teachers. As Plato (765) wrote, 'The chosen candidate to be minister of education, and those who choose him, should appreciate that this is by far the most important of all the supreme offices in the state.' Although our current government clearly does not consider this to be accurate, these words by Plato surely encapsulate the importance of the work of skilled, pedagogically informed and dedicated teachers. Aristotle prophesized how education is the cornerstone of a civilization, so why do we hear so frequently that schools should do 'this', add 'that' to the curriculum or carry out others' service roles? Why are teachers being used as 'back-fillers' for society's issues and problems even if, in reality, the action could and sometimes should be undertaken by other professionals from other disciplines, parents, carers or the state?

Teachers are multitaskers and have a great ability to change and be flexible, because when working with pupils flexibility is essential. When teachers' values, beliefs and identities are constantly asked to reshape and reform by ongoing social and political drivers, internal conflict between these can cause dilemmas such as a lack of professional self-worth and personal confidence

(Pillen et al. 2013). One of the authors actually saw a possible reaction in practice to this in a special school while they were carrying out data collection for a research study (Soan 2013). A pupil had the involvement of social care and health professionals as well as educationalists in planning their holistic development. On at least three occasions across a period of 3 years, when a colleague from another discipline/agency said that the school needed to implement a new intervention or strategy for this pupil, there was no questioning or debate from the SEN lead and class teachers, just a 'yes, we can do that'. The school was expected to then purchase the new intervention and learn to use it (if not already in the school). They did not question, resist or add their professional expertise or knowledge – just changed their practice. As part of this 'group' as a researcher, when I questioned the findings of a health report, resulting in the group asking for a second opinion, we were told we would be wasting money because the second doctor would agree with the original assessment. Not only does this raise questions about the self-worth of individual teachers, but also a lack of regard from others working in different, but 'collaborative', partner agencies/services. Yes, this is only one example, but could this be indicating an unspoken hierarchy of the position of teachers from other service agencies? The *SEND Review* Green Paper (HM Government 2022b: 67) and the *Special Educational Needs and Disabilities (SEND) and Alternative Provision (AP) Improvement Plan* (HM Government 2023) have recognized that health, social care and education 'professionals' and systems need to collaborate more effectively, but changing mindsets and collaborative working are complex processes, especially when working across different disciplines (Boddison and Soan 2021).

Who is a teacher and why do they teach?

Some seek to become a teacher because they want to make a difference, to influence and encourage the next generation; some join the profession because this is what their family do, and others because it is a career that fits in with their life plan. But being a teacher is a total life craft or vocation where your school and the pupils dominate your 'pedagogical life' (Hansen and Laverty 2013: 224). Hansen and Laverty (2013: 227) state that:

> 'Teachers assume responsibility for creating, directing and coordinating educative influences that occur more naturally elsewhere in human community and life ... they humanize by revealing to students the unfathomable capacity and creativity of people. They show students how meaningful human life can be if a person inhabits it as fully as he or she can.'

Jerrim and Sims (2018: 5) found similar views: 'For more than 90% of primary and lower-secondary teachers in England, the chance to contribute to society and to aid the development of pupils were also key reasons why they chose to enter the teaching profession.' From these descriptions it can be seen how important it is for teachers to enjoy working with children and young people, and to be passionate about sharing knowledge and their wisdom. As Dewey

(1984: 370) wrote, a teacher needs to be learned and to demonstrate this 'in learning from all the contacts of life' and welcoming the need for 'continuous readjustment' (Hansen and Laverty 2013: 229). Thus, a teacher is an individual eager to be a lifelong learner, an investigator who has a passion for seeing children and young people achieve the best they can by using their skills and interests. They see the importance of social, emotional and physical growth and development as equal to cognitive development and are able to adapt to the needs of individual pupils, as they want society to replicate.

The authors assert that these tasks can only be achieved by a teacher if they have a secure grounding in child development, sociology, psychology, philosophy, history of education, teaching pedagogy and content knowledge. Without this wealth of knowledge and understanding, teaching becomes a 'technical' role, where strategies are implemented due to fashion or requirement and where skills are learnt in a specific location, frequently impossible to replicate in other education contexts, because every pupil and school ethos is different. Teachers in this position can easily implement a technique or intervention because they are told to, but do not understand why and for what purpose. Their ability to change and to be flexible demonstrates teachers' desire to do the best possible for their pupils. For us, this is when you can see the in-depth and masterly training required to be a teacher, but because of the type and length of training currently promoted by government many find this impossible to achieve. It is not the individual teacher's 'problem', but reflects systemic and societal misconceptions about what teaching is. So, is this lack of in-depth pedagogical understanding one of the possible reasons why still in 2019, only 41 per cent of teachers said there is appropriate training in place for all teachers to work with pupils who have what society labels a 'special educational need' (HM Government 2022b)? Why is there a lack of confidence in teaching all children and young people whatever their learning need, and acknowledgement that the initial teacher training and early career frameworks need to be reviewed yet again (HM Government 2022b)? Do not forget the first special educational needs Code of Practice was published in 1994, providing sufficient time for 'generationally' significant systems change to have occurred. Of course, we are not underestimating what has been achieved towards inclusive education by teachers and society, but why do teachers still feel so insecure when it comes to working with pupils with neurodiversity or other constraints to their learning, and why is it such a persistent ongoing issue?

Could this indicate a fundamental problem with the initial teacher education (ITE) curriculum, its duration and foundations for continual development and the collective political understanding of what a teacher is and what knowledge and understanding they need to start and develop their careers? Even in the latest *Improvement Plan* teachers are only mentioned directly 19 times in 101 pages (HM Government 2023). Also, when writing about increasing the capacity of specialists, it is only educational psychologists and speech and language therapists (although essential) that the government highlights in the *Improvement Plan* (HM Government 2023) and not teachers or SENCos. Additionally, the SENCo qualification is to become an undergraduate qualification (NVQ Level 5), leaving a direct progressive pathway for specialization 'up to the individual'. In their response to this news the CEO of nasen (the National Association for Special Educational Needs) writes about the removal of the NASENCo (National Award for Special Educational Needs Coordinators) from being a statutory requirement:

> 'we recognise the quality of this Masters level award and the depth of knowledge and understanding that it delivers, and we would encourage the current providers of the NASENCO Award to maintain their offer for those wishing to study SEND and inclusion at a higher level'
>
> (nasen 2023)

So, are teachers and SENCos really considered by the government to be professionals requiring specialist pedagogy?

Dewey (see Chapter 3), Vygotsky (Chapter 3) and Bruner (Chapter 3) all proclaim the importance of teachers being constantly agile, using their core pedagogical foundations to help them understand and constantly adapt their practice. As Hansen and Laverty (2013: 226) say:

> Experienced teachers know that real learning often entails tension, anxiety, moments of uncertainty, and the disconfirmation of expectations. They know that what succeeds with a particular student in a particular situation, may fail in a different context. The art of teaching is understanding how and when to make use of the science of teaching. 'What works' – that is, what research indicates is efficacious in practice – *is never* self-justifying in education. [emphasis added]

If teaching is not just a technical role which can follow a 'what works' approach, what is it?

Is teaching a profession?

We suggest that all involved in the world of education would assert that teachers are professionals, 'fully engaged in professional practice and entitled to the benefits that should (but generally do not, in their case) accrue to professionals (such as physicians, lawyers)' (Reagan 2013: 210). Others, because of honest misunderstandings about what teachers really do, frequently consider teaching as an occupation (Labaree 2004).

First, therefore, it is important to state that in agreement with Reagan (2013) we consider that the concepts of 'profession' and 'professionalism' are socially constructed and as such are not static, but change over time as society changes. Thus, there cannot be one single definition of teacher professionalism because as a concept it is 'fluid and dynamic' (Englund 1993; Alexander 2010; Elton-Chalcraft and Cooper 2022: 505) – like inclusion! Alexander (2010: 450–1) warns that the term 'teacher professionalism' fails to recognize 'where feelings matter … and where subtlety and realism puncture the notions of "one-size-fits-all" and "good primary practice"'.

Despite this lack of an agreed definition, there have been many models designed using key economic, political and educational factors of the time to

Table 6.1 The government requirements of the 'teaching profession'

DfEE (1998) Green Paper, *Teachers: Meeting the Challenge of Change* The teaching profession need to ...	DfE (2011) Teachers' Standards (latest update December 2021) The teacher must ...
• have high expectations of themselves and of all pupils	• set high expectations which inspire, motivate and challenge pupils
• accept accountability	• promote good progress and outcomes by pupils
• take personal and collective responsibility for improving their skills and subject knowledge	• demonstrate good subject and curriculum knowledge • plan and teach well-structured lessons
• seek to base decisions on evidence of what works in schools in the UK and internationally	• make accurate and productive use of assessment
• work in partnership with other staff in schools	• manage behaviour effectively to ensure a good and safe learning environment
• welcome the contribution that parents, business and others outside a school can make to its success	• fulfil wider professional responsibilities
• anticipate change and promote initiative	• adapt teaching to respond to the strengths and needs of all pupils

identify how teaching can be called a profession and teachers, professionals. One of these models, shown in Table 6.1, was used to express the views of the New Labour government in the 1998 Green Paper, *Teachers: Meeting the Challenge of Change* (DfEE 1998). For comparison we have presented the current Teachers' Standards (DfE 2011, updated 2021) and the expectations stated in 1998, and it is interesting to notice how closely aligned they are.

The Preamble written in the current Teachers' Standards (DfE 2011, updated 2021: 10) mirrored in many ways the earlier model, showing how the 1998 model has been influencing more recent attempts at defining teacher professionalism.

> Teachers make the education of their pupils their first concern, and are accountable for achieving the highest possible standards in work and conduct. Teachers act with honesty and integrity; have strong subject knowledge, keep their knowledge and skills as teachers up-to-date and are self-critical; forge positive professional relationships; and work with parents in the best interests of their pupils
>
> (DfE 2011, updated 2021)

But do such Standards or requirements (Table 6.1) make teachers professionals? There is not a completely satisfactory answer to this question, although we would argue that as teachers are required to behave in a 'professional fashion', whether within the school or in wider society, teaching can perhaps be considered a profession by society.

Before leaving this part of the discussion it is important to be clear of the difference between professionalism and professionalization. The former term refers to the internal management of the profession and how each member carries out their role, while the latter is more concerned with the external criteria. The professionalization of teaching by the current Conservative government can be explicitly seen in the recent schools White Paper, *Opportunity for All: Strong Schools with Great Teachers for Your Child* (HM Government 2022a) where there is a focus on the external criteria of teachers' 'status, salary, specialization, and control' (Noddings 2001: 102 in Reagan 2013: 210). Evidence of this view can be seen throughout the White Paper, and in two other government initiatives, the first being the establishment of the Chartered College of Teaching in 2017, which was set up, amongst other aims, to raise the status of the teaching profession and to 'guide' career-long professional development (Shaw and Shirley 2022: 22). The second, announced first in January 2021 (DfE 2011, updated 2021), is:

> the Institute of Teaching *[which]* will be England's flagship teacher development provider, delivering cutting-edge training, including targeting disadvantaged areas of the country. *[The government state that this Institute]* will build the evidence-base on effective teacher development, driving standards of teacher training even higher.
> (HM Government 2022a: 21)

But is the professionalization of teaching positive, and if so, who for? Buyruk (2018) defines teaching as a semi-profession that progresses in the way of professionalization, and that while this can bring teacher autonomy it can also be used to define and control their work outside of politics. He says that 'For instance, governments are using Continuous Professional Development (CPD) as a new way of achieving broader educational reforms (Day and Sachs, 2004)' (Buyruk 2018: 3). We fully agree with Day and Sachs' (2004) comment regarding CPD, as can be seen in policies such as the Schools Mental Health training (Gov.uk 2023). Work such as that by Lawn and Grace (2011) states that such professionalization reforms have actually alienated and deskilled teachers, within an increasingly bureaucratic school system. Following on this argument, Buyruk (2018) goes on to suggest that 'teachers have lost their autonomy and control over their own labour processes with the separation of planning and application as a result of developing new management strategies, advancements in technology, growing curriculum packages, standardisation and tests'. Could this be another possible reason why teachers become unable and unwilling to remain in the role long term?

For us, likewise the increased emphasis on the professionalization of teachers for the benefit of national political and economic gains is completely contrary to how we perceive the role and responsibilities of teachers and teaching.

Perhaps 'teaching profession' and 'teacher professionalism' are too restrictive to capture the essence of teaching and a teacher? Without doubt we feel teaching is a whole-life activity, such as that described by Green (1985: 4) as the 'conscience of craft' to be 'a felt presence as well as reverberating influence in the life of another person' (Hansen and Laverty 2013: 223), and where personal philosophy, attitudes, beliefs and values all contribute to the complex craft of teaching (Elton-Chalcraft and Cooper 2022: 507). So perhaps teaching is a masterly craft, and teachers are craftspeople valued in an inclusive, equitable society, where as scientist-practitioners they teach children logical and critical thinking skills, a valuable asset in this world of disinformation. Indeed, we only have to look back to 1959 and the book called *Primary Education* published by HMSO to find the head of a primary school described as a 'practised craftsman' and that 'Responsibility for promoting the craft of teaching does not stop with the ... young schoolmaster or school mistress' but with a good head who is a good teacher themselves (HMSO 1959: 92–3).

Initial teacher education and continuing teacher development

While we have suggested that teaching is a masterly craft and thus teachers are master craftspeople, we do not consider everyone has the same opinion or views of what masterly crafts are. Others view crafts as something you can gain by being observed and by observing (Gove 2010) (in addition to subject knowledge we suspect), and although this is undoubtedly true, taking initial teacher education (ITE) or initial teacher training (ITT) out of 'college' or universities for the majority of time is not understanding the 'master' aspect of the craft, despite what Gibb (2014) strongly declared. During Michael Gove's famous 2010 speech he said:

> we will reform teacher training to shift trainee teachers out of college and into the classroom. We will end the arbitrary bureaucratic rule which limits how many teachers can be trained in schools, shift resources so that more heads can train teachers in their own schools and make it easier for people to shift in mid-career into teaching.

Such actions will ensure there are more unqualified and context-specific trained teachers in schools, helping to resolve the ongoing teacher retention issue (but perhaps only in the short term). We propose that this 'fix' will not enable the effective teaching of all pupils throughout the system long term, as teachers who have observed and copied the expert teachers in one school will, when relocating, recognize that this 'what works' knowledge cannot always be replicated elsewhere. Left feeling 'deskilled' and perhaps even following a school ethos they do not agree with will mean that teachers will simply either learn the 'rules' of this new setting, leaving them disempowered, or will choose to leave the profession because their values and self-worth have been destroyed.

The importance of linking theory to practice is not disputed, but linking practice to theory is equally important. Theory is 50 per cent of this pairing and therefore should be 50 per cent of a school-led or postgraduate teaching programme. The length of the programme should provide sufficient time for trainee teachers to reflect, to review and to practise their craft. This is not the case in England, with a typical 36-week postgraduate (PGCE) programme requiring trainees to be in school for 24 of those weeks, leaving only 12 for university teaching, learning and supervision. While 60 Masters-level credits are gained, these are only a third of a Master's degree. With School Direct, a 1-year programme, only 30 days on average are given to university 'guidance'.

Do these 'quick' to qualification routes really provide all our children and young people with sufficiently skilled and knowledgeable teachers to help them cope and prosper in a dynamic and quickly changing twenty-first-century society? Particularly for those with additional constraints to their learning, who deserve more than a medical label. We believe that the current government see the 'short-term' impact of the changes put in place across the last decade and are now adding to this patchwork of teacher training a reinvigorated package of post-qualification courses to continue covering over the grazes and ever-increasing gaps!

We totally agree with what the Rt Hon Nadhim Zahawi, former Secretary of State for Education (HM Government 2022a: 8), said the government are going to offer post initial qualification:

> At the heart of these ambitions is the need for an excellent teacher for every child in classrooms across England. Improving the quality of teaching is the single most important in-school factor in improving outcomes for children, especially for children from disadvantaged backgrounds and those with special educational needs and disabilities (SEND). We know that great teachers are made, not born. That is why we are delivering the single biggest programme of teacher development ever undertaken in this country and investing further in the skills and futures of the professionals who are central to our mission.

But would it not be most effective to review the whole system and really consider what initial teacher training (or more appropriately initial teacher education) needs are to ensure high-quality learning experiences are offered to all pupils whatever their needs and wherever they live in England? The most recent government directives to initial teacher training (ITT) providers and employers of newly qualified teachers (QTS) are the ITT Core Content Framework (DfE and EEF 2019b) and the Early Career Framework (ECF) (DfE and EEF 2019a). They were designed to support trainees' development in behaviour management, pedagogy, curriculum, assessment and professional behaviours, and are presented in eight sections so that they are congruent with the Teachers' Standards (DfE 2011, updated 2021) post initial teacher training. These documents do define terms used such as 'expert colleagues', and the 'learn that' and 'learn how to' tables are clearly presented (DfE and EEF 2019b). But beside the fact that, as explained in Chapter 5, not all schools have to fulfil the same

Table 6.2 Proportion of pupils with an autism spectrum disorder EHC plan, by primary type of need, as of January of each year (HM Government 2022b)

2010	2011	2012	2013	2014	2015	2016	2017	2018	2019	2020	2021
0.53%	0.56%	0.59%	0.62%	0.65%	0.70%	0.72%	0.76%	0.82%	0.89%	1.00%	1.11%

Table 6.3 Proportion of pupils with a speech, language and communication need EHC plan, by primary type of need, as of January of each year (HM Government 2022b)

2010	2011	2012	2013	2014	2015	2016	2017	2018	2019	2020	2021
0.37%	0.38%	0.38%	0.39%	0.39%	0.40%	0.39%	0.40%	0.42%	0.46%	0.51%	0.59%

obligations regarding the Early Career Framework, the ITT Core Content Framework and the ECF both fail to include what we consider should be a third column in their tables, with the heading 'why learn'. This we suggest is the most important 'knowledge' teachers need *to begin to* obtain during their ITT, not just post-ITT. Learning 'what' and 'how': the 'what works' part of teaching is helpful and necessary for national consistency (what) and development (how).

We argue though that the most crucial aspect of understanding teaching and being able to develop teaching skills and knowledge is 'why', disrupting Gove's (2010) and Gibb's (2014) ideas and views. Knowing 'why' a teacher needs to 'learn that' and 'learn how' is crucial, and although quality ITE providers will include the 'why' in their specific curriculum, this is we suspect not included by all. Without understanding *'why'* they need to gain specific skills and knowledge – for example the ability to be flexible, to understand pupils' individual differences, children's stages of development and needs – trainee teachers' skills will be at best insecure and easily replaced with the 'what works' or 'folk cookbook' (see Chapter 3) approaches alone. Such an approach will probably be 'good enough' for 80 per cent of the pupils in a classroom, but what happens to Warnock's (1978) 20 per cent (18 plus 2) when a teacher without this underpinning understanding teaches a pupil who does not understand the 'what works' approach or will not comply with the behaviour standards expected? How can a teacher without understanding of 'why' this pupil might be responding to their teaching in this way alter and adapt their teaching to include this pupil in the lesson, enabling them to have a positive learning experience (Soan 2021)? Is this deficit the reason why the ITT framework and early career framework are requiring yet another review (HM Government 2023)?

The most recently published data detailing the level and type of teaching qualification illustrates this well, with only just under 45,000 teachers having a Bachelor of Education (BEd) (a specific teaching degree) – with 6,893 having a postgraduate certificate of education (a 36-week teaching qualification) and the remaining 441,394 with a subject degree (or higher) (no further details provided) (Gov.uk 2022).

Perhaps it might be argued that this is one of several reasons why numbers of pupils with an EHC plan with the primary need of autism spectrum disorder (ASD) or speech, language and communication need (SLCN) have increased proportionately more than pupils with other neurodiversity between 2010 and 2021 (Tables 6.2 and 6.3).

Although only a tentative hypothesis, there is statistical evidence to illustrate how the 'quick' route to teaching or the 'within school' type of teacher training is growing at the same time that the higher education institution route (full teaching degree of 3 or 4 years) is decreasing (see Tables 6.4 and 6.5). As mentioned earlier, is the government's need to 'produce' more teachers as quickly as possible actually at the expense of an in-depth understanding of important teaching pedagogy such as child development, and social and psychological development? Could a different approach to initial teacher education built over a period of time a workforce who have really 'mastered' their craft

Table 6.4 QTS national statistics for all routes into teaching (Gov.uk 2022)

Year	Higher education No.	%	Total school-led No.	%	Postgraduate total No.	%	PG teaching apprenticeship* No.	%	High potential (Teach First) No.	%
2012/13	20864	87	3484	88	28595	87				
2013/14	18742	91	9900	93	27433	91				
2014/15	15258	90	12721	93	26607	92				
2015/16	13983	90	14413	93	28396	91				
2016/17	12188	90	14879	93	27067	91				
2017/18	13217	90	14661	93	27878	91				
2018/19	13600	89	15349	93	28949	91	113	75	1200	91
2019/20	13150	90	16164	92	29314	91	272	76	1625	92
2020/21	16675	85	18696	81	35371	87	675	51	1648	92

Note: * not clear whether these figures are included in postgraduate total or not

Why Become a Teacher **101**

Table 6.5 Difference in numbers of trainee teachers qualifying between 2012/13 and 2018/19 and between 2012/13 and 2020/21

Year	Higher education No.	Total school-led No.	Postgraduate total No.	PG teaching apprenticeship No.	High potential (Teach First) No.
2012/13	20,864	3484	28,595	Nil	Nil
2018/19	13,600	15,349	28,949	113	1200
2020/21	16,675	18,696	35,371	675	1648
Total difference between years (2012/13 & 2018/19)	−7264 (35% decrease)	+11865 (341% increase)	+344 (1% increase)		
Total difference between years (2012/13 & 2020/21)	−4189 (20% decrease)	+15212 (437% increase)	+6776 (24% increase)	+562 (497% increase)	+448 (37% increase)

(Reagan 2013)? Could such action contribute to improving teachers' confidence to include all pupils and thus avoid the highly expensive (in time, funding and resources) separate SEND system?

On researching earlier descriptions and requirements of teachers in England, three statements in particular resonated with the argument for quality training for teachers. The first, speaking about required changes after the Second World War, is about providing quality teachers with the 'right' knowledge for current societal needs: 'it is the quality of the teachers, and of the teaching they give, that matters more in the long run than logistics' (HMSO 1959: iii). This made explicit that in practice this meant that all teachers (in primary and secondary) must be graduates as 'the quality of every teacher is of first importance' (HMSO 1959: 8), while they were not expected to have a degree prior to the Second World War. There is no intention at all to make comparisons between the Second World War and the global pandemic, but do these devastating experiences which impacted on all in society provide us with an opportunity to 'relook and revision' what education for our children and young people should look like? Do the concerns about the survival of our planet and the significant positive technological advances achieved in recent years require society to rethink the objectives for a school curriculum? Should it be a curriculum which focuses on the planet and humanity's survival, as well as our children and young people's mental, cognitive and physical development and well-being, not just on creating a workforce which continues to be focused on the growth of economic profit? If the answer to this question is yes, or might be, then there is an argument for evaluating the curriculum and level of demand for initial and post teacher development. Back in 1959, HMSO seemed to recognize the importance of the role of the teacher and the level of demand required to be a good teacher:

> [Teachers], above all other qualities, [must possess] enough resilience to deal with the energy and far-reaching demands of the children, and enough resources to meet their extremely wide range of intellectual and imaginative power.
>
> It is scarcely possible for any teacher to cover the whole width and variety of all these children's interests with ready information and equal concern and success. But to do so remains his aim. He cannot do better than remain a student-teacher in the literal sense of that term.
>
> (HMSO 1959: 77)

Perhaps even more surprising was the then government's concern that teachers were worried that if they asked for advice from other professionals (e.g. health) for a pupil with special education needs, it might be 'interpreted as a desire to have a child removed from their school' (HMSO 1959: 108) – indicating that teachers at that time felt it was their role to teach all children. This document goes on to say that this is a misconception and that in 'no case will the advice be given to remove a child if he can receive a sound education in the school where he is' (HMSO 1959).

Teacher retention

As has already been demonstrated in this chapter, teacher retention is the most demanding issue for the government at the current time with regards to providing every pupil aged 5–16 with an education. Despite varied efforts to resolve this during the past decade, teachers continue to leave at a level which demands the continuing recruitment of more teachers from the UK and abroad.

> However, 21.7% of newly qualified entrants to the sector in 2017 were not recorded as working in the state sector two years later. The five year out-of-service rate for 2014 entrants was 32.6%, the highest rate during the current series, which dates back to 1997. The ten year out-of-service rate for 2009 entrants was 38.8%; this is also the highest rate since 1997. These declines in teacher retention over time mean that more new teachers are required to replace them.
>
> (Long and Danechi 2022: 14)

Such a constant demand must quite clearly impact on quality, a fact noted by Russell Hobby (General Secretary of the National Association of Head Teachers) on 30 June 2016: 'Official statistics mask the reality that school leaders are still sometimes forced to appoint staff who are less experienced or able than they would like because of a lack of applications for a post; it is about quality, not just the numbers in post' (Scott 2016).

In support of this message were the DfE national statistics which showed that only 75 per cent of teachers who qualified in 2012 were still in post in 2015. The Reporting Year 2021 statistics show that there has been a slight statistical increase in the 2012 figure (although there are more teachers in service currently than there were in 2015, which will impact on percentage levels):

- Almost 9 in 10 (87.5 per cent) teachers who qualified in 2020 were still teaching one year after qualification.
- Almost 8 in 10 (77.0 per cent) teachers who qualified three years ago are still teaching.
- Almost 7 in 10 (68.8 per cent) teachers who qualified five years ago are still teaching.
- Almost 6 in 10 (59.7 per cent) teachers who qualified ten years ago are still teaching. (Gov.uk 2022)

In 2015 there was a 10 per cent increase in the number of teachers without qualified teacher status (QTS) (from 20,300 to 22,500): '3.1 per cent of teachers in all primary/nursery schools do not have QTS, and at secondary it is 5.9 per cent. Free schools have the highest proportion of those without QTS (12.5 per cent at primary; 10.3 per cent at secondary)' (30 June 2016) (Gov.uk 2022).

The latest government figures (Reporting Year 2021) state that most teachers held qualified teacher status (97 per cent) but note that this figure included those that were still 'undertaking further qualifications during their employment to gain qualified teacher status' (Gov.uk 2022). This last statement seems to imply that the actual percentage of unqualified teachers might be higher than the stated 3 per cent as reporting 'qualified teachers' might include those that are working in schools under the 'Schools-led' training routes.

More concerns are being voiced from other reputable sources such as the NfER:

> Teacher retention rates, having improved substantially in 2020 due to economic uncertainty and lockdown, also appeared to be returning towards pre-pandemic levels in 2021. The evidence therefore seems clear that significant teacher supply challenges are re-emerging after two years of having eased somewhat due to the pandemic. Tackling teacher supply effectively to avoid shortages that are re-emerging and having a significant impact on schools requires policy action to improve the attractiveness of the teaching profession.
>
> (Worth and Faulkner-Ellis 2022: 16)

Employment of others in schools?

One other factor that has changed significantly in education, impacting on teachers' role and responsibilities, are the other positions that have arisen in schools in recent decades to try to support both the shortfall in teacher numbers and increase of teachers' workload. Government data shows that as of November 2021 only 48 per cent (465,526 full-time equivalent) of people working in state-funded schools in England were teachers (Gov.uk 2022), seeing a rise of nearly 2 per cent (456,900 full-time equivalent) since 2011. In comparison, between 2011/12 and 2020/21 while administrative and auxiliary staff and technicians have slightly decreased in number, 'other support staff' have increased by the full-time equivalent of 24 per cent. Staggeringly, the number of teaching assistants has risen from 345,505 (full-time equivalent 221,481) to 390,925 (full-time equivalent 275,812), representing a 13 per cent increase in total number and 25 per cent increase in full-time equivalent. Why is this? Are they filling in providing much-needed classroom cover for teacher shortfall, or are they there to work with pupils who teachers find 'difficult to manage' with additional needs such as a special educational need (see Chapter 3)?

Of course, it is important to recognize the positive work that teaching assistants and other support workers such as pastoral support workers actually can and do carry out. As in the majority of other workforce situations, the success of any team is dependent on how well they are managed, supported and trained, as well as ensuring that the expectations of the role are both viable and beneficial for the recipients. Nevertheless, we feel that during the past decade the increase in support roles like teaching assistants, learning/behaviour mentors and pastoral care workers have altered the role of teachers – quite substantially we suspect in secondary and larger primary schools and academies. Rice O'Toole's (2020) study, for example, explored whether the employment of pastoral support staff (PSS) who worked with pupils with social, emotional and mental health (SEMH) needs was changing the role and responsibilities of teachers. This research showed that there was a need for administrative staff to support pastoral care teachers and professionals. However, it also identified that employing non-teaching, unqualified support staff to undertake the pastoral care work means that vulnerable pupils are in danger of spending an increasing amount of time out of classrooms, with fewer opportunities to develop the skills and strategies required to help them learn. The study found that divorcing the holistic (academic and pastoral) role of teachers (McLean Davies et al. 2015) in an effort to decrease workloads has led some teachers to feel that a really positive element of their role has been removed. One of the study's respondents wrote, 'I think pastoral care is a core part of being a teacher. We are here to educate the whole child and teach them how to be decent citizens, good friends, reliable employees and in time strong parents' (Rice O'Toole and Soan 2021: 9). Others however felt that it was positive that they did not have to deal with all of the behavioural, learning and social needs of the pupils, with 74 per cent of the study's participants stating that teacher training did not prepare them to fulfil pastoral roles (Rice O'Toole 2020). This latter response provides evidence once again that there is a possible lack of understanding about *why* teachers need to see how providing pastoral care (and indeed being able to teach those with all types of learning needs) enables their pupils to develop cognitively as well as socially and emotionally. Thus, the short-term 'fix' due to necessity could once again be undermining the craftsmanship required for teachers to be able to work with a pupil's holistic development, and in some situations allows the most vulnerable to be taught and cared for by the least qualified.

This is not the final picture, as during the past two decades schools have been required to organize and be accountable for their own business finances and running costs. This means that schools now tend to have at least a school business manager (SBM) – part or full time (DfE 2022) – who, depending on the size of the school(s), can be paid anything between £25,000 and £65,000+ (full time). The Department for Education (2022: 12–22) states that a SBM and their team (in some cases) have different ways of managing these elements of school life:

> A primary school is more likely than a secondary school to completely outsource the following: human resources (42% vs. 13%); information and communications technology (ICT) (55% vs. 15%); finance support (47% vs. 33%); buildings maintenance services (33% vs. 16%), and school improvement services (45% vs. 27%). In most MATs, finance support, HR, legal, school improvement, payroll, ICT, and insurance are provided centrally through a top slice or on a charged basis. This is consistent across all MAT types.

This means that as soon as budgets are given to schools, a significant amount of that funding is immediately top sliced to ensure that the school remains a viable business – but how well does this serve the staff and pupils? This does not become an issue until educational decisions are made by those that are not teachers. Is this happening, and if so, how does it make teachers feel?

Conclusion

Arguably, everyone teaching in schools has to be able to manage ongoing change and conflict due to political directives. Teachers have seen their teaching practice challenged, demand for evidence of pupil progress dramatically increased and their teaching competence constantly monitored and appraised, causing them to be fearful of inspection and job insecurity. It is therefore understandable that recruiting and retaining teachers is becoming increasingly hard due to poor work/life balance and well-being, the stress of meeting targets and finding the role generally unsatisfying (DfE 2018). These struggles are, it is proposed, leading teachers to become risk-averse, overcompliant and even disillusioned (Wood et al. 2021). Teachers, especially senior leaders and SENCos, are now always having to balance between serving many masters, managing parents/carers and families as if they are customers and service users. Is it time, as Dewey asks in the book *The Public and its Problems* (Dewey 1984: 235–372), for the public to rescue the school education system 'from its less than noble controllers' (Johnston 2013: 108)?

Even though it is difficult to compare country to country, we recommend that despite all of the tensions that persist with teaching and teachers in England currently, our political leaders (and hence the general public) should consider and learn from the way Finland both values and trains its teachers, as described by Sahlberg (2015):

> Young athletes, musicians and youth leaders, for example, often have the emerging characteristics of great teachers without having the best academic record. What Finland shows is that rather than get 'best and the brightest' into teaching, it is better to design initial teacher education in a way that will get the best from young people who have natural passion to teach for life.
>
> …
>
> A good step forward would be to admit that the academically best students are not necessarily the best teachers. Successful education systems are more concerned about finding the right people to become career-long teachers.

And

> In fact, Finnish primary school teacher education programmes that lead to an advanced, research-based degree are so popular among young Finns that only one in 10 applicants is accepted each year. Those lucky students then have to study for five to six years before they are allowed to teach a class of their own.

Is such a system affordable in England today, or can the nation risk not to undertake this stand for high-quality education for all pupils, taught by world-class master craft teachers?

7 The Twenty-First-Century English Education System: Choosing a New Pathway

Introduction

This chapter draws together the discussions already shared in this book, and endeavours to present a new viable option for our state education system in these times of austerity, rapid change and development. We would never protest that we have all the answers or are experts in knowing how an equitable twenty-first-century education system should be constructed. Our decades of experience as professionals and service users have given us the evidence to express the view that the constant redesigning of the 'same old' is neither sufficient, affordable nor good enough for our children and young people. We believe that there have been many poorly considered and destructive decisions made about teaching and learning, especially inclusive and equitable education, by our political leaders in recent decades. These we feel have not been sufficiently focused on who are our future – our children – but instead on neoliberal ideology and party politics (see Chapter 2). Our desire would be for this text to ignite a national discussion and debate involving all who wish to participate, so that we do not keep failing our children and young people as they try to prepare for adult life in an increasingly complex society. As the recent House of Lords Children and Families Act 2014 Committee stated in its report (House of Lords 2022: 94), 'Every year that passes without a well-functioning SEND system is another year of a child's education that is failing.'

Education is *the* key, but our system is outdated, fragmented and inequitable and does not provide for a modern child's holistic development and skills. As the first two special educational needs Codes of Practice (DfE 1994; DfES 2001) state, we need to explicitly recognize through the curriculum and the design of the school, including its calendar, that the interactions between within-person aspects and environmental factors are complex and therefore need to be flexible. We should not expect pupils to change to adapt to a system (see Chapter 2) that is based on bureaucracy, targets and competition, and is so obviously unrelated to their own lived experiences.

We are not alone in these views, with UNESCO (2021: 11) stating that:

> Education systems have wrongly instilled a belief that short-term prerogatives and comforts are more important than longer-term sustainability. They have emphasized values of individual success, national competition and economic development, to the detriment of solidarity, understanding our interdependencies, and caring for each other and the planet.
>
> A new social contract for education must be anchored in two foundational principles: (1) the right to education and (2) a commitment to education as a public societal endeavour and a common good.

Importantly, in line with our thinking, UNESCO express how 'education' should form the foundations of the work of societies in shaping 'social, economic, and environmental justice' (UNESCO 2021: 11). It should unite our society in collective endeavours and prepare all, and particularly the young, for 'environmental, technological, and social changes on the horizon' (UNESCO 2021: 11). In order to achieve this, children and young people need to receive an education curriculum which has a holistic view of development enveloping all areas of child development (physical, emotional, social and academic), based on sound theoretical underpinnings and teachers who are skilled in their craft and their science of teaching.

To demonstrate how this can be achieved, the remainder of this chapter focuses on how key critical factors contribute to the construction of a viable, efficient and motivating education system. Key principles evolved from these factors will then be offered as a starting point for our readers to debate. This will unashamedly reflect our convictions about the type of education system we believe will unite our society and prepare especially the young for future 'environmental, technological, and social changes' (UNESCO 2021: 11) and enable them to be happy individuals with self-belief and respect for all others. These, alongside the challenge offered to policymakers and school leaders to embrace Robinson's framework (see Chapter 4), can be used effectively to operationalize educational action and thus improvement. From these firm theoretical underpinnings strategies, interventions and daily teaching practices can be developed and used in ways that can enable *all* children to make progress in *all* areas of their development.

Our vision is an education system based on civil societal consensus (Edwards 2008), separated from party politics and 'philanthropic governance' (Olmedo 2014; House of Lords 2022) which currently causes constant change, conflict, inequity of opportunities for children and young people and inconsistent messages to parents, carers and practitioners. As Edwards (2008: 27) says, the inability of politics to change the inequities caused by our economic system impacts negatively on being able to have 'more cooperation not competition, more collective action not individualism, and a greater willingness to work together to change the fundamental structures that keep most people poor so that all of us can live more fulfilling lives'. We believe that a society's future, our children and young people, should be at the core of all other sections of society, as stated by UNESCO (2021: 11), and that all children must have access to the best possible education, independent of wealth or social status, tailored to their individual interests and talents. It must be clarified that we are not just speaking about academic learning here, but about all skills and roles required for society to function fairly, efficiently and effectively.

What is affordable?

It is indisputable that economically England and many other nations are going to be financially vulnerable in the forthcoming years, due to many national and global factors. Politicians frequently claim that they have increased spending significantly in areas like education, but have they really? Much of that funding is spent on the upkeep of school buildings and grounds, on human resource issues and salaries for business colleagues rather than on teaching staff and resources directly relevant for pupils' learning and development, of course. It is argued that the 'business' elements of a school are essential to ensure pupils are safe, warm and well-fed, but should this be part of the 'education' budget? Or should the education budget be based solely on paying teachers' salaries, on continuing craft development and on teaching resources (including technology), with the important structural and business aspects funded through our appropriately resourced civil local authorities?

We would argue that such an approach would enable principals, head teachers and executive leaders to focus on their craft – teaching and learning – and less on the business aspects of their context. This could then provide opportunities to be more flexible about where and how teaching takes place, ensuring all young children and pupils are able to learn in an environment in which they are comfortable, creating equity across a local authority and potentially consolidating costs (Armstrong and Ainscow 2018; Bubb et al. 2019).

What is clear is that it is 'unaffordable' for a society not to have an education system which is able to provide all its future citizens with the self-confidence, knowledge, interpersonal and professional skills to contribute to the economic maintenance of their nation if it wants to continue to claim it is aiming to be inclusive. Continuing to promote an education system with a myriad of different roots in its structure perpetuates social inequity, inequality and injustice, let alone the 'waste' of talent and aspirations.

Does the public need to rescue the school education system 'from its less than noble controllers' (Johnston 2013: 108)?

Since the removal of Sir Gavin Williamson from his position as Secretary of State for Education in September 2021 there have been four further changes in this post (Zahawi, Donelan, Cleverly, Malthouse) before the current Education Secretary of State, Gillian Keegan, was 'appointed' on 25 October 2022. This 'Carousel of education secretaries' (Walker 2022) drew the following response from the joint general secretary of the National Education Union:

> This is one of the most important jobs in government, though you wouldn't think so given the way the role has been treated as an afterthought in recent years.
>
> Children and young people are paying the price for this constant upheaval and the lack of grip and understanding on the many issues facing the education service.

It is evident that there is a funding and staffing crisis across the whole of childhood provision, with the Children's Commissioner calling for a 'transformative' new model for early education and childcare in her *Vision for Childcare* report (Children's Commissioner 2022). In this it is clear that parents and carers are reporting that the current system is not working for them or their children. The report states that parents and carers would prefer to draw on their families and friends to care for their children when they could, as this made them feel 'happier and more supported' (Children's Commissioner 2022: 8). If this was not possible and they had to use professional services, they valued 'strong and positive relationships' with the people involved and for the 'childcare to be local, familiar and reliable' (Children's Commissioner 2022: 8). Schools (and colleges and universities) are in a similar position as that stated in this Early Years report with lack of funding, inconsistent collaborative relationships (wraparound services), low staff recruitment and poor retention and morale. If education is not valued or promoted sufficiently to meet the needs of parents/carers or children through national party politics or business then perhaps a broader, local service driven by civic decision needs to be constructed and developed so that all citizens get a voice in what is a key, if not the most crucial element of every progressive, inclusive society.

Inclusion and inclusive education

England has continued to this current time to promote and support inclusive education, in principle at least, since the agreement reached at the World Conference in Salamanca in June 1994 that called for the inclusion of all disabled children to become the norm. The adopted framework for action resulting from this agreement had as its guiding principle the requirement that all children should be accommodated in ordinary schools 'regardless of their physical, intellectual, social, emotional, linguistic, or other conditions' (CSIE 2020). This view was reflected in the first and subsequent Codes of Practice (DfE 1994; DfES 2001; DfE and DoH 2015) as one of their fundamental principles. Indeed, 'location' was and continues to be a significant factor when considering funding and provision for pupils with a 'special educational need' or disability. This 'view' of what inclusion means is mainly considered by professionals as 'outdated' in our current era, even though there is not an actual agreed definition provided in national policy.

Of course, inclusion did not just suddenly appear in 1994, and in the United Kingdom it was the 1972 Education Act which gave all children a right to education, whatever their disability, for the very first time (Warnock and Norwich 2010). It was this Act that stated that new principles of universal education were required, thus abolishing the concept of an ineducable child. In response to this, the government commissioned the Committee of Inquiry into the Education of Handicapped Children and Young People in 1974 [language used at the time]. This resulted in the now famous Warnock Committee report (Warnock 1978) which greatly influenced the 1981 Education Act. This commenced the pathway from the educational (and social) segregation of children towards integration, and hoped to commit to history negative medical terms used to describe children's differences, replacing them with the term 'special educational needs', under which sat four categories of need (DfE 1994; DfES 2001; DfE and DoH 2015). However it had the unintended outcome of creating a separate system of funding, resources, training and provision running alongside the generic state-funded education system. This has undoubtedly contributed to the undermining of teachers' confidence in being able to teach all pupils, created avenues for conflict between families and professionals, hindered the development of inclusive education and been extremely expensive and divisive.

Even though positive changes and developments towards integration did take place, undoubtedly as a consequence of the Warnock Committee report (Warnock 1978) (see Chapter 2), Baroness Warnock herself saw and explicitly voiced that it was 'time for a radical review' over a decade ago (Warnock and Norwich 2010: 11). She and others (such as Dyson 2001) recognized that you cannot have conflicting systems, where one tries to treat all children equally and another treats them differently. Despite the rhetoric at the time, the recently revised *Special Educational Needs and Disability Code of Practice* (DfE and DoH 2015) (England only) has done very little to deal with these difficulties and prevents the embedding of further truly inclusive educational practice.

Why not SEND?

It is our view that to continue to become as inclusive as possible the separate, expensive and divisive 'special educational needs and disability', 'additional' and 'different' terms and system should be ended, and individual pupil need reinstated as a whole-school responsibility. In this way all teachers will know they are teachers of all pupils, and parents and carers will not have the bureaucracy to confront to get what 'they see their child needs' through various layers of legal and statutory systems.

Quality initial teacher education (ITE) and continuing teacher development (CTD)

It is therefore not possible to continue to provide and promote such a rapid, shallow and diminished programme for initial teacher education (e.g. PGCE) if we are serious about ensuring our adults of the future can be critical, resourceful and lifelong learners. An early career framework (DfE and EEF 2019) which is not required by all is again a weak attempt to build resilience and substance in our teaching population, as cheaply as possible. With such an approach there are dangers of:

- poor retention of teaching staff, unable to sustain the stresses and strains of school life
- professional 'staleness' as teachers only feel 'safe' to stay in one environment for their careers (or until a new senior leader arrives) because they know what is required and can follow the school's rules
- the continuation of a teaching force in which many feel unable to teach all children and therefore rely on the separate SEND system and 'othering'
- the continuation of a 'what works' approach to teaching, which frequently fails when a pupil does not 'get' the 'what works' approach
- failure to promote and explicitly demonstrate inclusion and equity in practice.

These factors have become even further amplified in recent decades as just providing information to pupils becomes less important as part of the role of teachers in our current technological times. Teachers need to be able to teach all pupils, but in order to do this they need the right skills and access to core pedagogical principles through significant education thinkers such as Bruner, Vygotsky and Dewey (see Chapter 3) for confidence to be achieved. They need to enable their pupils and students to become critical and flexible thinkers, able to generate new creative ideas based on solid, research-based evidence. Teachers constantly need to encourage an individual's self-acceptance and confidence, as well as honed interpersonal skills – skills too frequently underrated (see Chapter 4). They need to be able to be effective communicators and collaborative, respectful partners, and be able to share specialist knowledge and demonstrate curiosity (Robinson 2018). To achieve this, teachers also need to understand and be specialists in these complex areas. All of this work can be emotionally and intellectually draining, and to sustain such practice teachers need to have access to professional supervision (Reid and Soan 2015, 2018; Monsen et al. 2021) and continue to be nurtured and developed through ongoing CTD as needed for requirements of society and the world. As we said in Chapter 2:

> This we believe will contribute to the reprofessionalizing of teaching based not only on subject content expertise, but embracing what some see as specialized and rarefied knowledge around the history and philosophy of teaching–learning, child and adolescent development (physical, cognitive, affective, behaviour,

language, psychosocial, social-emotional, mental health/well-being and so on), evidence-based or informed teaching approaches and strategies (covering the full range of learners), the management and organization of an inclusive classroom and school, and the roles and responsibilities of others (parents, carers, external specialists).

Though expensive, skilled teachers are the foundations for a truly equitable education system. Expensive, undoubtedly – but in the long term, we would argue value for money, as an inclusive, equitable system with skilled teachers able to provide a quality education for all would not require a separate, bureaucratic and divisive SEND approach for the vast majority. For the children and young people who require specialist education (whether short or long term) or health and care support, higher-level learning (such as Masters and doctorates) would be the expectation for those staff members who work and care for these most vulnerable in society. The provision, schools and residential environments can be seen as a continuum of the one whole education system, providing what a child needs for as long as they need it, working as professional teams (including the voices of the children and parents/carers).

Partnership working and respecting others' professional expertise

For four decades at least governments have written in special education policy that different agencies and professionals should collaborate and work together to meet the needs of the children and young people they work with and for (Anning et al. 2010; Edmond and Price 2012). Yet in 2022 there is not a consistent picture of collaborative working across the country, as illustrated by a House of Lords Committee report (House of Lords 2022: 17):

> Truly joined up working between education, health and social care remains unrealised. Health and social care are often absent from the picture, and families struggle against an overwhelming tide of bureaucracy in a system lacking coherence.

In fact, we would argue that we remain in the same position that Nancarrow et al. reported on following their thematic analysis of literature back in 2013. They found that practitioners focused on fulfilling their own professional system requirements, which were so frequently constrained by lack of staffing and funding, rather than on the needs of pupils. This undoubtedly remains the case and thus we propose that an integrated Children, Young People and Families Service (or what seems sensible at the time) be established, integrating education, social care and health staff involved with children and young people. This would promote truly multi-professional working, ending the silo working which dominates today, and would provide a mechanism to focus coherently on the needs of children and young people, their families and schools.

It is not defensible for national leaders to just keep on saying to education, social care and health colleagues to 'work collaboratively' and expect it to be done. Practitioners need to respect and value others' expertise and contributions. Integrated, multi-professional geographical teams, which have a clear mandate, sound management and governance, are probably the best way of achieving such collaboration and for making an impact on children and young people.

Couper and Soan (2021) suggest a few principles to follow when planning to collaborate with others. They say that the first steps should be to understand the purpose for collaboration and to build trust and respect between the individuals who will be working together. A plan of action should then be produced clearly identifying what all consider will benefit the pupil. Then, with a focus on the pupil's need, the plan should be implemented, during which time the professionals should communicate with each other confidently and honestly, asking for advice and support when needed. Such openness should lead to productive collaboration. Too often there are collaborations for friendship and steps proposed which are too large to achieve. Collaborations need to be productive, purposeful with clear goals and focused on the needs of the child or young person. It is for these reasons that we strongly recommend that public service professionals need to experience collaborative working throughout their initial education programmes and be given time to build respectful and trusting relationships with colleagues from other disciplines and professions.

Curriculum

The English national curriculum has been amended and updated numerous times since its introduction by the Education Reform Act 1988. To begin with it was inflexible and too prescriptive to enable inclusive practice, and newly qualified teachers became deskilled if they did not have a provided plan to teach a lesson. The school day was and remains, in many cases, very focused on English, mathematics and science lessons, with little thought for pupils' physical, creative and social development.

With schools' success measured by league tables and examination results, too often the pupils who do not grasp a new mathematical or language concept as quickly as 'expected' are given more of the same, as if repetition will without fail lead to understanding and success! Even worse, they miss out on playtime, physical activities or arts and crafts – all valuable to growing and developing minds. As the Office for Standards in Education, Children's Services and Skills (Ofsted 2022: section 1.3) itself reports: 'We must keep stressing the value of early education: from speech development to socialisation; physical dexterity to counting.'

It is interesting that academies and private schools (sometimes called public schools) do not have to follow the national curriculum, although currently they do have to teach relationships and sex education, religious education and a broad and balanced curriculum including English, mathematics and science.

Here again we see inequity and greater choice for those that have access to an academy because of location or can afford a private school education. Frequently, in private schools sports, dance and physical education take place daily, with opportunities to develop interpersonal skills through extracurricular clubs and experiences. While academic learning is highly valued, drama, the arts and personal development are given equal priority. Class sizes are smaller than those found in the majority of state schools and pupils may well have to pass an entrance examination before being accepted into the school. How can our children and young people experience equity if one system is good enough for them while others have greater opportunities?

We believe England needs a state education system which values the importance of: play, social engagement and physical and sensory development; the growth and maintenance of behavioural and emotional self-regulation; critical thinking and collaborative problem-solving; life skills and a sense of community and global cohesion (see Chapter 3) – in fact, a **collective curriculum** which all schools are expected to adhere to irrespective of funding arrangements.

With technological developments there is the opportunity for schools, especially if working collaboratively with neighbouring schools, to enable pupils with complex needs to access teaching and learning through a blended or flexible individualized curriculum with staff specifically employed to support them, not in addition to their class teaching, but as a standard role within a school. This would enable pupils who find large social groups too difficult to manage to access full-time learning and small group size activities and clubs, and provide parents/carers with the assurance that their child will still receive a quality education. Schools need to be able to respond immediately to the diverse needs of our population – a curriculum taught and provided through a range of different pathways but with the same goals as valued by the collective, our society. Although it is not possible, or even desirable, to determine in this book what such a curriculum should look like in daily practice, the following case studies will hopefully help operationalize Figure 7.1, showing the six principles found at the end of this chapter, as well as Robinson's framework (see Chapter 4).

We have identified a few strategic goals which might appear in a collective curriculum. These goals are for each child or young person to be able to develop age-appropriate interpersonal skills/good communication, self-belief, the importance of sustainability and the environment, digital competence and core academic skills.

A collective curriculum

Two sample pathway case studies

> 1 *Mavis (not her real name) is nearly 5 and has just joined a school which is deepening its curriculum with regard to the environment and sustainability. She has limited speech, poor social and physical skills (e.g. use of tools – cutlery, crayons) and poor comprehension. Mavis has not attended nursery and has not had the opportunity to play with other children.*
>
> The school decides that the pathway Mavis requires is to have time to get to know her environment and to increase language acquisition and

comprehension through play and engagement with the natural environment. Mavis will not be asked (but would not be stopped if she wanted) to work in a whole-class session, and will be able to engage in only small-group activities in order to help her build her confidence, trust the adults around her and enable her to begin to form relationships with her peers. Outside play, opportunities to use large tools and play equipment (to help develop gross motor skills) would be her main activities of the day. Mavis would be introduced to the selection, preparation and eating of finger foods, linking social skills to healthy eating. She would also have book sharing and drawing sessions, increasing her ability to focus and concentrate, as well as opportunities to rest throughout the day. Thus, although she would be in school full time, the expectations would focus on her needs using the curriculum and school goals as guidelines only. Progress would be monitored constantly (as it is now in Early Years) and new pathways implemented as appropriate.

2 *Henry (not his real name) has just been placed in foster care a long way from his birth family and peers. Although academically Henry meets all expected progress, he finds it difficult to be in a whole class and will leave when the noise and pressure of his situation become too much. He has not been able to make any new friends as yet but does not want to start at a new school. He has settled well in his foster home, and one of the carers is able to be home-based full time.*

When the school started to develop a pathway collaboratively with his social worker and foster carers, Henry's main strengths and interests were considered key to his engagement. The school offered Henry a flexible timetable incorporating digital learning, social digital engagement with one or two other peers at the school (with adult support), as well as opportunities to physically participate in lessons he enjoyed or did well at, if and when he felt able. A mentor teacher would be provided, and they would meet (physically or online) every day to ensure progress, and Henry's confidence and trust could be increased day on day. Such a programme could be fluid depending on his personal situation and attendance in school increased when Henry felt ready. In this way they hoped to ensure Henry's academic progress would not be compromised by his move, and that his self-esteem and peer interactions would be able to develop at his own speed. This pathway would also take into consideration when he had contact with birth family members or had local authority reviews, enabling work to be completed at non-conventional times or on another planned date. Henry's educational expectations would not be lower, but his personal situation would be acknowledged and supported, helping him learn to manage more difficult as well as more stable times.

As we move forward, we must not limit a child's learning environment by location, time or subject, but encourage their interests and talents whatever they may be.

Conclusion

To bring about profound change, the future school's organizing principles should centre on inclusion and collaboration. Excellence, achievement, quality, measurement, and progress are also valuable commitments that can be realigned in ways that include rather than marginalize.

(UNESCO 2021: 97)

Of course, liberating our state education system will not be a simple task, and immense changes will need to be implemented. It will mean the restructuring of the whole school system to include provision and timetabling which meet the fluid needs of our pupils. The funding of schools across England, and of course our inspection system (Ofsted), training routes and the curriculum, will all need to be radically reviewed – difficult, of course, but not impossible if that is what society sees is required.

There are without doubt many positives as well. Teachers will need to receive the underpinning understanding and theory they require (see Chapter 3) to work with all pupils, so commitment and work satisfaction, it is surmised, will all improve; parents and carers will have a better chance of equitable provision for their children; and the layers of administration required to run the 'SEND' system will be obsolete. Importantly, it could have a positive impact on other education professionals such as educational psychologists. No longer will they be required to be locked into producing assessment after assessment required for EHC plans, but will be able to work alongside schools and teachers in the classroom giving direct and individual advice and support. With jointly coordinated and funded partner health and social care services, it will be possible to provide holistic care and support in schools, removing the need for parents and carers to take whole days off work to attend clinics for their child's speech and language or occupational therapy sessions. Equally, pupils will not miss school, and teachers and other professionals will be able to collaborate more easily and effectively.

We know these suggestions are confronting and amazingly difficult for any nationwide education system to achieve, but with a long-term (at least 15 years) plan where actions are tackled in a sequential manner and not derailed by constant political changes in policy, we believe it is worth igniting a discussion and debate now. Such a plan will, we suggest, improve the craftmanship of teaching and thus teachers' motivation and commitment to the profession. It will necessitate collaborative working across disciplines and provide efficient time and funding resourcing of pupil provision. It will break the layers of bureaucracy for parents and carers and deepen meaningful relations between schools and their communities.

Most importantly, it will put the responsibility of educating our children and young people more directly into the hands of society, and hopefully aid the further growth and embedding of inclusion.

We end this book with as much passion and belief in providing an education system fit for all our children and young people as we had when we started our careers. Every child is priceless and worth the time, energy and economic investment in providing them with an equitable, inclusive and high-quality education, taught by teachers who believe in their craft.

It is hoped that the following list of principles (as well as Robinson's (2018) framework) and Figure 7.1 will aid in rigorous, child-focused discussions and debates, identifying the areas of the curriculum, the school environment and continuing teacher development that are required in each school. Not every strategy or intervention will work for every child, just as the ethos of every school will not be right for every child in a diverse and inclusive society. If the core of school education is based on understanding child development, teacher expertise and the needs of a society, then the surrounding layers of curriculum, assessment and interpersonal skills will fold smoothly around it, creating a well-balanced and solution-focused learning environment for all.

Six Principles for an equitable and inclusive education system respectful of all, responsible for all

Principle 1

School academic and social responsibility

- Schools and other educational establishments work together across local authorities and not in competition with each other – having shared outcomes/goals to achieve.
- Schools work in partnership with other statutory agencies: i.e. an integrated Child and Young People's Service.
- Schools work in partnership with parents/carers and families.
- School policies are to be clearly written and terms well defined (inclusion, coproduction and equity).

For example:

Our definition of inclusion is a process constantly evolving as people's views and expectations change and develop. Inclusion can be said to occur when diversity in all its shapes and forms is positively perceived by all in a community, and the individual feels safe, happy, respected and an equally valued member of that community.

Inclusive education can be defined as providing an educational environment where all who attend the provision can access, participate and engage in learning opportunities and experiences and all social activities, enabling them to achieve and develop as confident, positive adults. Inclusive education is not about a location, a 'need' or disability, but about providing a teaching–learning environment where all children and young people can learn and develop as positively as possible. One pupil might need a specialist environment for a term or a year, due to illness, loss or trauma, while another might need a much smaller, protective environment longer term. Inclusive education is therefore about meeting the needs of a pupil and not about putting everyone into one school together.

Equity is different to equality. Equality means every pupil should have access to the same teaching–learning opportunities. Equity means ensuring each pupil has access to the same teaching–learning experiences and opportunities by providing some pupils with more personalized and individualized input, support and resources so they can achieve and develop on their own terms (each according to need).

Co-production is a relatively new term being used in educational policy. It is a recent 'buzzword' which is frequently misrepresented. For us, co-production should be incorporated in all stages of a partnership project or support package. For example, a pupil's annual EHC plan review should be completed by all stakeholders during a meeting, with the final decisions and actions agreed only after every person has had their views and wishes at least listened to and discussed. All too frequently a pupil's plan for the next year is completed by professionals, and parents/carers and the pupil are asked just to agree to what the professionals propose. Full co-production implemented at each stage of development is difficult, complex and time-consuming, and as such may be very problematic to implement positively in all schools and for all pupils. Perhaps a realistic term such as 'consultation with partners' or 'shared production' would be clearer and help to manage parents, and carers' expectations.

Principle 2

Respect teaching as a craft and therefore teachers as professionals/craftspeople through full degree- and Masters-level initial teacher education and continuing craftsmanship development, including the scientist practitioner model.

Principle 3

A comprehensive, non-prescriptive collective curriculum

- Motivational and support children to take on challenges
- Fluid and flexible
- Valuing and encouraging school-readiness (Crehan 2016)
- Inclusive
- Digital/physical presence.

Principle 4

Equitable, fair access and engagement with the curriculum and to the educational community

Principle 5

Whole-school approaches, policies and strategies should be for all pupils

Principle 6

Progress measures

- These are valued ensuring that **evidence** collected is 'related to the presence, participation, and achievement of all students' (Ainscow 2020: 10).
- Performance is measured on the outcomes of the children as individuals, not as classes or schools.

Figure 7.1 Potential enforcers of inclusion in a liberated English state education system to meet parents' expectations

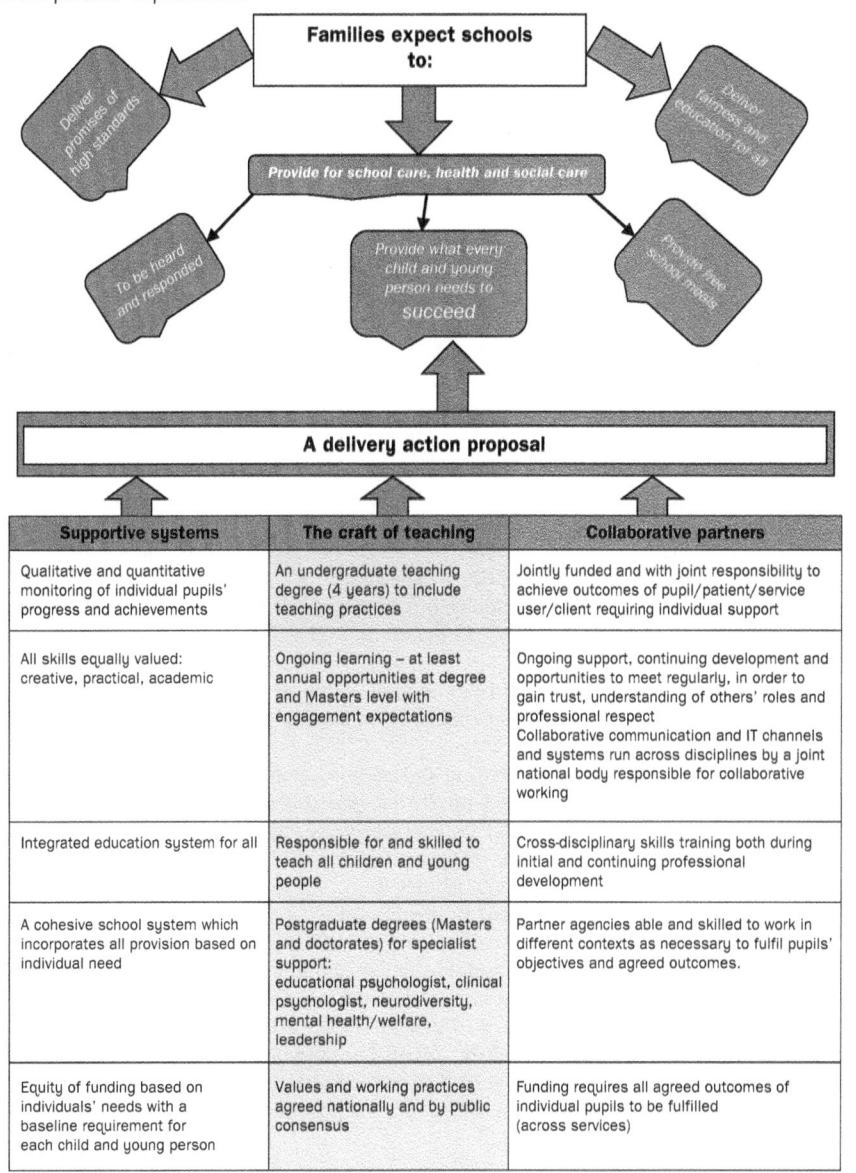

Families expect schools to:
- Deliver promises of high standards
- Deliver fairness and education for all
- Provide for school care, health and social care
- To be heard and responded
- Provides free school meals
- Provide what every child and young person needs to succeed

A delivery action proposal

Supportive systems	The craft of teaching	Collaborative partners
Qualitative and quantitative monitoring of individual pupils' progress and achievements	An undergraduate teaching degree (4 years) to include teaching practices	Jointly funded and with joint responsibility to achieve outcomes of pupil/patient/service user/client requiring individual support
All skills equally valued: creative, practical, academic	Ongoing learning – at least annual opportunities at degree and Masters level with engagement expectations	Ongoing support, continuing development and opportunities to meet regularly, in order to gain trust, understanding of others' roles and professional respect Collaborative communication and IT channels and systems run across disciplines by a joint national body responsible for collaborative working
Integrated education system for all	Responsible for and skilled to teach all children and young people	Cross-disciplinary skills training both during initial and continuing professional development
A cohesive school system which incorporates all provision based on individual need	Postgraduate degrees (Masters and doctorates) for specialist support: educational psychologist, clinical psychologist, neurodiversity, mental health/welfare, leadership	Partner agencies able and skilled to work in different contexts as necessary to fulfil pupils' objectives and agreed outcomes.
Equity of funding based on individuals' needs with a baseline requirement for each child and young person	Values and working practices agreed nationally and by public consensus	Funding requires all agreed outcomes of individual pupils to be fulfilled (across services)

References

Chapter 1

Kelly, B. and Perkins, D.F. (2012) *Handbook of Implementation Science for Psychology in Education*. Cambridge; New York: Cambridge University Press.

Warnock, M. and Norwich, B. (2010) *Special Educational Needs: A New Look*, ed. L. Terzi, 2nd edn. London; New York: Continuum International.

Chapter 2

Academies Act (2010) *Academies Act 2010*. Statute Law Database. Available at: https://www.legislation.gov.uk/ukpga/2010/32/contents (Accessed: 19 July 2022).

Ainscow, M. and César, M. (2006) Inclusive education ten years after Salamanca: Setting the agenda, *European Journal of Psychology of Education*, 21(3): 231–8. https://doi.org/10.1007/BF03173412.

Ainscow, M., Slee, R. and Best, M. (2019) Editorial: The Salamanca Statement: 25 years on, *International Journal of Inclusive Education*, 23(7–8): 671–6. https://doi.org/10.1080/13603116.2019.1622800.

Argyris, C. (1999) *On Organizational Learning*, 2nd edn. Oxford; Malden, MA: Blackwell Business.

Argyris, C. and Schön, D.A. (1974) *Theory in Practice*. Jossey-Bass Higher and Adult Education Series. San Francisco, CA: Jossey-Bass.

Armstrong, D. (2005) Reinventing 'Inclusion': New Labour and the Cultural Politics of Special Education, *Oxford Review of Education*, 31(1): 135–51. https://doi.org/10.1080/0305498042000337237.

Armstrong, D., Armstrong, A.C. and Spandagou, I. (2011) Inclusion: By choice or by chance?, *International Journal of Inclusive Education*, 15(1): 29–39. https://doi.org/10.1080/13603116.2010.496192.

Armstrong, F. (2007) Disability, education and social change in England since 1960, *History of Education*, 36(4–5): 551–68. https://doi.org/10.1080/00467600701496849.

Avramidis, E. and Norwich, B. (2002) Teachers' attitudes towards integration/inclusion: A review of the literature, *European Journal of Special Needs Education*, 17(2): 129–47. https://doi.org/10.1080/08856250210129056.

Ball, S.J. (2016) Neoliberal education? Confronting the slouching beast, *Policy Futures in Education*, 14(8): 1046–59. https://doi.org/10.1177/1478210316664259.

Baltodano, M. (2012) Neoliberalism and the demise of public education: The corporatization of schools of education, *International Journal of Qualitative Studies in Education*, 25(4): 487–507. https://doi.org/10.1080/09518398.2012.673025.

Bamberger, A., Morris, P. and Yemini, M. (2019) Neoliberalism, internationalisation and higher education: Connections, contradictions and alternatives, *Discourse: Studies in the Cultural Politics of Education*, 40(2): 203–16. https://doi.org/10.1080/01596306.2019.1569879.

References

Barton, L. (1988) *The Politics of Special Educational Needs*, ed. Len Barton. Disability, Handicap and Life Chances series, 4. London: Falmer.

Baxter, J. and Floyd, A. (2019) Strategic narrative in multi-academy trusts in England: Principal drivers for expansion, *British Educational Research Journal*, 45(5): 1050–71. https://doi.org/10.1002/berj.3550.

Bines, H. (2000) Inclusive standards? Current developments in policy for special educational needs in England and Wales, *Oxford Review of Education*, 26(1): 21–33. https://doi.org/10.1080/030549800103836.

Blandford, S. (2013) The impact of 'Achievement for All' on school leadership, *Educational Management Administration & Leadership*, 41(1): 45–62. https://doi.org/10.1177/1741143212462701.

Booth, T. (1996) A perspective on inclusion from England, *Cambridge Journal of Education*, 26(1): 87–99. https://doi.org/10.1080/0305764960260107.

Booth, T. and Ainscow, M. (2011) *Index for Inclusion: Developing Learning and Participation in Schools*, 3rd edn, substantially revised and expanded. Bristol: Centre for Studies on Inclusive Education.

Cameron, R.J. (Sean) and Monsen, J.J. (2005) Quality psychological advice for teachers, parents/carers and LEA decision makers with respect to children and young people with special needs, *Educational Psychology in Practice*, 21(4): 283–306. https://doi.org/10.1080/02667360500344864.

Capper, Z.L. (2020) A cultural historical activity theory analysis of educational psychologists' contributions to the statutory assessment of children and young peoples' special educational needs post-2014 Children and Families Act. Doctoral thesis, University of Birmingham.

Children and Families Act (2014) *Children and Families Act 2014*. Queen's Printer of Acts of Parliament. Available at: https://www.legislation.gov.uk/ukpga/2014/6/contents/enacted (Accessed: 1 June 2022).

Cigman, R. (2007) A question of universality: Inclusive education and the principle of respect, *Journal of Philosophy of Education*, 41(4): 775–93. https://doi.org/10.1111/j.1467-9752.2007.00577.x.

Clarke, E. and Visser, J. (2019) Is a good teaching assistant one who 'knows their place'?, *Emotional and Behavioural Difficulties*, 24(4): 308–22. https://doi.org/10.1080/13632752.2019.1625207.

Code of Practice (1994) *The Education (Special Educational Needs Code of Practice) (Appointed Day) Order 1994*. Queen's Printer of Acts of Parliament. Available at: https://www.legislation.gov.uk/uksi/1994/1414/made (Accessed: 8 July 2022).

Daniels, H., Thompson, I. and Tawell, A. (2019) After Warnock: The effects of perverse incentives in policies in England for students with special educational needs, *Frontiers in Education*, 4: 36. doi: 10.3389/feduc.2019.00036. Available at: https://www.frontiersin.org/articles/10.3389/feduc.2019.00036 (Accessed: 19 July 2022).

Department for Children, Schools and Families (DCSF) (2008) *Personalised Learning – A Practical Guide*. London: DCSF. Available at: https://dera.ioe.ac.uk/8447/7/00844-2008DOM-EN_Redacted.pdf (Accessed: 19 June 2021).

Department for Education and Skills (DfES) (2001) *Special Educational Needs Code of Practice*. London: DfES.

Department for Education (DfE) (1994) *Code of Practice on the Identification and Assessment of Special Educational Needs*. London: DfE. Available at: https://eric.ed.gov/?id=ED385033 (Accessed: 8 July 2022).

Department for Education (DfE) (2011) *Support and Aspiration: A New Approach to Special Educational Needs and Disability – Consultation*. Policy paper. Available at:

https://www.gov.uk/government/publications/support-and-aspiration-a-new-approach-to-special-educational-needs-and-disability-consultation (Accessed: 17 July 2022).

Department for Education (DfE) and Department of Health and Social Care (DoH) (2015) *Special Educational Needs and Disability Code of Practice: 0 to 25 years*. London: DfE and DoH. Available at: https://assets.publishing.service.gov.uk/government/uploads/system/uploads/attachment_data/file/398815/SEND_Code_of_Practice_January_2015.pdf (Accessed: 18 January 2021).

Doran, G.T. (1981) There's a SMART way to write management's goals and objectives, *Management Review*, 70(11): 35–6.

Education Act (1981) *Education Act 1981*. Queen's Printer of Acts of Parliament. Available at: https://www.legislation.gov.uk/ukpga/1981/60/enacted (Accessed: 30 June 2022).

Education Act (1993) *Education Act 1993*. Queen's Printer of Acts of Parliament. Available at: https://www.legislation.gov.uk/ukpga/1993/35/contents/enacted (Accessed: 8 July 2022).

Education Act (2011) *Education Act 2011*. Queen's Printer of Acts of Parliament. Available at: https://www.legislation.gov.uk/ukpga/2011/21/contents/enacted (Accessed: 10 June 2021).

Education and Skills Committee (2007) *Special Educational Needs: Separation of Assessment of Need from Funding of Provision*. London: Audit Commission. Available at: https://publications.parliament.uk/pa/cm200607/cmselect/cmeduski/memo/specialedneeds/ucm2802.pdf (Accessed: 2 March 2023).

Education Endowment Foundation (EEF) (2018) *Closing the Attainment Gap*, EEF website. Available at: https://educationendowmentfoundation.org.uk/support-for-schools/bitesize-support/closing-the-attainment-gap (Accessed: 12 March 2022).

Education Reform Act (1988) *Education Reform Act 1988*. Statute Law Database. Available at: https://www.legislation.gov.uk/ukpga/1988/40/contents (Accessed: 2 June 2022).

Frederickson, N. and Cline, T. (2010) *Special Educational Needs, Inclusion and Diversity*, 2nd edn, reprinted. Maidenhead: McGraw-Hill [u.a.].

Frederickson, N. and Cline, T. (2015) *Special Educational Needs, Inclusion and Diversity*, 3rd edn. Maidenhead: McGraw-Hill Education, Open University Press.

Giroux, H.A. (2005) The terror of neoliberalism: Rethinking the significance of cultural politics, *College Literature*, 32(1): 1–19.

Hallett, F. (2022) Can SENCOs do their job in a bubble? The impact of Covid-19 on the ways in which we conceptualise provision for learners with special educational needs, *Oxford Review of Education*, 48(1): 1–13. https://doi.org/10.1080/03054985.2021.1898357.

Hellawell, B. (2018) 'There is still a long way to go to be solidly marvellous': Professional identities, performativity and responsibilisation arising from the SEND code of practice 2015, *British Journal of Educational Studies*, 66(2): 165–81. https://doi.org/10.1080/00071005.2017.1363374.

HM Government (2022) *SEND Review: Right Support, Right Place, Right Time*, consultation. Available at: https://www.gov.uk/government/consultations/send-review-right-support-right-place-right-time (Accessed: 8 July 2022).

HM Government (2023) *Special Educational Needs and Disabilities (SEND) and Alternative Provision (AP) Improvement Plan: Right Support, Right Place, Right Time*. London: Department for Education and Department of Health and Social Care. Available at: https://assets.publishing.service.gov.uk/government/uploads/system/uploads/attachment_data/file/1139561/SEND_and_alternative_provision_improvement_plan.pdf (Accessed: 2 March 2023).

HM Treasury (2003) *Every Child Matters*. Policy paper. Available at: https://www.gov. uk/government/publications/every-child-matters (Accessed: 17 July 2022).

Hodkinson, A. (2010) Inclusive and special education: Inclusive and special education in the English educational system: Historical perspectives, recent developments and future challenges, *British Journal of Special Education*, 37(2): 61–7. https://doi. org/10.1111/j.1467-8578.2010.00462.x.

Hodkinson, A. (2019) *Key Issues in Special Educational Needs and Inclusion*, 3rd edn. Education Studies – Key Issues. Thousand Oaks, CA: SAGE Publications.

Hodkinson, A. and Burch, L. (2019) The 2014 special educational needs and disability code of practice: Old ideology into new policy contexts?, *Journal of Education Policy*, 34(2): 155–73. https://doi.org/10.1080/02680939.2017.1412501.

Hornby, G. (2015) Inclusive special education: Development of a new theory for the education of children with special educational needs and disabilities, *British Journal of Special Education*, 42(3): 234–56. https://doi.org/10.1111/1467-8578.12101.

House of Commons Education Committee (2019) *Special Educational Needs and Disabilities: First Report of Session 2019*. Available at: https://publications.parliament. uk/pa/cm201919/cmselect/cmeduc/20/20.pdf. (Accessed: 17 February 2023).

Lamb, B. (2009) *Lamb Inquiry: Special Educational Needs and Parental Confidence: Report to the Secretary of State on the Lamb Inquiry Review of SEN and Disability Information*. Nottingham: DCSF Publications. Available at: https://dera.ioe.ac. uk/9042/1/Lamb%20Inquiry%20Review%20of%20SEN%20and%20Disability%20Information.pdf (Accessed: 17 February 2023).

Lauchlan, F. and Greig, S. (2015) Educational inclusion in England: Origins, perspectives and current directions, *Support for Learning*, 30(1): 69–82. https://doi.org/10.1111/1467-9604.12075.

Lehane, T. (2017) 'SEN's completely different now': critical discourse analysis of three 'Codes of Practice for Special Educational Needs' (1994, 2001, 2015), *Educational Review*, 69(1): 51–67. https://doi.org/10.1080/00131911.2016.1237478.

Lindsay, G. (2003) Inclusive education: A critical perspective, *British Journal of Special Education*, 30(1): 3–12. https://doi.org/10.1111/1467-8527.00275.

Lindsay, G., Wedell, K. and Dockrell, J. (2020) Warnock 40 years on: The development of special educational needs since the Warnock Report and implications for the future, *Frontiers in Education*, 4. https://doi.org/10.3389/feduc.2019.00164.

Lucal, B. (2015) Neoliberalism and higher education: How a misguided philosophy undermines teaching sociology, *Teaching Sociology*, 43(1): 3–14.

MacBeath, J.E.C., Galton, M., Steward, S., MacBeath, A. and Page, C. (2006) *The Costs of Inclusion: A Study of Inclusion Policy and Practice in English Primary, Secondary and Special Schools*. Cambridge: Faculty of Education, University of Cambridge.

Mccafferty, P. (2010) Forging a 'neoliberal pedagogy': The 'enterprising education' agenda in schools, *Critical Social Policy*, 30(4): 541–63. https://doi.org/10.1177/0261018310376802.

McKinlay, I. (1996) The Education Act 1993: Working with health services to implement the code of practice, *Child: Care, Health and Development*, 22(1): 19–30. https://doi. org/10.1111/j.1365-2214.1996.tb00419.x.

Ministry for Children (2017) *Youth Justice Family Group Conferences*. Oranga Tamariki – Ministry for Children website. Available at: https://www.orangatamariki.govt.nz/youth-justice/family-group-conferences/ (Accessed: 19 July 2022).

Monbiot, G. (2016) Neoliberalism – the ideology at the root of all our problems, *Guardian*, 15 April. Available at: http://www.theguardian.com/books/2016/apr/15/neoliberalism-ideology-problem-george-monbiot (Accessed: 23 January 2021).

Monsen, J.J., Ewing, D.L. and Kwoka, M. (2014) Teachers' attitudes towards inclusion, perceived adequacy of support and classroom learning environment, *Learning Environments Research*, 17(1): 113–26. https://doi.org/10.1007/s10984-013-9144-8.

Monsen, J. and Frederickson, N. (2004) Teachers' attitudes towards mainstreaming and their pupils' perceptions of their classroom learning environment, *Learning Environments Research*, 7(2): 129–42. https://doi.org/10.1023/B:LERI.0000037196.62475.32.

Naraian, S. (2021) Making inclusion matter: Critical disability studies and teacher education, *Journal of Curriculum Studies*, 53(3): 298–313. https://doi.org/10.1080/00220272.2021.1882579.

National Statistics (2022) *Education, Health and Care Plans: Reporting Year 2022*. Gov.uk website. Available at: https://explore-education-statistics.service.gov.uk/find-statistics/education-health-and-care-plans (Accessed: 19 July 2022).

Norwich, B. (1995) Statutory assessment and statementing: Some challenges and implications for educational psychologists, *Educational Psychology in Practice*, 11(1): 29–35. https://doi.org/10.1080/0266736950110104.

Norwich, B. (2008) Special schools: What future for special schools and inclusion? Conceptual and professional perspectives, *British Journal of Special Education*, 35(3): 136–43. https://doi.org/10.1111/j.1467-8578.2008.00387.x.

Norwich, B. (2019a) From the Warnock Report (1978) to an Education Framework Commission: A novel contemporary approach to educational policy making for pupils with special educational needs/disabilities, *Frontiers in Education*, 4. Available at: https://www.frontiersin.org/articles/10.3389/feduc.2019.00072 (Accessed: 19 July 2022).

Norwich, B. (2019b) The case for a broader policy framework for special needs and inclusive education, in R. Webster (ed.) *Including Children and Young People with Special Educational Needs and Disabilities in Learning and Life: How Far Have We Come Since the Warnock Enquiry – and Where Do We Go Next?* London; New York: Routledge, Taylor & Francis Group (Routledge focus), pp. 71–6.

Norwich, B. and Eaton, A. (2015) The new special educational needs (SEN) legislation in England and implications for services for children and young people with social, emotional and behavioural difficulties, *Emotional and Behavioural Difficulties*, 20(2): 117–32. https://doi.org/10.1080/13632752.2014.989056.

Pinney, A. (2002) In need of review? The Audit Commission's report on statutory assessment and statements of special educational needs, *British Journal of Special Education*, 29(3): 118–22. https://doi.org/10.1111/1467-8527.00253.

Powell, J. and Booker, R. (1987) Needs, provision and the wider context in the 1981 education act: A challenge to current practice, *Educational Psychology in Practice*, 3(3): 34–9.

Ravet, J. (2011) Inclusive/exclusive? Contradictory perspectives on autism and inclusion: the case for an integrative position, *International Journal of Inclusive Education*, 15(6): 667–82. https://doi.org/10.1080/13603110903294347.

Roberts-Holmes, G. and Moss, P. (2021) *Neoliberalism and Early Childhood Education: Markets, Imaginaries and Governance*. Contesting Early Childhood. New York: Routledge.

Robinson, V.M. (2018) *Reduce Change to Increase Improvement*. Thousand Oaks, CA: Corwin Press.

Robinson, D., Moore, N. and Hooley, T. (2018) Ensuring an independent future for young people with special educational needs and disabilities (SEND): A critical examination of the impact of education, health and care plans in England, *British Journal of Guidance & Counselling*, 46(4): 479–91. https://doi.org/10.1080/03069885.2017.1413706.

Runswick-Cole, K. (2007) 'The Tribunal was the most stressful thing: more stressful than my son's diagnosis or behaviour': The experiences of families who go to the Special Educational Needs and Disability Tribunal (SENDisT), *Disability & Society*, 22(3): 315–28. https://doi.org/10.1080/09687590701259674.

Save the Children (2011) *The UK Poverty Rip-Off: The Poverty Premium 2010*. London: Save the Children. Available at: https://resourcecentre.savethechildren.net/document/uk-poverty-rip-poverty-premium-2010/ (Accessed: 1 June 2022).

Souto-Otero, M. (2013) Neo-liberalism and continuing vocational training governance in the UK: An examination of three theoretical accounts, *Educational Review*, 65(1): 20–35. https://doi.org/10.1080/00131911.2011.632815.

Special Educational Needs and Disability Act (2001) *Special Educational Needs and Disability Act 2001*. Statute Law Database. Available at: https://www.legislation.gov.uk/ukpga/2001/10/contents (Accessed: 8 July 2022).

Stevenson, N. (2015) Revolution from above in English schools: Neoliberalism, the democratic commons and education, *Cultural Sociology*, 9(4): 534–49. https://doi.org/10.1177/1749975515573266.

Tomlinson, S. (2012) The irresistible rise of the SEN industry, *Oxford Review of Education*, 38(3): 267–86. https://doi.org/10.1080/03054985.2012.692055.

Tomlinson, S. (2017) *A Sociology of Special and Inclusive Education: Exploring the Manufacture of Inability*. London; New York: Routledge.

UNESCO (1994) *The Salamanca Statement and Framework for Action on Special Needs Education – UNESCO Digital Library*. Available at: https://unesdoc.unesco.org/ark:/48223/pf0000098427 (Accessed: 17 March 2022).

United Nations General Assembly (UNGA) (1989) *The United Nations Convention on the Rights of the Child*. Available at: https://www.unicef.org.uk/what-we-do/un-convention-child-rights/ (Accessed: 27 May 2020).

Warnock, M.H.M. (1978) *Special Educational Needs: Report of the Committee of Enquiry into the Education of Handicapped Children and Young People*. London: HMSO. Available at: https://webarchive.nationalarchives.gov.uk/ukgwa/20101007182820/http:/sen.ttrb.ac.uk/attachments/21739b8e-5245-4709-b433-c14b08365634.pdf (Accessed: 17 February 2023).

Warnock, M. (2005) Special educational needs: A new look, in M. Warnock, B. Norwich and L. Terzi (eds) *Special Educational Needs: A New Look*. London: Bloomsbury Publishing, pp. 11–46.

Warnock, M. and Norwich, B. (2010) *Special Educational Needs: A New Look*, ed. L. Terzi, 2nd edn. London; New York: Continuum International.

Waters, M. and Brighouse, T. (2021) *About Our Schools: Improving on Previous Best*. Williston: Crown House Publishing.

Webster, R. and Blatchford, P. (2019) Making sense of 'teaching', 'support' and 'differentiation': The educational experiences of pupils with Education, Health and Care Plans and Statements in mainstream secondary schools, *European Journal of Special Needs Education*, 34(1): 98–113. https://doi.org/10.1080/08856257.2018.1458474.

Wheldall, K., Merrett, F. and Colmar, S. (1987) 'Pause, Prompt and Praise' for parents and peers: Effective tutoring of low progress readers, *Support for Learning*, 2(1): 5–12.

Whittaker, P. and Hayes, R. (2019) *Essential Tips for the Inclusive Secondary Classroom*. Abingdon; New York: Routledge.

Woods, K. and Farrell, P. (2006) Approaches to psychological assessment by educational psychologists in England and Wales, *School Psychology International*, 27(4): 387–404. https://doi.org/10.1177/0143034306070425.

Chapter 3

Ainscow, M., Farrell, P. and Tweddle, D. (2000) Developing policies for inclusive education: A study of the role of local education authorities, *International Journal of Inclusive Education*, 4(3): 211–29. https://doi.org/10.1080/13603110050059150.

Almond, N. (2021) *Quality First Teaching Checklist: The 10 Most Effective Strategies for Primary Schools*. Third Space Learning website. Available at: https://thirdspacelearning.com/blog/quality-first-teaching/ (Accessed: 5 July 2021).

Arikan, S. (2009) Rousseau and Vygotsky: Zone of Proximal Development, *Serenarikan's Blog*, 17 March. Available at: https://serenarikan.wordpress.com/2009/03/17/rousseau-and-vygotsky-zone-of-proximal-development/ (Accessed: 20 March 2021).

Bernaus, M. and Gardner, R.C. (2008) Teacher motivation strategies, student perceptions, student motivation, and English achievement, *The Modern Language Journal*, 92(3): 387–401. https://doi.org/10.1111/j.1540-4781.2008.00753.x.

Billington, T., Gibson, S., Fogg, P., Lahmar, J. and Cameron, H. (2022) Conditions for mental health in education: Towards relational practice, *British Educational Research Journal*, 48(1): 95–119. https://doi.org/10.1002/berj.3755.

Blatchford, P., Bassett, P., Brown, P., Martin, C., Russell, A. and Webster, R. (2009) *Research Brief: Deployment and Impact of Support Staff project*. Report DCSF-RB148. London: Department for Children, Schools and Families. Available at: https://discovery.ucl.ac.uk/id/eprint/10096858/1/Blatchford_DISS_project_summary.pdf (Accessed: 21 October 2021).

Blatchford, P., Webster, R. and Russell, A. (2012) *Challenging the Role and Deployment of Teaching Assistants in Mainstream Schools: The Impact on Schools: Final Report on the Effective Deployment of Teaching Assistants (EDTA) Project*. London: UCL Institute of Education. Available at: https://discovery.ucl.ac.uk/id/eprint/10096860/1/Blatchford_EDTA_project_final_report.pdf (Accessed: 21 October 2021).

Bogart, K.R., Logan, S.W., Hospodar, C. and Woekel, E. (2019) Disability models and attitudes among college students with and without disabilities, *Stigma and Health*, 4(3): 260–3. https://doi.org/10.1037/sah0000142.

Borg, S. (1998) Data-based teacher development, *ELT Journal*, 52(4): 273–81. https://doi.org/10.1093/elt/52.4.273.

Bosanquet, P. and Radford, J. (2019) Teaching assistant and pupil interactions: The role of repair and topic management in scaffolding learning, *British Journal of Educational Psychology*, 89(1): 177–90. https://doi.org/10.1111/bjep.12231.

Bronfenbrenner, U. (1986) Ecology of the family as a context for human development: Research perspectives, *Developmental Psychology*, 22(6): 723–42. https://doi.org/10.1037/0012-1649.22.6.723.

Bronfenbrenner, U. (1996) *The Ecology of Human Development: Experiments by Nature and Design*. Cambridge, MA: Harvard University Press.

Brown, J.S., Collins, A. and Duguid, P. (1989) Situated cognition and the culture of learning, *Educational Researcher*, 18(1): 32–42. https://doi.org/10.2307/1176008.

Bruner, J.S. (1977) *The Process of Education*. Cambridge, MA: Harvard University Press.

de Boer, A., Pijl, S.J. and Minnaert, A. (2011) Regular primary schoolteachers' attitudes towards inclusive education: A review of the literature, *International Journal of Inclusive Education*, 15(3): 331–53. https://doi.org/10.1080/13603110903030089.

Department for Children, Schools and Families (DCSF) (2008) *Personalised Learning – A Practical Guide*. London: DCSF. Available at: https://dera.ioe.ac.uk/8447/7/00844-2008DOM-EN_Redacted.pdf (Accessed: 19 June 2021).

Department for Education (DfE) and Department of Health and Social Care (DoH) (2015) *Special Educational Needs and Disability Code of Practice: 0 to 25 years*. London: DfE and DoH. Available at: https://assets.publishing.service.gov.uk/government/uploads/system/uploads/attachment_data/file/398815/SEND_Code_of_Practice_January_2015.pdf (Accessed: 18 January 2021).

Dewey, J. (1998) *Experience and Education*, 60th anniversary edn. West Lafayette, IN: Kappa Delta Pi.

Education Endowment Foundation (EEF) (2018) *Making Best Use of Teaching Assistants: Guidance Report*. London: Education Endowment Foundation. Available at: https://educationendowmentfoundation.org.uk/education-evidence/guidance-reports/teaching-assistants (Accessed: 2 August 2022).

Frederickson, N. and Cline, T. (2015) *Special Educational Needs, Inclusion and Diversity*, 3rd edn. Maidenhead: McGraw-Hill Education, Open University Press.

Gray, C. and MacBlain, S. (2015a) An Introduction to Learning Theories, in *Learning Theories in Childhood*, 2nd edn. Los Angeles: SAGE, pp. 15–24. Available at: https://us.sagepub.com/en-us/nam/learning-theories-in-childhood/book244107 (Accessed: 17 February 2023).

Gray, C. and MacBlain, S. (2015b) Bruner and Discovery Learning/Constructivism, in *Learning Theories in Childhood*, 2nd edn. Los Angeles: SAGE, pp. 129–48. Available at: https://us.sagepub.com/en-us/nam/learning-theories-in-childhood/book244107 (Accessed: 17 February 2023).

Greeno, J.G. and Middle School Mathematics through Applications Project Group (1998) The situativity of knowing, learning, and research, *American Psychologist*, 53(1): 5–26. https://doi.org/10.1037/0003-066X.53.1.5.

Gunner, E. (2014) *The Importance of Differentiation for Children with Special Educational Needs*. Special Needs Jungle, 2 May. Available at: https://www.specialneedsjungle.com/importance-differentiation-children-special-educational-needs/ (Accessed: 6 June 2021).

Hattie, J. (2009) *Visible Learning: A Synthesis of over 800 Meta-Analyses Relating to Achievement*. London; New York: Routledge.

Hattie, J. (2012) *Visible Learning for Teachers: Maximizing Impact on Learning*. London; New York: Routledge.

Hattie, J. and Clarke, S. (2019) *Visible Learning: Feedback*. Abingdon; New York: Routledge.

Hattie, J. and Larsen, S.N. (2020) *The Purposes of Education: A Conversation between John Hattie and Steen Nepper Larsen*. Abingdon; New York: Routledge.

Hattie, J. and Zierer, K. (2018) *10 Mindframes for Visible Learning: Teaching for Success*. London; New York: Routledge.

Henry, A. and Thorsen, C. (2018) Teacher–student relationships and L2 motivation, *Modern Language Journal*, 102(1): 218–41. https://doi.org/10.1111/modl.12446.

Hildebrand, D. (2018) John Dewey, in E.N. Zalta (ed.) *The Stanford Encyclopedia of Philosophy*, Winter 2018. Metaphysics Research Lab, Stanford University. Available at: https://plato.stanford.edu/archives/win2018/entries/dewey/ (Accessed: 12 April 2021).

Humphrey, N. and Symes, W. (2013) Inclusive education for pupils with autistic spectrum disorders in secondary mainstream schools: Teacher attitudes, experience and knowledge, *International Journal of Inclusive Education*, 17(1): 32–46. https://doi.org/10.1080/13603116.2011.580462.

Humphreys, S. and Jimenez, B. (2018) The evolution of personalised learning – from different, to differentiated and now to universally designed, *Global Journal of Intellectual & Developmental Disabilities*, 5(4): 65–6.

Kelly, B. and Perkins, D.F. (2012) *Handbook of Implementation Science for Psychology in Education.* Cambridge; New York: Cambridge University Press.

Lauchlan, F. and Boyle, C. (2007) Is the use of labels in special education helpful?, *Support for Learning*, 22(1): 36–42. https://doi.org/10.1111/j.1467-9604.2007.00443.x.

Lave, J. and Wenger, E. (1991) *Situated Learning: Legitimate Peripheral Participation.* Cambridge: Cambridge University Press. https://doi.org/10.1017/CBO9780511815355.

MacBlain, S. (2014) *How Children Learn.* Los Angeles: SAGE Publications.

Maynard, D.-M.B., Jules, M.A. and Marshall, I.A. (2022) Unearthing the common core for reflective teacher training in Antigua and Barbuda, England, and Canada, *Power and Education*, 15(1): 17577438221109916. https://doi.org/10.1177/17577438221109916.

Monsen, J.J., Ewing, D.L. and Kwoka, M. (2014) Teachers' attitudes towards inclusion, perceived adequacy of support and classroom learning environment, *Learning Environments Research*, 17(1): 113–26. https://doi.org/10.1007/s10984-013-9144-8.

Monsen, J. and Frederickson, N. (2004) Teachers' attitudes towards mainstreaming and their pupils' perceptions of their classroom learning environment, *Learning Environments Research*, 7(2): 129–42. https://doi.org/10.1023/B:LERI.0000037196.62475.32.

Navarro, J.L. and Tudge, J.R.H. (2022) Technologizing Bronfenbrenner: Neo-ecological Theory, *Current Psychology* [Preprint]. https://doi.org/10.1007/s12144-022-02738-3.

Navarro-Mateu, D., Franco-Ochoa, J., Valero-Moreno, S. and Prado-Gascó, V. (2019) To be or not to be an inclusive teacher: Are empathy and social dominance relevant factors to positive attitudes towards inclusive education?, *PLOS ONE*, 14(12), p. e0225993. https://doi.org/10.1371/journal.pone.0225993.

Nugent, T.T. (2009) The impact of teacher–student interaction on student motivation and achievement. Ed.D dissertation, College of Education, University of Central Florida, Orlando, FL. Available at: https://www.proquest.com/docview/305102755/abstract/EA76DA76CC3C4418PQ/1 (Accessed: 3 August 2022).

Oliver, M. (1990) *The Politics of Disablement.* Critical Texts in Social Work and the Welfare State. Basingstoke: Palgrave Macmillan.

Radford, J., Bosanquet, P., Webster, R. and Blatchford, P. (2015) Scaffolding learning for independence: Clarifying teacher and teaching assistant roles for children with special educational needs, *Learning and Instruction*, 36: 1–10. https://doi.org/10.1016/j.learninstruc.2014.10.005.

Reusser, K. and Pauli, C. (2015) Co-constructivism in educational theory and practice, in J.D. Wright (ed.) *International Encyclopedia of the Social & Behavioral Sciences*, 2nd edn. Oxford: Elsevier, pp. 913–17. https://doi.org/10.1016/B978-0-08-097086-8.92026-9.

Robinson, V.M. (2018) *Reduce Change to Increase Improvement.* Thousand Oaks, CA: Corwin Press.

Rogoff, B. (1990) *Apprenticeship in Thinking.* New York: Oxford University Press.

Rose, R. and Howley, M. (2007) Special educational needs (SEN) as a concept, in *The Practical Guide to Special Educational Needs in Inclusive Primary Classrooms.* London: SAGE, pp. 1–9. Available at: https://uk.sagepub.com/sites/default/files/upm-assets/13922_book_item_13922.pdf (Accessed: 26 February 2023).

Sahli Lozano, C., Brandenberg, K., Ganz, A.S. and Wüthrich, S. (2022) Accommodations, modifications, and special education interventions: Influence on teacher expectations, *Educational Research and Evaluation*, 27(5–8): 396–419. https://doi.org/10.1080/13803611.2022.2103571.

Scarpa, M.P. and Trickett, E.J. (2022) Translating ecology: Similarities and differences in the ecological images of Bronfenbrenner and Kelly, *Translational Issues in Psychological Science*, 8(2): 185–96. https://doi.org/10.1037/tps0000315.

References

Seifert, K. and Sutton, R. (2009) *Educational Psychology*, 2nd edn. Gainsville, FL: University Press of Florida.

Slavin, R.E. and Madden, N.A. (2006) Reducing the gap: Success for all and the achievement of African American students, *Journal of Negro Education*, 75(3): 389–400.

Soan, S. and Hutton, E. (2021) *Universal Approaches to Support Children's Physical and Cognitive Development in the Early Years*. Abingdon; New York: Routledge.

Swain, J., French, S., Barnes, C. and Thomas, C. (eds) (2014) *Disabling Barriers – Enabling Environments*, 3rd edn. Los Angeles: SAGE.

TES (2021) Spot the difference, *TES Magazine*, 16 April: 18–23.

Thomas, G. and Loxley, A. (2022) *Deconstructing Special Education and Constructing Inclusion*, 3rd edn. Maidenhead: Open University Press.

Tomlinson, S. (2012) The irresistible rise of the SEN industry, *Oxford Review of Education*, 38(3): 267–86. https://doi.org/10.1080/03054985.2012.692055.

Tomlinson, S. (2017) *A Sociology of Special and Inclusive Education: Exploring the Manufacture of Inability*. London; New York: Routledge.

Tomlinson, S. (2021) A sociology of special and inclusive education: Insights from the UK, US, Germany and Finland, in A. Köpfer, J.J.W. Powell, and R. Zahnd (eds) *Handbuch Inklusion international: Globale, nationale und lokale Perspektiven auf Inklusive Bildung [International Handbook of Inclusive Education: Global, National and Local Perspectives]*. Opladen; Berlin; Toronto: Verlag Barbara Budrich, pp. 59–74. https://doi.org/10.3224/84742446.

Tomlinson, S. and Hewitt, S. (2021) Disability, Education, and Work in a Global Knowledge Economy, in R.L. Brown, M. Maroto and D. Pettinicchio (eds) *The Oxford Handbook of the Sociology of Disability*. New York: Oxford University Press. https://doi.org/10.1093/oxfordhb/9780190093167.013.46.

Tudge, J.R.H., Navarro, J.L., Merçon-Vargas, E.A. and Payir, A. (2021) The promise and the practice of early childhood educare in the writings of Urie Bronfenbrenner, *Early Child Development and Care*, 191(7–8): 1079–88. https://doi.org/10.1080/03004430.2020.1844193.

Vygotsky, L.S. (1978) *Mind in Society: The Development of Higher Psychological Processes*. Cambridge, MA: Harvard University Press. https://doi.org/10.2307/j.ctvjf9vz4.

Warnes, E., Done, E.J. and Knowler, H. (2021) Mainstream teachers' concerns about inclusive education for children with special educational needs and disability in England under pre-pandemic conditions, *Journal of Research in Special Educational Needs*, 22(1): 31–43. https://doi.org/10.1111/1471-3802.12525.

Warnock, M.H.M. (1978) *Special Educational Needs: Report of the Committee of Enquiry into the Education of Handicapped Children and Young People*. London: HMSO. Available at: https://webarchive.nationalarchives.gov.uk/ukgwa/20101007182820/http:/sen.ttrb.ac.uk/attachments/21739b8e-5245-4709-b433-c14b08365634.pdf (Accessed: 17 February 2023).

Waters, M. and Brighouse, T. (2021) *About Our Schools: Improving on Previous Best*. Williston: Crown House Publishing.

Webster, J. (2018) *Differentiating for Success in an Inclusive Classroom*, ThoughtCo website. Available at: https://www.thoughtco.com/differentiation-instruction-in-special-education-3111026 (Accessed: 6 June 2021).

Webster, R. and Blatchford, P. (2013) *The Making a Statement Project: Final Report: A Study of the Teaching and Support Experienced by Pupils with a Statement of Special Educational Needs in Mainstream Primary Schools*. London: UCL Institute of Education. Available at: https://discovery.ucl.ac.uk/id/eprint/10096862/1/Webster_MAST_study_final_report.pdf (Accessed: 21 October 2021).

Webster, R. and Blatchford, P. (2017) *The Special Educational Needs in Secondary Education (SENSE) Study*. London: UCL Institute of Education. Available at: https://discovery.ucl.ac.uk/id/eprint/10096865/1/Webster_SENSE_study_final_report.pdf (Accessed: 17 February 2023).

Webster, R. and Blatchford, P. (2019) Making sense of 'teaching', 'support' and 'differentiation': The educational experiences of pupils with Education, Health and Care Plans and Statements in mainstream secondary schools, *European Journal of Special Needs Education*, 34(1): 98–113. https://doi.org/10.1080/08856257.2018.1458474.

Weselby, C. (2014) *What is Differentiated Instruction? Examples of How to Differentiate Instruction in the Classroom*, ResilientEducator website. Available at: https://resilienteducator.com/classroom-resources/examples-of-differentiated-instruction/ (Accessed: 6 June 2021).

Woodland, S., Kahler, M., Blue Star, J. and Fielding, B. (2021) Borrowing Bronfenbrenner: An argument for increasing the intersection of diverse theoretical and applied models, *Child Care in Practice*, online: 1–15. https://doi.org/10.1080/13575279.2021.1924120.

Chapter 4

Allingham, S. (2021) Time to refocus on the children, *Early Years Educator*, 23(4): 10–11. https://doi.org/10.12968/eyed.2021.23.4.10.

Andrew, A., Cattan, S., Dias, M.C. et al. (2020) *Family time use and home learning during the COVID-19 lockdown*, IFS Report R178. London: Institute for Fiscal Studies. https://doi.org/10.1920/re.ifs.2020.0178.

Argyris, C. (1993) *Knowledge for Action: A Guide to Overcoming Barriers to Organizational Change*. Joint publication in the Jossey-Bass Management series and the Jossey-Bass Social and Behavioral Science series. San Francisco, CA: Jossey-Bass.

Argyris, C. (1999) *On Organizational Learning*, 2nd edn. Oxford; Malden, MA: Blackwell Business.

Argyris, C. and Schön, D.A. (1974) *Theory in Practice*. Jossey-Bass Higher and Adult Education Series. San Francisco, CA: Jossey-Bass.

Argyris, C. and Schön, D.A. (1992) *Theory in Practice: Increasing Professional Effectiveness*. The Jossey-Bass Higher and Adult Education series. San Francisco, CA: Jossey-Bass.

Benzeval, M., Borkowska, M., Burton, J. et al. (2020) *Briefing Note COVID-19 Survey: Home Schooling*, Understanding Society Working Paper Series 2020–12. Colchester: Understanding Society study, Institute for Social and Economic Research. Available at: https://www.understandingsociety.ac.uk/research/publications/526136 (Accessed: 1 June 2022).

Blundell, R., Cribb, J., McNally, S., Warwick, R. and Xu, X. (2021) *Inequalities in Education, Skills, and Incomes in the UK: The Implications of the COVID-19 Pandemic*. London: Institute for Fiscal Studies. Available at: https://doi.org/10.1920/BN.IFS.2021.BN0321.

Bolton, P. (2021) *Education Spending in the UK*. Research briefing. House of Commons Library. Available at: https://commonslibrary.parliament.uk/research-briefings/sn01078/ (Accessed: 12 March 2022).

Bradach, J.L. (1998) *Franchise Organizations*. Boston, MA: Harvard Business School Press.

References

Brown, J.L., Jones, S.M., LaRusso, M.D. and Aber, J.L. (2010) Improving classroom quality: Teacher influences and experimental impacts of the 4rs program, *Journal of Educational Psychology*, 102(1): 153–67. https://doi.org/10.1037/a0018160.

Centre for Social Justice (2007) *Breakthrough Britain: Ending the Costs of Social Breakdown*. London: Centre for Social Justice. Available at: https://www.basw.co.uk/resources/breakthrough-britain-ending-costs-social-breakdown-0 (Accessed: 1 June 2022).

Children and Families Act (2014) *Children and Families Act 2014*. Queen's Printer of Acts of Parliament. Available at: https://www.legislation.gov.uk/ukpga/2014/6/contents/enacted (Accessed: 1 June 2022).

Department for Education and Morgan, N. (2016) *Educational Excellence Everywhere*. London: DfE. Available at: https://assets.publishing.service.gov.uk/government/uploads/system/uploads/attachment_data/file/508447/Educational_Excellence_Everywhere.pdf (Accessed: 30 December 2021).

Department for Education (DfE) (2011) *The National Strategies 1997 to 2011*. Policy paper. London: Department for Education. Available at: https://www.gov.uk/government/publications/the-national-strategies-1997-to-2011 (Accessed: 24 December 2021).

Department for Education (DfE) (2016) *DfE Strategy 2015 to 2020: World-Class Education and Care*. London: Department for Education. Available at: https://www.gov.uk/government/publications/dfe-strategy-2015-to-2020-world-class-education-and-care (Accessed: 19 June 2021).

Department for Education (DfE) and Department of Health and Social Care (DoH) (2015) *Special Educational Needs and Disability Code of Practice: 0 to 25 years*. London: DfE and DoH. Available at: https://assets.publishing.service.gov.uk/government/uploads/system/uploads/attachment_data/file/398815/SEND_Code_of_Practice_January_2015.pdf (Accessed: 18 January 2021).

Edmond, C. (2017) *These Rich Countries have High Levels of Child Poverty*. World Economic Forum website. Available at: https://www.weforum.org/agenda/2017/06/these-rich-countries-have-high-levels-of-child-poverty/ (Accessed: 1 June 2022).

Education Endowment Foundation (EEF) (2018) *Closing the Attainment Gap*, EEF website. Available at: https://educationendowmentfoundation.org.uk/support-for-schools/bitesize-support/closing-the-attainment-gap (Accessed: 12 March 2022).

Education Reform Act (1988) *Education Reform Act 1988*. Statute Law Database. Available at: https://www.legislation.gov.uk/ukpga/1988/40/contents (Accessed: 2 June 2022).

Elliot Major, L., Eyles, A. and Machin, S. (2020) *Generation COVID: Emerging Work and Education Inequalities*. CEPCOVID-19-011. London: Centre for Economic Performance, LSE. Available at: https://cep.lse.ac.uk/_new/publications/abstract.asp?index=7462 (Accessed: 1 June 2022).

Farquharson, C., Sibieta, L., Tahir, I. and Waltmann, B. (2021) *2021 Annual Report on Education Spending in England*. London: Institute for Fiscal Studies. https://doi.org/10.1920/re.ifs.2021.0204.

Fullan, M. (2010) *All Systems Go: The Change Imperative for Whole System Reform*. Thousand Oaks, CA: Corwin Press.

Fullan, M. (2013) *Motion Leadership in Action: More Skinny on Becoming Change Savvy*. Thousand Oaks, CA: Corwin Press.

Fullan, M. and Earl, L. (2002) United Kingdom national literacy and numeracy strategies – large scale reform, *Journal of Educational Change*, 3(1): 1–5. https://doi.org/10.1023/A:1016596004904.

Fullan, M., Rolheiser, C., Mascall, B. and Edge, K. (2005) Accomplishing large scale reform: A tri-level proposition, in F. Hernandez and I.F. Goodson (eds) *Social Geographies of Educational Change*. Dordrecht: Kluwer Academic Publishers, pp. 1–13. https://doi.org/10.1007/1-4020-2495-9_1.

Hargreaves, A. and Fink, D. (2000) The three dimensions of reform, *Educational Leadership*, 57(7): 30–3.

Hattie, J. (2009) *Visible Learning: A Synthesis of over 800 Meta-Analyses Relating to Achievement*. London; New York: Routledge.

HM Government (2022) *SEND Review: Right Support, Right Place, Right Time*, consultation. Available at: https://www.gov.uk/government/consultations/send-review-right-support-right-place-right-time (Accessed: 8 July 2022).

Kelly, B. and Perkins, D.F. (2012) *Handbook of Implementation Science for Psychology in Education*. Cambridge; New York: Cambridge University Press.

Kennedy, E.-K. and Monsen, J. (2016) Evidence-based practice in educational and child psychology: Opportunities for practitioner-researchers using problem-based methodology, *Educational & Child Psychology*, 33(3): 11–25.

Leithwood, K., Harris, A. and Hopkins, D. (2008) Seven strong claims about successful school leadership, *School Leadership & Management*, 28(1): 27–42. https://doi.org/10.1080/13632430701800060.

Magadi, M. and Middleton, S. (2007) *Severe Child Poverty in the UK*. London: Save the Children. Available at: https://resourcecentre.savethechildren.net/document/severe-child-poverty-uk/ (Accessed: 1 June 2022).

Monsen, J., Woolfson, L.M. and Boyle, J.T. (eds) (2021) *Why Do Teachers Need to Know about Psychology?: Strengthening Professional Identity and Well-Being*. Personal, social and emotional perspectives for educators. London; New York: Bloomsbury Academic.

National Equity Panel (2010) *An Anatomy of Economic Inequality in the UK: Report of the National Equality Panel*. London: Government Equalities Office and Centre for Analysis of Social Exclusion, LSE. Available at: https://eprints.lse.ac.uk/28344/1/CASEreport60.pdf (Accessed: 18 February 2023).

National Statistics (2022) *Education, Health and Care Plans: Reporting Year 2022*. Gov.uk website. Available at: https://explore-education-statistics.service.gov.uk/find-statistics/education-health-and-care-plans (Accessed: 2 June 2022).

Palardy, G.J. and Rumberger, R.W. (2008) Teacher effectiveness in first grade: The importance of background qualifications, attitudes, and instructional practices for student learning, *Educational Evaluation and Policy Analysis*, 30(2): 111–40. https://doi.org/10.3102/0162373708317680.

Pearlman, S. and Michaels, D. (2019) Hearing the voice of children and young people with a learning disability during the Educational Health Care Plan (EHCP), *Support for Learning*, 34(2): 148–61. https://doi.org/10.1111/1467-9604.12245.

Robinson, V.M. (1993) *Problem-Based Methodology: Research for the Improvement of Practice*. Oxford: Pergamon Press.

Robinson, V.M. (2011) *Student-Centered Leadership*. Jossey-Bass Leadership Library in Education. San Francisco, CA: Jossey-Bass.

Robinson, V.M. (2018) *Reduce Change to Increase Improvement*. Thousand Oaks, CA: Corwin Press.

Robinson, V.M.J., Hohepa, M. and Lloyd, C. (2009) *School Leadership and Student Outcomes: Identifying What Works and Why: Best Evidence Synthesis Iteration*. Wellington: Ministry of Education.

Robinson, V.M. and Lai, M.K. (2006) *Practitioner Research for Educators: A Guide to Improving Classrooms and Schools*. Thousand Oaks, CA: Corwin Press.

Robinson, V.M.J., Lloyd, C.A. and Rowe, K.J. (2008) The impact of leadership on student outcomes: An analysis of the differential effects of leadership types, *Educational Administration Quarterly*, 44(5): 635–74. https://doi.org/10.1177/0013161X08321509.

Robinson, V.M.J. and Timperley, H.S. (2013) School improvement through theory engagement, in M. Lai and S. Kushcer (eds) *A Developmental and Negotiated Approach to School Self-Evaluation.* Advances in Program Evaluation. Bingley: Emerald Group Publishing Limited, pp. 163–77. https://doi.org/10.1108/S1474-7863(2013)0000014010.

Sales, N. and Vincent, K. (2018) Strengths and limitations of the Education, Health and Care plan process from a range of professional and family perspectives, *British Journal of Special Education*, 45(1): 61–80. https://doi.org/10.1111/1467-8578.12202.

Save the Children (2011) *The UK Poverty Rip-Off: The Poverty Premium 2010.* London: Save the Children. Available at: https://resourcecentre.savethechildren.net/document/uk-poverty-rip-poverty-premium-2010/ (Accessed: 1 June 2022).

Taylor, M., Dees, J.G. and Emerson, J. (2004) The question of scale: Finding the appropriate strategy for building on your success, in J.G. Dees, J. Emerson and P. Economy (eds) *Strategic Tools for Social Entrepreneurs: Enhancing the Performance of Your Enterprising Nonprofit.* New York: John Wiley and Sons, pp. 235–66.

UNICEF (2007) *Child Poverty in Perspective: An Overview of Child Well-Being in Rich Countries.* Innocenti Report Card 7. Florence: UNICEF Innocenti Research Centre. Available at: https://www.unicef-irc.org/publications/445-child-poverty-in-perspective-an-overview-of-child-well-being-in-rich-countries.html (Accessed: 1 June 2022).

Waltmann, B., Tahir, I., Sibieta, L., Farquharson, C. and Britton, J. (2020) *2020 Annual Report on Education Spending in England.* London: Institute for Fiscal Studies. https://doi.org/10.1920/re.ifs.2020.0183.

Warnock, M.H.M. (1978) *Special Educational Needs: Report of the Committee of Enquiry into the Education of Handicapped Children and Young People.* London: HMSO. Available at: https://webarchive.nationalarchives.gov.uk/ukgwa/20101007182820/http:/sen.ttrb.ac.uk/attachments/21739b8e-5245-4709-b433-c14b08365634.pdf (Accessed: 17 February 2023).

Wyse, D. and Bradbury, A. (2022) Reading wars or reading reconciliation? A critical examination of robust research evidence, curriculum policy and teachers' practices for teaching phonics and reading, *Review of Education*, 10(1): e3314. https://doi.org/10.1002/rev3.3314.

Chapter 5

Allen, R., Bibby, D., Parameshwaran, M. and Nye, P. (2016) *Linking ITT and WORK-FORCE DATA: (Initial Teacher Training Performance Profiles and School Workforce Census): Research Report.* n.p.: National College for Teaching and Leadership and DfE.

Angel Solutions (2022) *Analysis of Ofsted Inspection Outcomes by School Type.* London: Local Government Association (LGA). Available at: https://www.angelsolutions.co.uk/wp-content/uploads/2022/05/Analysis-of-Ofsted-Inspection-Outcomes-by-School-Type-2022-03-31.pdf (Accessed: 18 February 2023).

Black, P., Harrison. C., Lee, C., Marshall, B. and Wiliam, D. (2003) *Assessment for Learning: Putting It into Practice.* Maidenhead: McGraw-Hill.

Boddison, A. and Soan, S. (2021) The Coproduction illusion: Considering the relative success rates and efficiency rates of securing an Education, Health and Care plan when requested by families or education professionals, *Journal of Research in Special Educational Needs*, 22(2): 91–104. https://doi.org/10.1111/1471-3802.12545.

Bruner, J.S. (1966) *Toward a Theory of Instruction.* Cambridge, MA: Belknap Press of Harvard University Press.

References

Burgess, S. and Thomson, D. (2019) *Making the Grade*. London: Sutton Trust. Available at: http://suttontrust.com/wp-content/uploads/2019/12/MakingtheGrade2019.pdf (Accessed: 18 February 2023).

Children and Families Act (2014) *Children and Families Act 2014*. Queen's Printer of Acts of Parliament. Available at: https://www.legislation.gov.uk/ukpga/2014/6/contents/enacted (Accessed: 1 June 2022).

Daniels, H., Thompson, I. and Tawell, A. (2019) After Warnock: The effects of perverse incentives in policies in England for students with special educational needs, *Frontiers in Education*, 4: 36. doi: 10.3389/feduc.2019.00036. Available at: https://www.frontiersin.org/articles/10.3389/feduc.2019.00036 (Accessed: 19 July 2022).

Department for Education and Skills (DfES) (2001) *Special Educational Needs Code of Practice*. London: DfES.

Department for Education (DfE) (2011, updated 2021) *Teachers' Standards: Guidance for School Leaders, School Staff and Governing Bodies*. London: DfE.

Department for Education (DfE) (2015) *Special Educational Needs and Disability: Supporting Local and National Accountability*. London: DfE.

Department for Education (DfE) (2018) *Factors Affecting Teacher Retention: Qualitative Investigation: Research Report*. London: DfE. Available at: https://assets.publishing.service.gov.uk/government/uploads/system/uploads/attachment_data/file/686947/Factors_affecting_teacher_retention_-_qualitative_investigation.pdf (Accessed: 18 February 2023).

Department for Education (DfE) (2021a) *Induction for Early Career Teachers (England): Statutory Guidance for Appropriate Bodies, Headteachers, School Staff and Governing Bodies*. London: DfE. Available at: https://assets.publishing.service.gov.uk/government/uploads/system/uploads/attachment_data/file/972316/Statutory_Induction_Guidance_2021_final__002____1___1_.pdf (Accessed: 18 February 2023).

Department for Education (DfE) (2021b) *Learning Outcomes for Senior Mental Health Leads in Schools and Colleges*. London: DfE Available at: https://assets.publishing.service.gov.uk/government/uploads/system/uploads/attachment_data/file/995681/Learning_outcomes_for_senior_mental_health_leads_in_schools_and_colleges.pdf (Accessed: 18 February 2023).

Department for Education (DfE) (2022) *Special Educational Needs and Disability: An Analysis and Summary of Data Sources*. London: DfE. Available at: https://assets.publishing.service.gov.uk/government/uploads/system/uploads/attachment_data/file/1082518/Special_educational_needs_publication_June_2022.pdf (Accessed: 18 February 2023).

Department for Education (DfE) and Department of Health and Social Care (DoH) (2015) *Special Educational Needs and Disability Code of Practice: 0 to 25 years*. London: DfE and DoH. Available at: https://assets.publishing.service.gov.uk/government/uploads/system/uploads/attachment_data/file/398815/SEND_Code_of_Practice_January_2015.pdf (Accessed: 18 January 2021).

Dewey, J. (1929) *The Sources of a Science of Education*. The Kappa Delta Pi Lecture Series. New York: Horace Liveright.

Dolton, P., Marcenaro, O., De Vries, R. and She, P.-W. (2018) *Global Teacher Status Index 2018*. London: Varkey Foundation.

Earl, L., Fullan, M., Leithwood, K., Watson, N., Withjantzi, D., Levin, B. & Torrance, N. (2001) *Watching and Learning 2: OISE/UT Evaluation of the Implementation of the National Literacy and Numeracy Strategies*. Nottingham: DfEE Publications.

Fullan, M., Quinn, J., Drummy, M. and Gardner, M. (2020) *Education Reimagined: The Future of Learning*. A collaborative position paper between New Pedagogies for

Deep Learning and Microsoft Education. Available at: http://aka.ms/HybridLearning-Paper (Accessed: 18 February 2023).

Gee, G., Worth, J. and Sims, D. (2015) *Academies and Maintained Schools: What do we Know?*, election factsheet. National Foundation for Educational Research. Available at: https://www.nfer.ac.uk/publications/FFEE02/FFEE02.pdf (Accessed: 2 March 2023).

Gov.uk (n.d.) *Types of School*. Available at: https://www.gov.uk/types-of-school/academies (Accessed: 2 March 2023).

Gov.uk (2014) *Press Release: New Curriculum will make Education System 'Envy of the World'*. Available at: https://www.gov.uk/government/news/new-curriculum-will-make-education-system-envy-of-the-world (Accessed: 2 March 2023).

Gov.uk (2020) Press release: Voucher scheme launches for schools providing free school meals. Available at: https://www.gov.uk/government/news/voucher-scheme-launches-for-schools-providing-free-school-meals (Accessed: 11 August 2022).

Gov.uk (2021) *The Education Hub: What is an Academy and What are the Benefits?* Available at: https://educationhub.blog.gov.uk/2021/10/14/what-is-an-academy-and-what-are-the-benefits/ (Accessed: 2 March 2023).

Gov.uk (2022a) *Guidance: Elective Home Education and Children Missing Education: Submit your Data*. Available at: https://www.gov.uk/guidance/elective-home-education-and-children-missing-education-submit-your-data (Accessed: 6 March 2023).

Gov.uk (2022b) *School Workforce in England: Reporting Year 2021*, Gov.uk website. Available at: https://explore-education-statistics.service.gov.uk/find-statistics/school-workforce-in-england (Accessed: 18 February 2023).

Gov.uk (2023) *Guidance: Senior Mental Health Lead Training*. Available at: https://www.gov.uk/guidance/senior-mental-health-lead-training#overview (Accessed: 6 March 2023).

Gray, C. and MacBlain, S. (2015) Bruner and Discovery Learning/Constructivism, in *Learning Theories in Childhood*, 2nd edn. Los Angeles: SAGE, pp. 129–48. Available at: https://us.sagepub.com/en-us/nam/learning-theories-in-childhood/book244107 (Accessed: 17 February 2023).

Halpern, D. and Sanders, M. (2016) Nudging by government: Progress, impact, and lessons learned, *Behavioral Science & Policy*, 2(2): 53–6.

HM Government (2022) *Opportunity for All: Strong Schools with Great Teachers for Your Child*. London: HMSO.

HM Government (2023) *Special Educational Needs and Disabilities (SEND) and Alternative Provision (AP) Improvement Plan: Right Support, Right Place, Right Time*. London: Department for Education and Department of Health and Social Care. Available at: https://assets.publishing.service.gov.uk/government/uploads/system/uploads/attachment_data/file/1139561/SEND_and_alternative_provision_improvement_plan.pdf (Accessed: 2 March 2023).

Hodkinson, A. and Burch, L. (2019) The 2014 special educational needs and disability code of practice: Old ideology into new policy contexts?, *Journal of Education Policy*, 34(2): 155–73. https://doi.org/10.1080/02680939.2017.1412501.

Long, R. and Danechi, S. (2022) *Home Education in England*, Commons Library Research Briefing. House of Commons Library. Available at: https://researchbriefings.files.parliament.uk/documents/SN05108/SN05108.pdf (Accessed: 26 February 2023).

Mackley, A. (2021) Coronavirus: Universal Credit During the Crisis, Commons Library briefing paper 8999. House of Commons Library. Available at: https://researchbriefings.files.parliament.uk/documents/CBP-8999/CBP-8999.pdf (Accessed: 11 August 2022).

Millar, F. (2022) People are yearning for a new educational age, says Sir Tim Brighouse in his new book with Mick Waters, *The Guardian*, 1 January. Available at: https://www.theguardian.com/politics/2022/jan/01/sir-tim-brighouse-many-hold-gove-responsible-expert-educator-sets-out-whats-gone-wrong-with-britains-schools?CMP=fb_gu&utm_medium=Social&utm_source=Facebook&fbclid=IwAR0FbE4U8Q1PNbP1LGc8t-mEfXK4nHhV-qtVfRWbHl8SkR5wDHsBgfq5qm2Y#Echobox=1641030562 (Accessed: 18 February 2023).

Monsen, J., Woolfson, L.M. and Boyle, J.T. (eds) (2021) *Why Do Teachers Need to Know about Psychology?: Strengthening Professional Identity and Well-Being*. Personal, social and emotional perspectives for educators. London; New York: Bloomsbury Academic.

NASUWT (n.d.) *Policy Paper on Teacher Professionalism (England)*, NASUWT website. Available at: https://www.nasuwt.org.uk/advice/in-the-classroom/professionalism/teacher-training-professionalism-england-/policy-paper-on-teacher-professionalism-england.html (Accessed: 26 February 2023).

National Statistics (2022) *Education, Health and Care Plans: Reporting Year 2022*. Gov.uk website. Available at: https://explore-education-statistics.service.gov.uk/find-statistics/education-health-and-care-plans (Accessed: 19 July 2022).

Oates, T. (2011) Could do better: Using international comparisons to refine the National Curriculum in England, *Curriculum Journal*, 22:2: 121–50. DOI:10.1080/09585176.2011.578908.

Rice O'Toole, A.M. and Soan, S. (2021) Is the employment of pastoral support staff (PSS) working with students with social, emotional and mental health (SEMH) needs changing the role and responsibilities of teachers in London and South-East England?, *Pastoral Care in Education*, 40(2): 197–216. DOI: 10.1080/02643944.2021.1918227.

Schâringer, S. (2022) An exploration of perceptions of inclusion within one multi-academy trust in relation to the process of end of key stage two statutory testing within the current English educational climate. Unpublished thesis, Canterbury Christ Church University.

Schleicher, A. (2018) *World Class: How to Build a 21st-Century School System: Strong Performers and Successful Reformers in Education*. Paris: OECD Publishing. https://doi.org/10.1787/9789264300002-en.

Simon, J. (2014). Tough Young Teachers is a show that sounds like another TV gimmick – in fact it's anything but, *The Mirror*, 9 January. Available at: https://www.mirror.co.uk/tv/tv-previews/what-time-tough-young-teachers-3001901 (Accessed: 7 August 2022).

Sky Sports (2021) Marcus Rashford: Man Utd forward awarded MBE for campaign to end child food poverty, *Sky Sports* website, 9 November. Available at: https://www.skysports.com/football/news/11667/12464652/marcus-rashford-man-utd-forward-awarded-mbe-for-campaign-to-end-child-food-poverty (Accessed: 11 August 2022).

Smith, G., Sylva, K., Smith, T., Pm Sammons, P. and Omonigho, A. (2018) *Stop Start: Survival, Decline or Closure? Children's Centres in England, 2018*. London: Sutton Trust. Available at: https://www.suttontrust.com/wp-content/uploads/2018/04/Stop-Start-FINAL.pdf (Accessed: 18 February 2023).

Stevenson, N. (2015) Revolution from above in English schools: Neoliberalism, the democratic commons and education, *Cultural Sociology*, 9(4): 534–49. https://doi.org/10.1177/1749975515573266.

Stigler, J. and Stevenson, H. (1999). How Asian teachers polish each lesson to perfection, in *Child Growth and Development*, 6th edn. Maidenhead: McGraw-Hill, pp. 66–77.

Takala, M., Pirttimaa, R. and Tormane, M. (2009) Inclusive special education: The role of special education teachers in Finland, *British Journal of Special Education*, 36(3): 162–72.

TeacherToolkit (2018) What do the British public think about teachers?, *@TeacherToolkit*, 18 November. Available at: https://www.teachertoolkit.co.uk/2018/11/18/teacher-index-2018/ (Accessed: 26 February 2023).

Terzi, L. (2010) *Justice and Equality in Education*. London: Continuum.

UNESCO (1994) *The Salamanca Statement and Framework for Action on Special Needs Education – UNESCO Digital Library*. Available at: https://unesdoc.unesco.org/ark:/48223/pf0000098427 (Accessed: 17 March 2022).

UNESCO (2019) Futures of Education: Learning to Become. ED/2019/ERF/1. Available at: https://unesdoc.unesco.org/ark:/48223/pf0000370801 (Accessed: 6 March 2023).

UNESCO (2021) *Reimaging our Futures Together*. Paris: UNESCO. Available at: https://en.unesco.org/futuresofeducation/ (Accessed: 18 February 2023).

Warnock, M.H.M. (1978) *Special Educational Needs: Report of the Committee of Enquiry into the Education of Handicapped Children and Young People*. London: HMSO. Available at: https://webarchive.nationalarchives.gov.uk/ukgwa/20101007182820/ http:/sen.ttrb.ac.uk/attachments/21739b8e-5245-4709-b433-c14b08365634.pdf (Accessed: 17 February 2023).

West, A. (2022) Education and ignorance in the UK 80 years after Beveridge: The role of government and equality of opportunity, *Social Policy & Administration*, 56(2): 299–314. https://doi.org/10.1111/spol.12781.

Worth, J. and Faulkner-Ellis, H. (2022) *Teacher Labour Market in England: Annual Report 2022*. Slough: NFER.

Chapter 6

Alexander, R. (ed.) (2010) *Children, their World, their Education: Final Report and Recommendations of the Cambridge Primary Review*. Abingdon and New York: Routledge.

Boddison, A. and Soan, S. (2021) The Coproduction illusion: Considering the relative success rates and efficiency rates of securing an Education, Health and Care plan when requested by families or education professionals, *Journal of Research in Special Educational Needs*, 22(2): 91–104. https://doi.org/10.1111/1471-3802.12545.

Buyruk, H. (2018) Changes in teachers' work and professionalism in England: Impressions from the 'shop floor', *Malaysian Online Journal of Educational Sciences*, 6(2).

Day, C. and Sachs, J. (2004) Professionalism, performativity and empowerment: Discourses in the politics, policies and purposes of continuing professional development, in *International Handbook on the Continuing Professional Development of Teachers*. Maidenhead: Open University Press, pp. 3–33.

Department for Education and Employment (DfEE) (1998) *Teachers: Meeting the Challenge of Change*. London: HMSO.

Department for Education (DfE) (2011, updated 2021) *Teachers' Standards: Guidance for School Leaders, School Staff and Governing Bodies*. London: DfE.

Department for Education (DfE) (2018) *Factors Affecting Teacher Retention: Qualitative Investigation: Research Report*. London: DfE. Available at: https://assets.publishing.service.gov.uk/government/uploads/system/uploads/attachment_data/file/686947/Factors_affecting_teacher_retention_-_qualitative_investigation.pdf (Accessed: 18 February 2023).

Department for Education (DfE) (2022) *Survey of School Business Professionals, 2021*. Research report, Government Social Research. London: Department for Education.

Department for Education (DfE) and Education Endowment Foundation (EEF) (2019a) *Early Career Framework*. London: DfE.

Department for Education (DfE) and Education Endowment Foundation (EEF) (2019b) *ITT Core Content Framework, Teachers Standards*. London: DfE.

Dewey, J. (1984) *John Dewey: The Middle Works 1899–1924, Vol.9: Democracy and Education 1916*, ed. J.A. Boydston. Carbondale, IL: Southern Illinois University Press.

References

Elton-Chalcraft, S. and Cooper, H. (2022) Conclusion: Moving forward, in H. Cooper and S. Elton-Chalcraft, *Professional Studies in Primary Education*, 4th edn. London: Sage, pp. 502–16.

Englund, T. (1993) Are professional teachers a good thing? Paper presented at the Professional Actions and Cultures of Teaching Conference, London, Ontario.

Gibb, N. (2014) Teaching unions aren't the problem – universities are, *The Guardian*, 23 April. Available at: https://www.theguardian.com/commentisfree/2014/apr/23/teaching-unions-arent-problem-universities-schools-minister (Accessed: 18 February 2023).

Gov.uk (2022) *School Workforce in England: Reporting Year 2021*, Gov.uk website. Available at: https://explore-education-statistics.service.gov.uk/find-statistics/school-workforce-in-england (Accessed: 18 February 2023).

Gov.uk (2023) *Guidance: Senior Mental Health Lead Training*. Available at: https://www.gov.uk/guidance/senior-mental-health-lead-training#overview (Accessed: 6 March 2023).

Gove, M. (2010) Michael Gove, speech to the National College annual conference, 16 June, Birmingham. Available at: https://www.gov.uk/government/speeches/michael-gove-to-the-national-college-annual-conference-birmingham (Accessed: 18 February 2023).

Green, T. (1985) The formation of conscience in an age of technology, *American Journal of Education*, 94(1): 1–32.

Hansen, D.T. and Laverty, M. (2013) Teaching and pedagogy, in R. Bailey, R. Barrow, D. Carr and C. McCarthy (eds) *The SAGE Handbook of Philosophy of Education*. London: Sage, pp. 223–35.

HM Government (2022a) *Opportunity for All: Strong Schools with Great Teachers for your Child*. London: HMSO.

HM Government (2022b) *SEND Review: Right Support, Right Place, Right Time*, consultation. Available at: https://www.gov.uk/government/consultations/send-review-right-support-right-place-right-time (Accessed: 8 July 2022).

HM Government (2023) *Special Educational Needs and Disabilities (SEND) and Alternative Provision (AP) Improvement Plan: Right Support, Right Place, Right Time*. London: Department for Education and Department of Health and Social Care. Available at: https://assets.publishing.service.gov.uk/government/uploads/system/uploads/attachment_data/file/1139561/SEND_and_alternative_provision_improvement_plan.pdf (Accessed: 2 March 2023).

HMSO (1959) *Primary Education*. London: HMSO.

Jerrim, J. and Sims, S. (June 2018) *The Teaching and Learning International Survey (TALIS) 2018*. Research Brief. London: DfE.

Johnston, J.S. (2013) John Dewey and educational pragmatism, in R. Bailey, R. Barrow, D. Carr and C. McCarthy (eds) *The SAGE Handbook of Philosophy of Education*. London: Sage, pp. 99–110.

Labaree, D. (2004) *The Trouble with Ed Schools*. New Haven, CT: Yale University Press.

Lawn, M. and Grace, G. (2011) *Teachers: The Culture and Politics of Work*, 2nd edn. London: Routledge.

Long, R. and Danechi, S. (2022) *Teacher Recruitment and Retention in England*, House of Commons Library, Number 07222, 8 December. Available at: https://researchbriefings.files.parliament.uk/documents/CBP-7222/CBP-7222.pdf (Accessed: 18 February 2023).

McLean Davies, L., Dickson, B., Rickards, F., Dinham, S., Conroy, J. and Davis, R. (2015) Teaching as a clinical profession: Translational practices in initial teacher education – an international perspective, *Journal of Education for Teaching*, 41(5), 514–28. https://doi.org/10.1080/02607476.2015.1105537.

nasen (2023) *nasen Responds to the Publication of the SEND and Alternative Provision Improvement Plan*, nasen website, 2 March. Available at: https://www.wholeschoolsend.

org.uk/news/nasen-responds-publication-send-and-alternative-provision-improvement-plan (Accessed: 6 March 2023).

Noddings, N. (2001) The caring teacher, in V. Richardson (ed.) *Handbook of Research on Teaching*, 4th edn. Washington, DC: American Educational Research Association, pp. 99–105.

Pillen, M.T., Den Brock, P.J. and Beijaard, D. (2013) Profiles and change in beginning teachers' professional identity tensions, *Teaching and Teacher Education*, 34(5): 86–97. https://doi.org/10.1016/j.tate.2013.04.003.

Plato (1970) *Laws 765* (trans. T.J. Saunders). Harmondsworth: Penguin Classics.

Reagan, T. (2013) The professional status of teaching, in R. Bailey, R. Barrow, D. Carr and C. McCarthy (eds) *The SAGE Handbook of Philosophy of Education*. London: Sage, pp. 209–21.

Rice O'Toole, A.-M. (2020) The role of qualified teachers in the modern secondary school: Whose responsibility is pastoral care in secondary schools? Unpublished thesis, Canterbury Christ Church University.

Rice O'Toole, A.M. and Soan, S. (2021) Is the employment of pastoral support staff (PSS) working with students with social, emotional and mental health (SEMH) needs changing the role and responsibilities of teachers in London and South-East England?, *Pastoral Care in Education*, 40(2): 197–216. DOI: 10.1080/02643944.2021.1918227.

Sahlberg, P. (2015) Q: What makes Finnish teachers so special? A: It's not brains, *The Guardian*, 31 March. Available at: https://www.theguardian.com/education/2015/mar/31/finnish-teachers-special-train-teach (Accessed: 2 March 2023).

Scott, S. (2016) *Highest Teacher Leaving Rate in a Decade – and 6 Other Things we Learned about the School Workforce*. Schools Week website. Available at: https://schoolsweek.co.uk/highest-teacher-leaving-rate-in-a-decade-and-6-other-things-we-learned-about-the-school-workforce/ (Accessed: 18 February 2023).

Shaw, S. and Shirley, I. (2022) History of education, in H. Cooper and S. Elton-Chalcraft (eds) *Professional Studies in Primary Education*, 4th edn. London: Sage, pp. 3–30.

Soan, S. (2013) An exploration through a small number of case studies of the education provision for looked after children who have experienced early life abuse or neglect. Unpublished PhD thesis, University of Kent/Canterbury Christ Church University.

Soan, S. (ed.) (2021) *Why Do Teachers Need to Know about Diverse Learning Needs?: Strengthening Professional Identity and Well-Being*. London: Bloomsbury.

Warnock, M.H.M. (1978) *Special Educational Needs: Report of the Committee of Enquiry into the Education of Handicapped Children and Young People*. London: HMSO. Available at: https://webarchive.nationalarchives.gov.uk/ukgwa/20101007182820/http:/sen.ttrb.ac.uk/attachments/21739b8e-5245-4709-b433-c14b08365634.pdf (Accessed: 17 February 2023).

Wood, R., Jackson, C. with Bayliss, S. and Usher, N. (2021) The role of the teacher, in D. Maisey and V. Campbell-Barr (eds) *Why Do Teachers Need to Know About Child Development?: Strengthening Professionals Identity and Well-Being*. Personal, Social and Emotional Perspectives for Educators. London: Bloomsbury.

Worth, J. and Faulkner-Ellis, H. (2022) *Teacher Labour Market in England: Annual Report 2022*. Slough: NFER.

Chapter 7

Ainscow, M. (2020) Promoting inclusion and equity in education: Lessons from international experiences, *Nordic Journal of Studies in Educational Policy*, 6(1): 7–16. https://doi.org/10.1080/20020317.2020.1729587.

Anning, A., Cottrell, D., Frost, N., Green, J. and Robinson, M. (2010) *Developing Multi-Professional Teamwork for Integrated Children's Services*. Maidenhead: Open University Press.

Armstrong, P. and Ainscow, M. (2018) School-to-school support within a competitive education system: Views from the inside, *School Effectiveness, School Improvement*, 29(4): 614–33.

Bubb, S., Crossley-Holland, J., Cordiner, J., Cousin, S. and Earley, P. (2019) *Understanding the Middle Tier: Comparative Costs of Academy and LA-Maintained School Systems*. London: Sara Bubb Associates.

Centre for Studies on Inclusive Education (CSIE) (2020) The UNESCO Salamanca Statement, CSIE website. Available at: http://www.csie.org.uk/inclusion/unesco-salamanca.shtml (Accessed: 2 March 2023).

Children's Commissioner (2022) *Vision for Childcare*. London: Children's Commissioner. Available at: childrenscommissioner.gov.uk/wp-content/uploads/2022/10/cc-vision-for-childcare-oct-22.pdf (Accessed: 18 February 2023).

Couper, C. and Soan, S. (2021) Working together, in S. Soan (ed.) *Why Do Teachers Need to Know about Diverse Learning Needs?* London: Bloomsbury, pp. 99–118.

Crehan, L. (2016) *Cleverlands: The Secrets Behind the Success of the World's Education Superpowers*. London: Unbound.

Department for Education and Skills (DfES) (2001) *Special Educational Needs Code of Practice*. London: DfES.

Department for Education (DfE) (1994) *Code of Practice on the Identification and Assessment of Special Educational Needs*. London: DfE. Available at: https://eric.ed.gov/?id=ED385033 (Accessed: 8 July 2022).

Department for Education (DfE) and Department of Health and Social Care (DoH) (2015) *Special Educational Needs and Disability Code of Practice: 0 to 25 years*. London: DfE and DoH. Available at: https://assets.publishing.service.gov.uk/government/uploads/system/uploads/attachment_data/file/398815/SEND_Code_of_Practice_January_2015.pdf (Accessed: 18 January 2021).

Department for Education (DfE) and Education Endowment Foundation (EEF) (2019) *Early Career Framework*. London: DfE.

Dyson, A. (2001) Special needs in the twenty-first century: Where we've been and where we're going, *British Journal of Special Education*, 28(1): 24–9.

Edmond, N. and Price, M. (eds) (2012) *Integrated Working with Children and Young People*. London: Sage.

Edwards, M. (2008) 'Philanthrocapitalism' and its limits, *International Journal of Not-for-Profit Law*, 10(2): 22–9.

House of Lords (2022) *Children and Families Act 2014: A Failure of Implementation: Report of Session 2022–2023*. London: House of Lords Children and Families Act 2014 Committee. Available at: https://publications.parliament.uk/pa/ld5803/ldselect/ldchifam/100/100.pdf (Accessed: 18 February 2023).

Johnston, J.S. (2013) John Dewey and educational pragmatism, in R. Bailey, R. Barrow, D. Carr and C. McCarthy (eds) *The SAGE Handbook of Philosophy of Education*. London: Sage, pp. 99–110.

Monsen, J., Woolfson, L.M. and Boyle, J.T. (eds) (2021) *Why Do Teachers Need to Know about Psychology?: Strengthening Professional Identity and Well-Being*. Personal, social and emotional perspectives for educators. London; New York: Bloomsbury Academic.

Nancarrow, S., Booth, A., Ariss, S., Smith, T., Enderby, P. and Roots, A. (2013) Ten principles of good interdisciplinary teamwork, *Human Resources for Health*, 11(19): 1–11.

Ofsted (2022) The Annual Report of His Majesty's Chief Inspector of Education, Children's Services and Skills 2021/22. London: Ofsted. Available at: https://www.gov.uk/government/publications/ofsted-annual-report-202122-education-childrens-services-and-skills/the-annual-report-of-his-majestys-chief-inspector-of-education-childrens-services-and-skills-202122#looking-forward (Accessed: 18 February 2023).

Olmedo, A. (2014) *From England with love … ARK, heterarchies and global 'philanthropic governance'*, Journal of Education Policy, 29(5): 575–97. https://doi.org/10.1080/02680939.2013.859302

Reid, H. and Soan, S. (2015) *Supervision: A Business and Community Service for Colleagues in Schools*. Evaluation Report. Canterbury: Canterbury Christ Church University, Faculty of Education.

Reid, H. and Soan, S. (2018) Providing support to senior managers in schools via 'clinical' supervision: A restorative and purposeful professional and personal space, *Professional Development in Education*, 45(1): 59–72. DOI: 10.1080/19415257.2018.1427132.

Robinson, V.M. (2018) *Reduce Change to Increase Improvement*. Thousand Oaks, CA: Corwin Press.

UNESCO (2021) *Reimagining our Futures Together: A New Social Contract for Education*. Paris: UNESCO.

Walker, P. (2022) 'Carousel of education secretaries' as Kit Malthouse becomes fifth in a year, *The Guardian*, 7 September. Available at: https://www.theguardian.com/politics/2022/sep/07/kit-malthouse-becomes-tories-fifth-education-secretary-in-a-year (Accessed: 2 March 2023).

Warnock, M.H.M. (1978) *Special Educational Needs: Report of the Committee of Enquiry into the Education of Handicapped Children and Young People*. London: HMSO. Available at: https://webarchive.nationalarchives.gov.uk/ukgwa/20101007182820/http:/sen.ttrb.ac.uk/attachments/21739b8e-5245-4709-b433-c14b08365634.pdf (Accessed: 17 February 2023).

Warnock, M. and Norwich, B. (2010) *Special Educational Needs: A New Look*, ed. L. Terzi, 2nd edn. London; New York: Continuum International.

Index

academies 17, 73, 83–84, 104, 115
   MATs 84, 106
accountability 6, 13, 17, 25, 55, 58, 83, 94
   league tables 17, 29, 74, 76, 115
Alternative Provision (AP) 25
Annual Reviews *14–15*

Bruner, Jerome 33, 36, 39–42, 43, 44, 85, 93
   active discovery *40*
   instructional scaffolding *40*, 41

Centre for Social Justice (2007) 53
child development 45, 76, 92, 109
Children and Families Act 2014 *11*, *14*, 20, 58, 59–60, 80, 108
Children, Young People and Families Service 114
collaboration 22, 78
   collaborative working 61, 70, 91, 114–115, 116, 118
constructivism *40*
continuing/continuous professional development (CPD) 8, 95
continuing teacher development (CTD) 113
continuum of provision model 8, 27, 35
co-partners 59
co-production 22, 59, 78, 120
covid-19 50, 53, 79, 86
craftmanship of teaching 118
curriculum 49, 50, 103, 115
   collective 116, 120

Deployment and Impact of Support Staff project 48
deprofessionalized teaching 52
Dewey, John 33, 35–37, *40*, 42, 43, 44, 85, 92, 93, 107
   experiential learning 35, 37
   active reflection 36
differentiation 45, 49, 50, 51
disability
   policy *14*

Early Career Teachers Induction programme/framework 84, 97, 113
eco-systemic 33, 34
Education Act 1944 75
Education Act 1972 112
Education Act 1981 6, 7, 8, 9, *14*, 23
   inclusive 9
   innovative 9
Education Act 1993 9, 12, *15*
Education and Skills Committee (2007) *16*
Education, Health and Care (EHC) assessment and plans *19*, 20, 22, 23, 24, 59, 60, 77, 79, *98*, *99*, 100
education policy 28, 31, 62, 75
education reform 55, 58–59, 61
Education Reform Act 1988 27, 29, 61, 115
educational psychologists (EPs) 8, 10, 13, *14*, *15*, 18, 20, 24, 32, 46, 47, 52, 79, 118
equity 83, 119, 120
Every Child Matters (2003) 18
experiential learning 35
   experiential pupil-centred teaching 37

family group conference 12
Finland, education 107
free schools 17, 83
funding 9

Green Paper (HM Government, March 2023) 12, 24–25

Hattie, John 33, 34, 36, 42–44, 45, 46, 60
   differentiated teaching 43–44
   explicit teaching 43
   oral feedback 43
health and social care 20, 22
high needs funding 79
higher order thinking 55
House of Commons Education Committee (2019) 23, 24

identification dilemma 30
inclusion 9, 17, 29, 31, 73, 75, 76, 111, 121

definition 119
for all 2, 13
functional 8
locational 8
social 8
Inclusion Index 31
inclusive education 26, 27, 28, 29, 42, 47, 50, 52, 73, 74, 111
differentiation 45, 46, 47, 49, 51
individual education plan (IEP) 10, 13, 23
individualized approach 35, 42, 52
inequality
educational 53, 74
inequity 75, 77, 88, 109, 110, 116
initial teacher education (ITE) 92, 96, 97, 100, *101*, *102*, 106, 113
Institute of Teaching 95
integration 8, 26, 27
integrated working 2, 18

labels (SEND) 7, 9, 23, 30, 31, 32, 77, 81, 82
league tables 17, 29, 74
learning 66–69
learning support assistants (LSA) 13
local authority (LA) 12, 17, 18, 22, 23–24, 25, 29, 32, 79, 80, 84
local education authority (LEA) 8, 9, 10, 12, *15–16*, *19*, 79
local offer *19*

Making a Statement (MAST) study 48
Making Best Use of Teaching Assistants (2018) 49
marketization of education *16*, 17, 18, 28–29, 59–60, 73, 78, 80
medical 10, 112
medical models 9, 30, 32, 33–34
medicalized categories 9
multidisciplinary
approach/working 8, 18, 23

National Change programme 26
national collective curriculum 4, 116–117, 120
National Curriculum *16*, 27–28, 73–74, 75, 115
National Literacy Strategy 53, 54, 56, 74
analytic phonics (AP) 53, 54
systematic synthetic phonics (SSP) 53
National Numeracy Strategy 53, 56, 74
neoliberalism 28, 32, 52, 73, 74

occupational therapists 10, *15*, 20, 24, 46, 47
Office for Standards in Education, Children's Services and Skills (Ofsted) 115

parents/carers 12, *15*, 22, 25, 58, 76, 78, 80
communication with 18, 79
decision making *19*
parental choice 29, 78, 85–86
rights 10, *14–15*, 17, 80
views 10, 13, 23
pastoral support workers 105–106
pedagogy, quality of 29, 31, 35, 52, 75, 100
performance league tables 17
personal budgets *19*
personalization *16*, 24, 28, 42, 51, 52
Personalised learning – A Practical Guide (DCSF 2008) 44
professionalism 56, 95
professionalization, of teachers 31, 95, 114
progress 21, 48, 51, 74, 80
measures 120
provision (SEN) 17–18, *19*, 24, 27, 29, 30, 48
plan 21, 48
pupils 76, 79–80
rights *14*
participation *15*, *19*
well-being 74

qualified teacher status (QTS) 82, 104
Quality First teaching 32, 34, 44, 45, 61
Waves of intervention model 44–45, 46

reflective thinking 36
reflect cycle 42
reimagining 72, 87
Reimagining our Futures Together (2021) 72
rights
parents/carers 10, 17, 25
children 10, 17
Robinson, Viviane 52, 57–58, 60, 61–71
educational change 57–58, 62, 67–70
educational improvement 57, 58, 60, 62–67, 70, 71
theories-of-action 63–66, 68, 71
theories-in-use 63–66

Salamanca Statement 11, *14*, 27, 76
School Action (SA) 13, 78
School Action Plus (SA+) 13
schools 10, 13, 17, 20, 22, 23–24, 25, 27, 30, 50
  policies 119
  reform 55, 56, 58, 59, 61, 72
school advisors 8, 18
school business manager 106
School Direct 97
school leaders 54, 56, 60, 61, 62, 64–66, 68, 69, 70, 76, 83, 104, 107
scientist-reflective practitioners 42, 52, 93, 96
segregated 8
SEN provision 48
SEN Support *19*, 20, 22, 77, 79
SMART targets 10, 13, 21
special educational needs (SEN) 7
  categories/terminology *11*, *14*
  change 13
  policy 18, 30, 59, 73, 75, 78, 80
  provision 17–18, *19*, 29
  support 18, *19*
  system 18, 73, 75, 76, 81, 82, 83, 103, 108, 112
special educational needs and disability (SEND) 92
Special Educational Needs and Disabilities (SEND) and Alternative Provision (AP) Improvement Plan (HM Government, March 2023) 12, 58, 91, 92
Special *Educational* Needs and Disability Act 2001 12
Special educational needs and disability code of practice: 0–25 (DfE & DoH, 2015) *11*, 12, *19*, 20–21, 22, 23, 34–35, 45, 59, 78, 80, 112
Special Educational Needs and Disability Tribunal (SENDIST) 12
Special Educational Needs Code of Practice (DfE, 1994) 9, 11, 12, *14–15*
  graduated five-stage model 10, *14*
  Individual Education Plan (IEP) 10, 13
  SEN register 10, 13
Special Educational Needs Code of Practice (DfES, 2001) *11*, 12–13, *14–15*
special educational needs coordinator (SENCo) 13, 20–21, 23, 79, 83, 92, 107

Special Educational Needs Review Green Paper (2022) 91
Special Educational Needs Secondary Education project (SENSE) 48
special schools 8, *14–15*, 23
specialist provision/education 8, *14–15*, 51
specialist teachers (STs) 8, 10, 18, 20
speech and language therapists 10, *15*, 20, 24, 46, 47
state education system (English) 1, 24, 26, 28, 29, 44, 53, 56, 61, 72, 73, 76, 84, 85, 87, 114, 118, 120
statement of special educational needs 8, 10, 13, *14–16*, 60
  statutory assessment 9, 10, 13, *14–15*, 20
statutory assessment tests (SATs) 76, 78
supervision 113
Support and Aspiration: A New Approach to Special Educational Needs and Disabilities (DfE, 2011) 18, 24–25

targeted support 32
teachers *19*, 20, 23, 27, 29, 30, 36, 43, 47, 48, 50, 51, 52, 53, 54, 56, 58, 60–69, 73, 74, 77, 79, 82, 85, 90, 91–92, 96, 107, 113
  craft 91, 96, 106, 120
  identity 74, 90
  para-professional 75, 82
  professional 93, 120
  recruitment 55, 82
  retention 55, 77, 82, 95, 96, 104–105, 113
Teachers: Meeting the Challenge of Change (DfEE, 1998) 94
teacher training 9, 31, 32, 82, 83, 92, 97, 100, 107
teaching assistants (TA) 13, 17–18, 24, 27, 29, 47, 48, 49, 50, 81, 105
Teaching Standards 81, 94, 97
The Lamb Inquiry (2009) *16*
The National Strategies 1997–2011 (DfE, 2011) 56
theories-of-action 63
theory engagement 70, 71
tribunals *14*, 80

United Nations Convention on the Rights of the Child (UNGA 1989) *15*

United Nations Educational, Science and Cultural Organization (UNESCO) World Conference 11

Vision for Childcare Report (2022) 111
Vygotsky, Lev 33, 37–39, 42, 43, 44, 85, 93
  constructivism *40*
  Zone of Proximal Development (ZPD) *40*

Warnock, M. 3
  Warnock Committee Report (1978) 3, 6, 7, 8, 9, 11, 12, 13, *14*, 26, 30, 51, 112
Waves of intervention model 44–45, 46
workplace skills and competences 25

Zone of Proximal Development (ZPD) 38–39, 40